the case of the black family

the case of the black family

a sociological inquiry

by jerold heiss

columbia university press
new york and london 1975

Jerold Heiss is a Professor of Sociology at the University of Connecticut.

Copyright ©1975 Columbia University Press
Printed in the United States of America

Library of Congress Cataloging in Publication Data

Heiss, Jerold.
  The case of the black family: a sociological inquiry.

  Bibliography: p. 233
  Includes index.
  1. Negro families—United States.   I. Title.
E185.86.H43   301.42′1   74-34418
ISBN 0-231-03782-1

For My Parents
Sam and Rose Heiss

acknowledgments

It is a commonplace for authors to say, when they want to be gracious, "If not for X this book would never have been written." In this case the statement is literally true. The data upon which this study is based come from a secondary analysis of materials gathered by Robert L. Crain, and if it had not been for his generosity in making these data available to a person he had never even met, this book quite obviously would have been impossible. I wish to express my most heartfelt thanks to him.

My debt to C. Edward Noll is almost as great. It was from him that I learned of the existence of the data, and he introduced me to the SPSS system of computer programs, which represented the key to the efficient use of the material. His help throughout the course of the project contributed greatly to whatever merit this book has.

Doris Y. Wilkinson, Michael Gordon, Kenneth Hadden, and Albert K. Cohen read parts of the manuscript and thanks are due them for their useful comments.

A small grant from the University of Connecticut Research Foundation provided funds to cover equipment and supplies. The data analysis utilized the computer of the University of Connecticut Computer Center, which is partially supported by National Science Foundation Grant GJ-9. Special thanks are due computer operators John Nordstrom, Dianne Wise, Bill Angiletta, and Joan Littlefield, whose help made the many long hours at the Computer Center a little shorter.

I wish also to thank Sandra Golab for her help in the preparation of the manuscript, and John D. Moore and Karen Mitchell of Columbia University Press for their shepherding of the book through the publishing process.

Finally I wish to acknowledge the encouragement and forebearance of my wife and daughters. My gratitude to them is beyond measure.

JEROLD HEISS

Storrs, Connecticut
July, 1974

contents

Part One

The Consequences of
Black Family Structures

chapter one

the case
of
the black family

An indictment has been handed down against the black family; it has been held responsible for many of the problems of black people. Largely because of this, the family life of black Americans has become a subject of intense sociological interest after many years of relative neglect. Yet, although the matter has been debated endlessly, the case has never had a full hearing in the court of scientific research. Much of the writing on the subject is polemical, and though the more judicious writers have been building a body of relevant evidence it is not yet sufficient to permit a decision. Our first goal in writing this book is to bring together new and existing data which will allow a verdict on the accusations that have been made.

The usual charges against the black family have four components. First of all, they state that certain family characteristics are more common among blacks. Second, these traits are said to be typical of black families but not of white families. Third, it is suggested that these differences are not merely a result of the fact that the black group has more lower-status persons, more Southern-born people, etc. The differences are assumed to be more intrinsic to racial status. Fourth, and most crucially, it is claimed that these traits are causally related to outcomes which are undesirable. It is not merely that the black family is assumed to be different. The key aspect of the accusation claims that blacks would be "better off" if the differences in family form did not exist.

In most instances each aspect of the charge remains to be tested, and therefore before rendering a verdict it will be necessary for us to answer four questions in each case.

For those charges which prove to have some validity, we must take an additional step. It is not enough to know that a situation exists. We must inquire into the underlying reasons for it, just as a modern court is concerned with more than the facts of guilt and innocence. In this case we will ask, what causes these family traits, and why do they have these consequences?

Most of the previous work done on this topic focuses on the black family not for its intrinsic interest, but rather because it is thought to be implicated in a social problem. Of course, the problems approach is a legitimate one, but interest should not be limited to it. When we study the many other family systems which have commanded attention we go beyond such considerations. But as Adams (1971: 120) says, there are two tendencies in regard to the black family: "One is to ignore black families altogether; the other is to treat them as social problems."

What we have discussed so far is clearly in the problems tradition, but in addition, we will devote part of this book to nonproblem aspects of the black family. We will deal with it as another *case* which should be studied if we are to develop a general understanding of family systems. Much of the material will relate to the effects of family traits, but we will go beyond the effects relevant to the first goal of the study. For example, because it is part of the indictment we will attempt to determine whether maternal dominance is a barrier to achievement. In addition, we will investigate the relation between this family trait and personality, simply because the matter is of general sociological interest.

Both the problem-oriented and the nonproblem-oriented material will permit us to bring empirical data from black families to bear upon family theories which have not been adequately tested on any group. Despite salutary changes in recent years, it is still true that some family theories have been more discussed than tested, and our data will help us judge the validity of several of them. In addition, we will be able to add a new dimension to theories which have been extensively tested. Generally these have been worked out with the white family in mind, and they have been tested primarily on white, middle-class samples. We do not know the extent to which they hold for other groups, and a test utilizing data from black families seems particularly appropriate.

Ideally, if this book were to have the degree of integration we would like, all the material would relate to a single general theoretical perspective. This would be an excellent way to tie together rather heterogeneous material. However, this will not be possible, for none of the available theories has relevance for more than a few of the topics we wish to cover. The primary theoretical contribution of this volume will be found in the tests of the specific theories, and the major unifying element will be the set of charges.

A number of family traits—size, interaction patterns, stability, age at marriage, household composition, and kin relations—are considered to be of great practical and theoretical significance, and these will represent the central variables of the study.[1] Beyond this, the form of the book is dictated by the questions we wish to answer. Because they represent the first step in the test of the charges against the black family, in the next chapter we will consider the basic questions, what are the characteristics of black families, and do they differ from those of white families? With this matter settled, we then turn to a consideration of the effects of these characteristics within the black group. In the next group of chapters we will relate the central variables to a variety of dependent variables * and go as far as possible in explaining the effects we find. In the second part of the book we will complete the chain by inquiring into the antecedents of the central variables. Each part will be followed by a concluding chapter in which we bring together the various strands and relate them to our theoretical concerns.

These points will be elaborated as they come along in the data analysis. For now, let us go into some detail about the accusations. What charges have been made?

the indictment

Though variously stated, the essence of the general charge against the black family is that it is at least partially responsible for the economic,

---

* Terms that appear in the glossary are asterisked the first time they appear in the text.
1 The critics usually include high rates of illegitimacy, but this will not be a central concern of this book, for our data do not permit a totally unambiguous index.

social, and personal problems faced by black Americans. The Moynihan Report (Moynihan, et al., 1965: 30) puts it graphically:

> Obviously, not every instance of social pathology can be traced to the weakness of family structure. . . . Nonetheless, at the center of the tangle of pathology is the weakness of the family structure. Once or twice removed, it will be found to be the principal source of most of the aberrant, inadequate, or antisocial behavior that did not establish, but now serves to perpetuate the cycle of poverty and deprivation.

Frazier (1957: 636) is no less sweeping in his accusation, and the charge is similar:

> The widespread disorganization of family life among Negroes has affected practically every phase of their community life and adjustments to the larger white world. Because of the absence of stability in family life, there is a lack of traditions. Life among a large portion of the urban Negro population is casual, precarious, and fragmentary. It lacks continuity and its roots do not go deeper than the contingencies of daily living. This affects the socialization of the Negro child.

Proliferation of these citations is not necessary. The point that these views are not limited to an idiosyncratic few can perhaps be made by one additional quotation:

> The general formulation of the problem—that the socioeconomic system constrains the family in ways that lead to disorganization and that family disorganization then feeds back into the system to sustain and perpetuate social and economic disadvantage—is reasonably well accepted. . . . [Rainwater and Yancey, 1967: 309] [2]

The Specifications. Though these statements are abundantly clear, they are so general that they are almost immune to test. But this need not give us pause, for specifications of the charges are easily found.

The specific accusations all contend that certain traits are unusually common in black families and that these characteristics are causally related to outcomes defined as undesirable. In the eyes of the critics the most salient characteristics of the black family include: early age at

---

2 It must be noted that the other authors quoted above also place the *ultimate* cause of black problems outside the family.

marriage, large size, female dominance,[3] role segregation, multigenerational households, low levels of aid from kin, and marital instability. For example:

The selection of mates among Negroes has been achieved at a fairly early age, usually earlier among the lower socioeconomic classes than among the higher. In general, however, age at marriage is not a satisfactory measure of trends among Negroes because a very high proportion—about a fifth—of brides and grooms in any given year are entering a second or third marriage. The overall average age at marriage thus appears older than it really is for first marriages. [Bernard, 1966a: 82] [4]

Most nonwhite children under eighteen live in large families. . . . Crowding is the lot of slum families of whatever color, but it is more likely to occur— and it is likely to be more severe—among Negroes. [Ibid.: 130]

A fundamental fact of Negro American family life is the often reversed roles of husband and wife. Robert O. Blood, Jr. and Donald M. Wolfe, in a study of Detroit families, note that "Negro husbands have unusually low power," and while this is characteristic of all low income families, the pattern pervades the Negro social structure. [Moynihan, et al., 1965: 30]

This failure to engage in "chit-chat" is symbolic of the broader tendency for the Negro man to interact less with his wife. . . . In the leisure time aspects of marriage, less interaction takes place between Negro husbands and wives. [Blood and Wolfe, 1970: 63–64]

In 1960 a large proportion of all nonwhite families—14 per cent—were multigenerational. In fact, among nonwhite families with their own children of any age, only about half had no other members. The chances were great that all these multigenerational families were living under crowded conditions. [Bernard, 1966a: 130]

Although women in Pruitt-Igoe named close associates comparable in number to those of their white lower-class counterparts, their associations were apparently less permanent in nature, in that relatives and long-time friends made up a smaller proportion. . . . Because a broad social network constitutes a personal and family resource on which people can draw when they are in need, the comparative paucity of durable relations within the social networks identified by Pruitt-Igoeans underscores their lack of strong mediating and supporting associations. [Rainwater, 1970: 110]

3 Many authors tend to lump female-headed households and female-dominated homes in a general category of matriarchal structure. These are, obviously, different things, and the use of the single term is frequently confusing. Furthermore, matriarchy is not an appropriate term for either situation and we will generally avoid using it.
4 Inclusion of a quotation from an author does not necessarily imply that his or her work, as a whole, indicts the black family.

8 Consequences of Black Family Structures

The white family has achieved a high degree of stability and is maintaining that stability. By contrast the family structure of lower class Negroes is highly unstable, and in many urban centers is approaching complete breakdown. N.B. There is considerable evidence that the Negro community is in fact dividing between a stable middle-class group that is steadily growing stronger and more successful, and an increasingly disorganized and disadvantaged lower-class group. . . . The discussion of this paper is not, obviously, directed to the first group excepting as it is affected by the experiences of the second—an important exception. [Moynihan, et al., 1965: 5–6]

The critics further suggest that these assumed characteristics of the black family [5] cause economic and psychological effects which they consider undesirable. For example, an early age at marriage, large families, and absent fathers, are thought to increase the likelihood that a family will know poverty and deprivation. Most admit that general social conditions represent the first two strikes against black people, but it is supposedly the family itself that pitches the all-important third one.

On the psychological side, the focus is generally on the male. It is charged, for example, that psychological problems result when a boy grows up without a father or with an ineffectual one. Pettigrew (1964: 17, 21) puts it this way:

Recent psychological research vividly demonstrates the personality effects upon children of having been raised in a disorganized home without a father. One such study reveals that eight and nine year old children whose fathers are absent seek immediate gratification far more than children whose fathers are present in the home. . . . Regardless of race, children manifesting this trait also tend to be less accurate in judging time, less "socially responsible," less oriented toward achievement, and more prone toward delinquency. Indeed, two psychologists maintain that inability to delay gratification is a critical factor in immature, criminal, and neurotic behavior. The sex-identity problems created by the fatherless home are perpetuated in adulthood.

5 There is some question concerning whether this is supposed to be a general description or whether it is meant to apply to only one segment of the black group. Undoubtedly, most of the writers have in mind lower-status blacks, but the distinction is not consistently maintained. Moynihan's comment on marital instability shows this as does the lack of qualification in the other quotations. In our discussions we will avoid this problem by presenting, wherever appropriate and feasible, separate data for lower-status and higher-status blacks.

Among the other effects on children which have been attributed to the absent or ''denigrated'' father are: lowered intelligence scores, delinquency, high dropout rates, low school achievement, lessened resistance to the negative effects of racism (Moynihan, et al., 1965: 34 ff.); failure to learn the values and expectations of society (Lincoln, 1971: 346); susceptibility to schizophrenia, lack of marital aptitude (Bernard, 1966a: 125, 128–29); debilitating effects on personality development, exaggerated toughness, aggressiveness, cruelty, etc. (Bronfenbrenner, 1967: 914–15).

The other family traits also are supposed to have undesirable consequences, but let us stop for now. The point is clear, and additional details will be provided in the relevant chapters.[6]

data and methods

The new data which will be presented in this volume come from a secondary analysis of materials gathered by Robert L. Crain and the National Opinion Research Center in the summer of 1966. The original study (Crain, 1970, 1971; Crain and Weisman, 1972) was initially supported by the U. S. Civil Rights Commission, and it sought to determine the effects, if any, of attending integrated schools. Through the foresight of Dr. Crain, many questions were asked about the respondents' family life, and these items make the present study possible.

The population for the main sample is defined as all blacks living in metropolitan areas outside the South.[7] The sampling design is a multistage type usually referred to as a block-quota sample. This method is commonly used by survey research centers, and though it is not a completely random method it is considered to be both an adequate substitute and a necessary compromise. Cost considerations

6 It should be emphasized that these charges have not gone unchallenged. Billingsley (1968), Ladner (1971), Staples (1971a, 1971b), Ryan (1972), Scanzoni (1971), Herzog (1966), Hill (1972), would be included among the defenders of the black family.
7 The South is defined as the states of Delaware, Maryland, West Virginia, Virginia, North Carolina, South Carolina, Georgia, Florida, Kentucky, Tennessee, Alabama, Mississippi, Arkansas, Oklahoma, Louisiana, and Texas.

make it impossible to use probability sampling for surveys of this scope and complexity.

Within each of 25 metropolitan areas census tracts were randomly chosen, and within the chosen tracts 297 blocks were chosen by random procedures. Thus, to the level of blocks the method is strictly probabilistic. Below the level of blocks a quota-sample approach was used. In this method the interviewer is instructed to interview a certain number of people in each category of the quotas. For example, he might be told to interview 5 men and 5 women; 6 people under 30; 4 people over 30. He is not, however, instructed that he must interview a particular person who has been chosen randomly. This method introduces some bias into the sample. The interviewer will fill his quotas as easily as he can, and those who are easy to find and interview may be different from those who are not. A random procedure and the quota method will produce the same number of men, for example, but the quota sample will probably have fewer lower-class men, fewer busy men, fewer hostile men, etc.

We should not, however, exaggerate the deficiencies of the sample design. As it turns out, the sample and the population are quite close on traits which were not included as part of the quotas. The interviewers were instructed as to how many men, how many working women, and how many other women they should interview, but the sample they obtained is also quite close to census statistics on socioeconomic status. Crain and Weisman (1972) estimate that people with only a grammar-school education are underrepresented by some 3 to 5 percent, and the distribution by occupational level is quite close to census figures. Even without a correction for changes that occurred from the time of the census to the time of the study, the largest difference is only 6 percent.

Certainly the sample is not perfect, but we may have reasonable assurance that when we estimate population characteristics we will be reasonably accurate. Of course, more frequently we will be interested in the relationship between variables, and then sampling considerations will be less crucial.

The interviewers, all of whom were black, completed 1,651 interviews which were of sufficient quality for inclusion. This sample, however, requires correction, for the sampling design provided for oversampling in high-income areas and in metropolitan areas of less than 2,000,000 residents. This was done to ensure that the sample would include a sufficient number of people from integrated schools. Such a procedure does not cause any problem, for it is a simple matter to weight * the obtained sample to correct for the disproportionate numbers from the oversampled areas. However, the reader must remember that the weighted numbers (N's) * provided in the tables are on the average about 2.5 times the actual N, since the weighting procedure increased the N from 1,651 to 4,153.[8]

In addition to the data from this sample, we have material from a national survey of the general population which was conducted at about the same time as the study of blacks. Many questions were included in both studies, so it is possible to make comparisons between whites and blacks.

The sampling design of the national survey was the same one used in the survey of blacks. The only difference was that all noninstitutionalized residents of the United States over 21 were eligible for inclusion. From the 1,526 respondents we selected those who were Northern, metropolitan whites aged 21–45. This group numbers 343 and it is directly comparable to the blacks of the Crain sample. In addition, there were 53 blacks in the national survey who meet the age and residence requirements of this study. They were weighted 2.5, the average weight applied to the blacks in the Crain study, and added to the black sample for the black-white comparisons.

The first set of questions on the schedule deals with the residential history of the respondent, and this is followed by a number of questions relating to the family of origin: stability of parental home, number of siblings, several family-power items, data relating to the socioeconomic status of the parental home, etc. Then there are many items dealing with early interracial contacts and school experiences. After that, the focus turns to the respondent as an adult; his job and marital history, followed by a long list of attitudinal and behavioral items covering such topics as trustfulness, economic problems, racial attitudes, views about children, self-esteem, and secondary association participation. All in all, there were almost 500 questions and subquestions. Only occasionally did we have to sing the secondary analyst's

8 Since smaller metropolitan areas and higher-income neighborhoods were oversampled by a factor of 2, the weighting factor was 2 for larger metropolitan areas and lower-income neighborhoods. Thus each case was weighted, 1, 2, or 4.

lament, ''If they had only asked . . .'' The national survey was similar in content and organization and covered most of the same topics. It did not, however, dig as deeply on most issues.

In summary, this book will focus on several general issues. We will present data which bear upon the many charges that have been made against the black family. Does it have the traits it is purported to have, and are its characteristics related to undesirable outcomes? We will also study aspects of the black family which are of general theoretical interest. Do data from black families support or deny theories which have been worked out with the white family in mind? What are the antecedents of black family traits?

The data to be used in this study come from two broadly based surveys, one a sample of Northern metropolitan blacks and the second a general national sample. Both contain items relating to the family, personality items, measures of achievement, etc., and few areas of contemporary interest are overlooked.

This, then, is what we plan to do and what we plan to use. We turn now to our first concern: black-white differences in family structure.

chapter two

black family structure
in
comparative perspective

At this point in time, it may seem quite unnecessary to inquire into the basic characteristics of black families, but a close reading of the literature shows that much can be gained from such an investigation. Despite the recent increase in research on the black family, our knowledge of the relationship between race and family traits remains limited. There are a number of things "everybody knows" about the subject, but the data supporting what is commonly accepted are often weak and contradictory. For many characteristics, we are not even certain whether blacks and whites are similar or different, and when we can be fairly sure that a difference exists what lies behind it is usually not clear. It often remains possible that the relationship is spurious; * the difference may merely reflect the distribution in the two races of socioeconomic status or some similar variable. And when there is little doubt about the existence of a nonspurious difference, it is often possible that the trait is not characteristic of blacks but merely less rare among them.

We would expect that there would be some differences between white and black families. Even when social status is held constant in the usual ways, it is still likely that there will be variations in situational factors, values, and personal resources which will show up as differences in family structure.[1] At the same time, these differences should not be large. Blacks and whites of comparable education, income, and occupation have much in common, and this should be reflected in their family life.

---

1 In this study socioeconomic status (SES) is measured by respondent's education, occupation of the main wage earner, and family income. It must be emphasized that the usual methods of controlling for socioeconomic status will not produce comparable

age at marriage

The relationship between race and age at marriage is apparently changing. In earlier days whites were less likely to marry young, but more recently the gap seems to have diminished or disappeared (Bernard, 1966a: 82). For example, among women who married for the first time in the years 1920–29, 33 percent of the blacks and 19 percent of the whites were under 18. For the period 1950–54, the percentages were 26 and 18, and for 1965–70, 18 and 14.

For men the trend is similar. Of those married in 1920–29, 37 percent of blacks and 22 percent of whites were under 21. By 1950–54, the percentages were 28 and 25, and by 1965–70 they were 31 and 30 (U.S. Bureau of the Census, 1973b: Table 3). Clearly, whites and blacks are equally likely to marry young.[2]

Aside from the question of a black-white difference, the data are not consonant with the view that black marriages are typically early marriages. There is, of course, a definitional problem. We do not have a totally satisfactory answer to the question, at what age is the label "early marriage" no longer applicable? However, the ages of 18 for women and 21 for men have traditionally been the points at which the permission of parents has not been required, and if we use them it is clear from the data presented above that most black marriages do not occur when the partners are "too young." Furthermore, that conclusion does not require alteration in the case of people from lower-status backgrounds. In our sample, 28 percent of the women who had ever married did so before 18, and 37 percent of the men married before 21. For people of lower-status background the figures are 29 and 38.[3]

The data do not support the charges. Blacks and whites are not

---

groups when races are being compared. Blacks and whites who are equal in number of years of education, for example, may not be equal in status or earning power. At best, our techniques will reduce the status differences; they will not eliminate them (Jackson, 1973: 407).

2 The median ages for the two races are about the same. For those married in 1965–70 they were 20.6 and 20.5 for black and white women respectively. For men they were 22.8 and 22.6 (U.S. Bureau of the Census, 1973b: Table 3).

3 These figures in fact exaggerate the extent of early marriage. Some of the respondents are not yet married, and they are not included in these data. When they do marry they will add to the ranks of those who marry late.

very different in age at marriage, and most black marriages are not early marriages. Of course, this does not completely absolve youthful marriages. They still might cause problems when they occur, even if they do not occur very often. The data do say, however, that it is hardly likely that age at marriage will prove useful in explaining black-white differences on other variables.

fertility and family size

Extensive census data leave little doubt that for the country as a whole, black fertility is higher than white. Several indices point in this direction: in 1968 there were 118 live births per 1,000 black women aged 15–44, and the comparable rate for whites was 82. In 1973, the average black woman aged 15–44 who had ever been married had 2.8 children, as compared with 2.2 for whites. At every age level black women have had more children than white women (U.S. Bureau of the Census, 1971b; Table 92; 1973f: 5; 1973e: Table 12).

These figures, however, do not necessarily mean that the fertility rates of *comparable* whites and blacks are unequal. The residential and social characteristics of whites and blacks are markedly different, and this may be the cause of the differential fertility. It may be, for example, that the high fertility of blacks is due to the fact that they are more likely than whites to be of lower socioeconomic status, and people of low status tend to have larger families regardless of race.

The data show that socioeconomic characteristics do contribute to the differentials. For example, black women with less than four years of high school have much higher fertility than white women with equal education, but the gap is narrow for high-school graduates, and it is reversed among women who went to college (U.S. Bureau of the Census, 1973e: Tables, 17, 18). There is no doubt, though, that rates standardized * by education would show a black-white difference. It would, however, be a reduced difference. Similarly, 1969 data show that when family income is controlled, nonwhites [4] with incomes under $10,000 a year have higher fertility than comparable whites, but

4 Prior to 1970, census data were usually published for whites and "nonwhites." About 92 percent of the people in the nonwhite category are black.

beyond this amount nonwhites have slightly fewer children than whites (U.S. Bureau of the Census, 1971a: Table 15). If fertility rates were standardized on income, the difference between the races would persist in reduced form.

Region and size of place of residence also influence the size of the fertility differentials. In the South and in nonurban areas black fertility is much higher than that of whites, but outside the South, according to 1972 figures, blacks have only slightly higher birth rates. Roughly speaking, whites who do not live in the South average about 3.1 children.[5] The comparable figure for blacks is 3.5. In the South the figures are 2.9 and 4.4 (U.S. Bureau of the Census, 1973e: Tables 17, 18). Similarly, the black-white difference for 1970 was small in urbanized areas, 3.0 v. 3.6, but large in rural nonfarm and farm areas: 3.2 v. 5.1 and 3.5 v. 5.7 (U.S. Bureau of the Census, 1972a: Table 76).

Published data do not permit us to control for region, community size, and education simultaneously, so they cannot tell us about the difference between the races in the key group of Northern, urban, lower-status people. The data of our study, however, indicate that there is a noticeable difference in this segment. Ever-married black women aged 35–44 have borne on the average 3.9 children. Comparable white women have had 3.1 children. Among higher-status women, the means are less divergent: 2.9 for blacks and 2.5 for whites.[6]

Thus the charge finds some empirical support. Blacks generally have considerably higher fertility than whites. There are a few subgroups in which this is not so, and the difference is large only in certain segments of the population. But even if blacks and whites had the same distribution of social characteristics there would be a difference.

In absolute terms, it does not seem appropriate to characterize black fertility as high, and we find little to support claims that there has been an "extraordinary growth in Negro population"(Moynihan,

---

5 The base is ever-married women, ages 35–44.
6 The higher SES group has a score of 4 or above on a 9-point scale. By any absolute measure one does not have to be of very high status to qualify for the higher group. A person with a high school diploma, an income of $5,000 at 1966 value, and a semi-skilled job would qualify. Such people, however, are relatively rare in the black sample. The dividing line is about the median for the sample.

et al., 1965: 25). In fact, in recent years the proportion of the total population which is black increased only slightly, from 9.9 percent of the total in 1950 to 11.1 percent in 1970 (U.S. Bureau of the Census, 1973c: Table 4). And part of this increase is due to a narrowing of the gap in death rates.

All this does not entirely settle the issue. For some purposes a measure of family size is most appropriate, and number of children born is not a perfect index of family size. The data show, however, that the use of figures on family size does not change very much. In 1971 the average white family had 3.5 members, the average black family 4.3 (U.S. Bureau of the Census, 1972b: Table B). This difference is about the same as that observed between the general rates of white and black fertility.

Many blacks do live in families of considerable size. Bernard (1966a: 130) was correct when she stated that according to the 1960 census most nonwhite children under 18 lived in large families. Specifically, omitting family heads and their spouses, 63 percent of all nonwhites under 18 and 56 percent of urban nonwhites under 18 lived in families of 6 or more members. However, such a statement must be examined carefully. For one thing, a family of 6 typically would include 4 children, a number which was not considered excessive in the recent past. Also, we should note, as Bernard does not, that 36 percent of white children in urbanized areas lived in families this large (U.S. Bureau of the Census, 1964a: Table 4a). Black children are not the only ones to experience the "large" family. Furthermore, a large proportion of children may live in large families, but a smaller proportion of families are large.[7]

All of this is meant to indicate only that one must be careful not to exaggerate the absolute and relative size of the black family. We do not mean to suggest that whites and blacks are the same in this matter. In general we accept as proven the contention that black families are larger and blacks have higher fertility.

7 We do not have data on this point which are comparable to those presented above. Census figures do say, however, that only 38 percent of all nonwhite households "with own children of any age" contained 6 or more members (U.S. Bureau of the Census, 1964b: Table 17). For 1970, 35 percent of black families "with own children under 18," contained 6 or more members (U.S. Bureau of the Census, 1973d: Table 5).

maternal dominance

One of the most commonly held beliefs about the black family is that it is female dominated: women are supposed to wield an unusual amount of power. The existing systematic evidence is, however, quite contradictory. Blood and Wolfe (1970) found clear differences in decision-making power between black and white women in their 1955 data from a sample of blue-collar families in the Detroit area. (The blacks were characterized by a high percentage of wife-dominant families and a small proportion of egalitarian families. Each race had about the same number of husband-dominant families.) Aldous (1969) and Centers et al. (1971) also present data favoring the popular view, but the differences are small in both cases.

Several other studies, Middleton and Putney (1960), Mack (1970, 1971, 1974), TenHouten (1970), Hyman and Reed (1969) and Bridgette (1970) fail to find significant black-white differences in husband-wife power, but TenHouten and Bridgette report that black men exercise relatively low power over their children. There are also studies which show greater male power in the black group. King (1967) asked lower SES ninth-grade students in Jacksonville to report the relative power of their parents over large purchases, and the results show that black males have greater autonomy than whites. For other matters the results were variable. Baughman and Dahlstrom (Baughman, 1971), to close the circle, present data which consistently indicate greater power for black males—in general and in regard to the children.

Our data on this matter are the respondents' reports of the situation in their parents' family, and this leads into a difficulty. Because of the interest in long-term effects the questions had to be posed this way, but it prevents us from describing the current scene. However, if we limit our attention to the respondents who were under 28 at the time of the interview, we will be able to reduce the force of that problem. From them we can learn about black-white differences in the fifties and early sixties.

Table 2.1 contains the data, but before we consider them we should introduce the dependent variable, the maternal control score. This score is a composite made up of three items related to the time when the respondent was growing up: ''When you did something wrong, who usually punished you?'' ''Who kept track of the family money?'' ''Thinking back now, who do you think made the important decisions in your house when you were a child?'' [8] This measure seems to capture the essence of the critics' point better than a simple decision-making question would. Their idea seems to be that black women are the central persons in their families. They are said to have power over the children and control of resources as well as control over decisions. There is, in addition, an empirical justification for combining the items. The results of a factor analysis * show they reflect a single underlying trait.

Table 2.1.   Percentage Distribution of Maternal Control Scores by Race and Parental SES (PrSES) (Respondents Aged 21 to 28 from Intact Families)

	Total Sample		Lower PrSES		Higher PrSES	
Maternal Control Score	Black	White	Black	White	Black	White
0	12	36	11	37	13	34
1	31	35	33	37	31	36
2	32	18	30	10	34	20
3	25	11	27	16	22	9
N *	769	85	337	19	427	64
Gamma	.48		.48		.45	
Standardized gamma = .40						

* The black sample is weighted to adjust for disproportionate sampling. The white sample is unweighted.

The table indicates that there was a black-white difference of considerable size (gamma $[\gamma]$ * = .48), and it appears that the relationship is not due to the differential distribution of parental socioeconomic status (PrSES) [9] in the two racial groups. Some indication of this is

8 The score is a simple count of the frequency with which the respondent answered ''mother.''
9 Parental SES (PrSES) is measured by father and mother's education and occupation of father (or mother). Even more than for respondent's SES, the higher group is low on an absolute scale. The sample is very strongly skewed toward the lower levels. Forty percent of all black respondents are in the lowest category on the 9-point scale; i.e., neither parent went beyond grammar school, and the main wage earner was unskilled. The top 3 categories contain only 6 percent of the cases. The dividing line was placed at approxi-

seen in the second and third sections of Table 2.1. For people of lower-status background and for those in the higher category the gap between the races is as large as it is for the total sample. The implication is that if the races were equal in parental SES they would still differ in maternal control.

On the basis of these data, however, we cannot be certain of that conclusion. Within each of the parental SES groups the distribution of scores is different for the two races. The average black in the lower PrSES group, for example, has a lower score than the average white in that group. In other words, the tabular control * method that we have just used does not completely control for parental SES. This uncontrolled variance might possibly be the source of the black-white difference in maternal control.

This problem can be obviated by standardization. Here we ask the question, what would be the distribution of maternal control scores in the black sample if the blacks had the same distribution by parental SES score that the whites do? And by a weighting process [10] an exact answer can be provided. Then we take the new distribution of control scores and calculate a "standardized gamma."

In this case the standardized gamma is .40, a figure which is not much lower than the original gamma of .48. Even if blacks had the same status backgrounds as whites, there would be higher female control in the black group. The original correlation is not due to the differential distribution of parental SES.

Given the nature of the data we cannot reach a firm conclusion concerning racial variation in maternal control. This in itself is important, since so many previous authors assumed the point to be beyond question. Moreover, even if we put greater stock in the studies which

---

mately the median of the black group in order that we might have enough cases for some of the more complex comparisons. This was done after some experimentation which indicated that if we shifted the dividing line upward somewhat, nothing much would change. The exceptions to this are noted in the text.

10 To determine the standardized proportion of blacks who have a maternal control score of 0, for example, we first multiply the proportion of blacks in PrSES category 1 who have a maternal control score of 0 by the total number of whites in PrSES category 1. The same is then done for each of the other PrSES categories and the individual products are summed. This sum is divided by the N for whites. The resulting figure is the proportion of blacks who would have a maternal control score of 0 if the SES backgrounds of blacks were the same as those of whites.

show a difference, we find it difficult to accept the idea that the black family is female dominated. In our data only a fourth of the black women controlled in all three areas, and as Jackson (1973) has noted, in the Blood and Wolfe study the average score for black families is in the equalitarian range. In their 1970 reanalysis of their data, Blood and Wolfe say that the "modal pattern shifts from equalitarianism for white families to wife-dominance for Negro families" (1970: 61), but this is misleading. It is technically true, but it should be noted that an equal balance of power is almost as common: 39 percent of the black families are wife-dominant and 33 percent equalitarian. At best, then, the typical descriptions of the black matriarchy represent an exaggeration of the facts.

companionship

The evidence bearing upon black-white differences in companionship is very limited. There is, in fact, only one study (Blood and Wolfe, 1970) that contains directly relevant data, and it is limited to "informative companionship," the extent to which there is verbal communication between the spouses. On this measure there are clear differences. Blue-collar black men tell their wives what happened at work less often than do white men of comparable status. And, conversely, black women are less likely to tell their husbands their troubles after a bad day.

These data do not tell us anything about the extent of joint activity, and though there may be a "broader tendency for the Negro man to interact less with his wife" (Blood and Wolfe, 1970: 63), we do not see any evidence of it in the existing literature. Unfortunately, our data do not permit us to test the idea, for we do not have information on joint activity for the white respondents. The only conclusion possible is that no conclusion can be reached.

household composition

Closely related to the claims that black families are large is the charge that they tend to be extended in form: that they are likely to include more than two generations. Since this trait is supposed to have consequences beyond those associated with size, we will consider it separately.

It is not a simple matter to state how many black families are nuclear and how many extended, for definitions vary and the application of a definition often turns on the delicate question of who is the family head in a family containing several adults. For example, if an adult son is considered the head, his siblings will be considered ''other relatives,'' but if his father is the head he and his brothers and sisters are simply the children of the head. In the first case the household would be considered extended; in the latter nuclear. This problem is not solvable with the available data, so our figures must be considered rough estimates.

The 1970 census (U.S. Bureau of the Census, 1973d: Table 31) clearly shows that white families are more likely than black families to be nuclear in form. Seventy-five percent of black families fall into one of Billingsley's (1968) three nuclear categories: husband-wife; husband-wife children; man *or* woman and children. For whites the percentage is 90. About 25 percent of black families are extended, as compared with 10 percent of white families. There is, then, a difference, but we must stress that the large majority of families in both races are of the nuclear type. It hardly seems right to characterize black families as extended when only a fourth of them are in that category.

Our data for whites do not include family structure, so we cannot control for socioeconomic status in a black-white comparison, but we did not find support for the critics' claim that extended families are much more common among lower-status blacks than among blacks of higher status. When we use respondent's education as the index, the highest proportion of extended families is found in the best-educated group; but the differences are small.

The critics' description contains a germ of truth but no more than that. Extended families are more common among blacks. Nonetheless, most black families are nuclear, and lower-status blacks are not much more likely to live in extended households than are other blacks.

aid from kin

Given the difficulties that face many blacks, it would come as no surprise if we were to find that there is less assistance available from the kin group. A person who is fighting a battle for self-survival is not likely to be able to help relatives. As of now, however, there is little evidence to support this view. In fact, the only systematic data available oppose the notion (Hays and Mindel, 1973); but it must be noted that the sample used in that study consisted of only 25 matched pairs, and some of the findings are probably a result of the simple fact that more of the black families had relatives living with them. There is good reason to look into the matter further.

Our data indicate that blacks and whites differ in the extent to which they depend upon relatives for their start in the world. We found that 25 percent of the blacks who are currently married say relatives helped them find their first jobs, and 16 percent of whites report this ($\gamma = .27$). Controlling for education, however, reduced the relation. The difference between the races is only 4 percentage points in the group which did not graduate from high school and 7 points in the higher-educated group. It seems that the two races are quite similar in this matter.

It may be, however, that this particular item is somewhat atypical. Helping a relative find a job may not be very costly in time or money, two resources which are particularly scarce in a deprived and overburdened group. A more searching test of the availability of kin aid in the black community involves a question concerning the number of relatives who could be expected to help in some way if a serious emergency took place in the family. At the minimum such a situation would require a time expenditure, and quite frequently a financial cost would also be involved.

The data are consistent with the critics' view, for blacks say there are fewer relatives they could call on. The average number is 4.7 for blacks and 6.6 for whites. With socioeconomic status controlled, the relationship is reduced somewhat, but in each of the SES categories there is a clear difference between whites and blacks.

Without at all denying this variation, we should add a few words of clarification. It must not be assumed that large numbers of blacks had no one they could call on. Only 11 percent of the blacks are in this category as compared with 6 percent of the whites. The whites have a larger pool of relatives, but most blacks have someone. It should also be noted that the variation is mostly due to a difference in the availability of in-laws. For the total sample the difference between means is .7 for own relatives and 1.1 for in-laws. The percentage reporting "none" is the same for both races in regard to own relatives, but for in-laws there is a 17-point gap. Similar patterns appear when SES is controlled.

These findings certainly do not show much variation between the races in regard to kin availability, but at the same time they do suggest that there is a distinction. They lead us to reject the view that opposes the critics', the view which suggests that minority-group status leads to an increase in the saliency of kin because such status leads to increased need for mutual aid (Adams, 1970; Hays and Mindel, 1973). Blacks may approach whites in this matter, but they clearly do not exceed them. At the same time we cannot completely accept the critics' position, since that seems to be an exaggeration of the facts.

marital status

On the basis of previous research concerning marital status,[11] there is little doubt that black families are, as charged, more likely to be

---

11 There are acute terminological problems in this area, for many of the commonly used concepts suggest value judgments we do not wish to convey. There is no easy solution to this difficulty, particularly since we wish to avoid neologisms and euphemisms. All we can do is to use precisely defined terms and urge the reader not to add excess meaning to them. The following terms have these meanings when used to refer to the respondent's childhood family: A *broken home* or a *disrupted family* is one in which the respondent did not live with both his real parents until he was 16 because of parental divorce, separation, desertion, *or* death. An *unstable family* is one in which the cause of the break was not death. Similar terms are used in describing the respondent's marital history.

broken than are white families. Farley and Hermalin (1971) show, moreover, that this has probably been the case for some time, and other studies (Udry, 1966a, 1966b; Glick, 1970; Bernard, 1966b) make it clear that this is not merely a reflection of differences in socio-economic status. Even with SES controlled, the black-white differences remain.

Our data show that blacks are more likely to come from broken homes ($\gamma = .51$); are more likely to come from homes broken by conflict ($\gamma = .68$), and are more likely to have been brought up without

Table 2.2.   Percentage Distribution of Current Marital Status of Ever-Married Persons by Race and Education

Marital Status	Total Sample		Less than 12 Years of Education		12 or More Years of Education	
	Black	White	Black	White	Black	White
Married, not previously married	61	86	56	84	68	87
Widowed	2	1	3	0	2	1
Married, previously married	14	7	16	7	11	6
Divorced or separated	22	6	25	9	19	6
N *	3,654	301	2,002	68	1,652	232
Gamma	.57		.56		.51	
Standardized gamma = .49						

* The black sample is weighted to adjust for disproportionate sampling. The white sample is unweighted.

a father or stepfather ($\gamma = .49$). As in the previous studies, this cannot be explained as an artifact of SES. With parental SES controlled, the differences between the races are almost equally pronounced (standardized $\gamma = .46, .67, .44$ for the three measures).

Table 2.2 shows that the gap is not narrowing in the present generation. For the respondents there is considerable difference between whites and blacks in regard to broken-marriage rates ($\gamma = .57$) and it remains when education is controlled (standardized $\gamma = .49$).

This is only part of the story, however. To say that blacks have known greater marital disruption than whites is not quite the same as saying that the charge against the black family is proven. Some of the authors go far beyond the simple statement of a rate difference. The reader will recall Moynihan's use of the term ''approaching complete breakdown'' in speaking of the family system of lower-class Negroes, and though other authors are not as graphic in their descriptions, the picture one gets is that instability caused by conflict is the typical pattern of black lower-class families. Do the data support this charge?

The evidence of this study shows that 60 percent of the blacks, regardless of parental SES, lived with both their parents throughout their early years. Furthermore, about half of those who did not live with their parents failed to do so because of the death of a parent. Of the blacks from lower-status backgrounds, 80 percent did *not* have their families broken by divorce or separation before they were 16.

These figures are, however, not directly pertinent, for they refer to the previous generation. The destruction of the black family, it is suggested, is a recent, urban, lower-class phenomenon (despite the fact that Frazier [1939] was talking about the same thing 35 years ago).

The data for these respondents, all of whom are residents of Northern metropolitan areas, fail to support the idea of a collapse in the black family. Among those who did not finish high school, the lower education group of Table 2.2, 72 percent of those who have ever been married are presently married. Among those who have only a grammar-school education the percentage is 70; for the total sample it is 75. Certainly this is not a picture of domestic bliss, particularly when one considers that about 15 percent are not in their first marriage and some of those who are now married will in the future have a broken marriage.[12] Nonetheless, the image of a collapse is not appropriate here. By far the most common family arrangement is the husband and wife living together.[13] Again, it seems quite clear that the more extreme statements of the critics do not accurately describe the situation.

12 The oldest respondents with a grammar-school education have the lowest rate of marital stability: 66 percent are now married and only 46 percent are currently living with their first spouse.
13 It is true, however, that female-headed black families have become more common in recent years. National figures show that in 1960, 22 percent of black families were of this type. By 1974 the percentage had increased to 34 (U.S. Bureau of the Census, 1971b: Table 87; 1974: Table 52).

conclusion

In this chapter we have considered three of the central questions: Are certain traits more characteristic of the black family? Are any differences between the races spurious? Do any of these traits typify the black family? We would conclude that the evidence does not support all the critics' contentions regarding differences between black and white families. In recent years blacks and whites have shown the same pattern in regard to age at marriage, and we cannot be sure whether there is more maternal dominance in black families because the data are contradictory. In regard to the relative degree of companionship in black and white families, there are almost no systematic data. So at least 3 of the supposed differences are untrue or unproven.

Blacks do, however, have higher fertility and larger families; they are more likely to live in multigenerational households; and their marriages are less stable. In addition, they have fewer relatives to call on in an emergency.

Black-white differences in socioeconomic status, region, or some similar variable contribute to the variation on family traits, and it also tends to be true that the size of the gap varies in different segments of the population. In no case, however, can the differences between the races be explained by variation in socioeconomic status or demographic traits. The black-white differences are not spurious as far as we can tell. They do not disappear when these variables are controlled.

For *some* variables the critics are close to the truth in the first two elements of the charge. On all variables, however, they are wrong when they suggest that these traits are typical of black families. In general there seems to be an exaggeration of the data. Black families are somewhat more likely to have these traits, but most black families do not have them. The black family is characterized by these traits only in a relative sense.

All this notwithstanding, there is some variation in family structure. We will now attempt to determine if the differences make a difference.

chapter three

age
at
marriage

The controversy which has swirled around the black family has centered on the kind of material we considered in the previous chapter. Much of the literature bears solely on the relative frequency of certain family traits in the two racial groups. In fact, one could get the idea that the charges against the black family can be settled simply by determining whether or not these traits are more common among blacks. That is not the case; such materials do not answer the key question. The contention is that particular family traits contribute to the problems of black Americans. *To show that these traits are more common among blacks settles nothing unless it is also shown that they have the consequences they are assumed to have.* Logical argument, theory, and data from white samples will not do. It must be shown that these family traits have particular consequences in the black community, or the critics' case collapses. The next several chapters represent our attempt to test that case.

We start with one family trait which did not show black-white differences—age at marriage. Since blacks do not marry at an unusually early age, we already know the critics' full charge cannot be accepted. But it is still of interest to know if early marriage, when it occurs, has the consequences described by the critics.

Even among those who argue that age at marriage and marital outcome are associated, there is uncertainty concerning the casual patterns involved. Bernard's (1966a: 82–83) remarks typify the situation. On the one hand she says, "Youthful marriages, regardless of race, have a relatively poor prognosis. . . . Extreme youth is a handicap in marriage, but more so among those of low socio-economic class background." On the other hand, she goes on to suggest that age at marriage may not be the causal factor. People who marry young tend to have lower levels of employment, education, and church attendance, and since these are associated with marital problems the possibility exists that the relationship is spurious. We may ultimately have to face this problem. But first, is there in fact a relationship?

age at marriage and marital stability

The basic data unequivocally support the contention that age at marriage is associated with marital instability. As may be seen in Table 3.1, in all subgroups early marriages are much more likely to be broken by conflict. Half or more of the early marriages are now broken, but the rate for late marriages is, at a maximum, 28 percent. The gap between early and late marriages runs from 26 to 37 percentage points.

Table 3.1.   Rates of Marital Instability of Ever-Married Black Respondents by Age at Marriage, Sex and Parental SES

Age at Marriage	Total Sample	Lower PrSES	Higher PrSES
		Males	
Under 20 *	49	50	50
20 or 21	28	31	25
22 through 24	22	23	22
Over 24	16	17	13
Weighted N	1,430	734	666
Pearson correlation †	−.23	−.21	−.27
Partial correlation ‡	−.14	−.09	−.20
		Females	
Under 18 *	56	54	59
18 or 19	36	31	41
20 or 21	37	33	40
Over 21	28	28	28
Weighted N	1,855	992	812
Pearson correlation †	−.19	−.20	−.18
Partial correlation ‡	−.12	−.11	−.14

* For each sex the cutting points that were used divide the samples into approximately equal quartiles.
† A negative sign indicates the later the age at marriage the lower the rate of instability.
‡ Number of years since marriage is controlled.

This comparison is, however, "unfair" to people who married early, for they have been married longer, and therefore they have had longer exposure to the risk of a broken marriage. To get around this problem we calculated the partial correlations * between age at marriage and instability, with number of years since marriage held constant. These figures indicate that the uncontrolled data exaggerate the situation. The zero-order correlation * between age at marriage and marital stability is − .23 for men and − .19 [1] for women. The partial correlations are − .14 and − .12. A good part of the original relation is attributable to differences in length of marriage. At the same time, it becomes clear that the relationship between age at marriage and marital stability is not totally artifactual. Even with length of marriage controlled, early marriages appear to be poorer risks.

Now that we have established the existence of a relationship, we must look deeper. Appearances may be deceiving in this matter, since a third variable which is antecedent to both may lie behind the correlation of age at marriage and instability. It is crucial that we determine whether this is so, for if age at marriage does not have an independent effect upon stability, it is "guilty only by association," and that puts a very different light on the situation.

The potential associated biases * include several premarital traits: parental SES, stability of parental marriage, number of siblings, education, and region of residence. Each of them was added, in turn, as a control variable to the first-order partial * (number of years since marriage controlled), and the results are completely consistent. In no subgroup was there a significant reduction in the correlation. Early marriages would show less stability even if they were equivalent to later marriages in regard to these premarital social characteristics.

It still may be, of course, that the association between age at marriage and marital instability is spurious. One can never be sure that all the possible associated biases have been controlled, and in this case

---

1 Tests of statistical significance are not used as criteria for deciding whether or not associations are worthy of note. Because of the weighted sample, they would be difficult to calculate, but even if this were not so their use would not be indicated. The sample is large enough so that quite small correlations suggest a real difference in the universe. Instead of level of significance we focus on the size of the association. Generally, a correlation less than .10 is considered to be trivial. Correlations between .10 and .20 are viewed as indicating a small, but clear, association.

we know they have not been, since no personality or value items were used. Nonetheless, we have considered several social variables, and these include most of the ones that have been suggested. For the present the conclusion is that age at marriage may be the causal factor, and if it is not, the true cause is not one of the factors usually suggested.

Before we attempt to determine what it is about early marriages which lead to instability, let us consider whether the prognosis is equally bad for all early marriages or whether it is only in certain segments of the population that early marriages have higher rates of instability.

Bernard (1966a), it will be remembered, suggested that the greatest effect is in the lower socioeconomic status group, but the data indicate that this is not so. With years since marriage controlled, the partial correlations suggest that for males the association is primarily in the higher SES group; partial $r = .20$ for higher SES men and .09 for those of lower-status background. For females the relation is about the same in both groups, .14 and .11.

Somewhat surprising is the fact that the relation does not vary by sex. We would have expected the age at marriage to be more important for the men. As just noted, for the high-status males the correlation is higher than for other groups, but for low-status males it is lower (.09). Thus, there is not much difference between men and women in general. The first-order partial is .14 for men and .12 for women.

In general, then, there is support for the critics' charge that early age at marriage is associated with marital instability. Part of the relationship is artifactual, but when the artifact is removed a relationship remains. Contrary to some opinions (Burchinal quoted in Bernard, 1966a: 82–83) the relation is not due to the fact that people who marry early have certain premarital traits such as poverty, poor education, etc. Partialing out these variables has little effect on the correlation. Finally, it is a very stable relationship. It appeared in all subgroups and the magnitude tended to be consistent, except that it was unusually high for males of higher-status background.

Those are the facts of the matter, and we now turn to a search for an explanation. It seems likely that the answer lies in the early days of marriage, and there is a generalized description bearing on this to be found in the literature on white families. If we look at this material we may get some clues as to the reasons for the high rates of instability for young black marriages.

a portrait of the youthful bride and groom

Many writers on the white family suggest that one of the key facts about early marriages is that they are likely to be preceded by a pregnancy (Inselberg, 1962; de Lissovoy, 1973; Burchinal, 1959, 1960) and thus they are often not completely voluntary. This is thought to represent the first strike against the marriage. Parents are likely to disapprove; the couple feels trapped and burdened with the problems attendant on the birth of a child while still in the throes of working out the adjustments associated with the early days of marriage. This is exacerbated by the fact that the first child is not likely to be the last. Early marriages have high fertility rates (Kiser, et al., 1968: 117–18).

The economic plight of couples who marry young is also emphasized. Bartz and Nye (1970: 265) suggest that "early marriage results in lower social class placement. The principal mechanism is curtailed formal education with resultant occupational placement in unskilled, semi-skilled, and clerical occupations." It is not merely that people of lower-status background are more likely to marry young; the fact of young marriage ensures that any social mobility will be downward.

That, however, takes a longer-term view. From the beginning there are pressing financial problems. De Lissovoy (1973: 247) notes that "The fiscal picture of debts was depressing. One-third of the couples had debts requiring regular payments and over half had borrowed from finance companies at exhorbitant interest rates."

These economic problems lead the young couples to turn to their parents for help: "the outstanding economic characteristic noted virtually in all couples was the help patterns extended by the families of both husband and wife. The contributions to the couples came in the form of goods, money, and services" (ibid.). Inselberg (1962) found that these financial problems frequently led young couples back into the parental homes. Three-fourths of them had lived with parents or other relatives.

Aid from parents may represent the financial salvation of the young couple, but it is supposedly not an unmixed blessing. Inselberg (1962: 76) reports that

Establishing a working relationship with in-laws was another area presenting difficulties for many [young] wives. Responses of 50 percent of them to the sentence stem, "In-laws are," revealed either hostility or ambivalence as compared with 16 percent of the control wives. . . . Although none of the [young] couples in which the wives were having difficulties with in-laws were living with the husband's parents at the time of the interview, almost half of these couples had lived with the husband's parents prior to the study. This living arrangement could easily have precipitated conflicts. Also, parental disapproval may not have completely worn off and may be reflected in the strained relationships.

De Lissovoy's (1973: 250) data do not suggest that in-laws represent a major problem, but he too reports that wives had trouble with their in-laws: "Mothers-in-law while helpful and well-meaning were seen as intruding. This was especially noted after the birth of the first child."

On the other hand, relations between the husband and his in-laws tend to be good. Inselberg (1962) found no difference in ratings of in-law interaction between men who married young and those who married at an older age, and de Lissovoy (1973: 250) reports: "There was a considerable number of spontaneous expressions of gratitude by the husbands for help received. It was also possible to note cues that the husband and the wife's father were often very close."

Another characteristic of young marriages is the inability of the husband to accept some of the role prescriptions associated with his new status. De Lissovoy (1973: 248) states it succinctly: "The husbands remained 'boys' in a number of ways. They went 'out' with former 'buddies', stayed after school to play basketball and other sports. . . . The realization that a married status required a different orientation to life came slowly." (See also, Inselberg, 1962: 76.) This apparently was not characteristic of the wives. In fact their situation was quite the opposite: "The wives . . . felt 'dropped' by former friends and led rather lonely lives. While husband's former friends and classmates dropped in often, very few of the wives reported callers" (de Lissovoy, 1973: 248).

If this description holds for youthful black marriages but not for the marriages contracted at a later age, we would have the basis for an explanation of the relative instability of the early marriages. If they start out this way it would be no surprise that they often fail. In the discussion which follows, we will limit our attention to existing first marriages of less than 6 years' duration, and compare youthful and older marriages. Are there "danger signs" to be seen in this period?

Age at Marriage, Premarital Pregnancy, and Early Fertility. Our index of premarital pregnancy is quite inexact, and a large proportion of the cases fall into an "uncertain" category.[2] Therefore, we cannot really cast much light on the relationship between premarital pregnancy and early marriage. However, given the importance placed on this by other writers some consideration is necessary.

For males from both social-status groups and for lower-status women, those who marry *late* are more likely to be in the category, "marriage was definitely preceded by a pregnancy." At least 35 percent of them were clearly parents or parents to be at the time of marriage. For those who married young, the percentage is less than 15. Women of higher-status background show a different pattern. For these women the proportion who definitely became pregnant prior to marriage is between 10 and 15 percent regardless of age at marriage. Our crude measure suggests that for three of the subgroups, those who marry early are *less* likely to start off marriage with a child.

We would caution again that care must be taken here, for our measure may be more likely to "catch" the premarital pregnancies of those who marry late. For those who married young, if there was a premarital pregnancy it probably occurred soon before the marriage,

2 The index of premarital pregnancy was calculated by subtracting age of oldest child from present age to determine respondent's age at birth of first child, and then we compared this age with age at first marriage. By this method many cases can be classified as definitely no premarital pregnancy or definitely a premarital pregnancy. Other cases are, however, ambiguous. For example, if age at marriage is the same as age of birth of child, there may or may not have been a premarital conception. The respondent might have been married at the age of 19 years and one month, and the child could have been born just prior to the twentieth birthday, or the child might have been born before the wedding. In this case the chances of a premarital pregnancy are 138 out of 144, assuming a nine-month term, and therefore all such cases are classified as "probably premarital pregnancy." On the other hand, if the age at marriage is one year less than the age at birth of first child, there is still the possibility of a premarital pregnancy. In this situation the chances of a premarital pregnancy are only 45 out of 144, and such respondents are classified as "probably no premarital pregnancy."

and thus it would be an uncertain case. In marriages which came at a later age the premarital conception sometimes occurred many years before the first marriage. At any rate it is clear that in many cases premarital pregnancy did not lead to early marriage, and many early marriages are not preceded by pregnancy.

Given these relationships, it does not seem likely that premarital pregnancy is a significant factor in the association between early marriage and marital instability.

Whatever the situation in regard to premaritally conceived children, it is clear that the general relation between age at marriage and number of children is rather weak in the first five years. In general, couples who marry young do not have significantly higher fertility; the partial correlation is only $-.05$ (with years since marriage held constant). For women of higher-status background, however, the difference is much greater: partial $r = -.50$. Fertility is generally high, an average of 1.5 children in these marriages of less than 6 years' duration, except for high-status women who marry late. They have about half the average number of children.

In general, it appears that those who marry young do not have the responsibility for significantly more children in the early years of marriage, but that is not true for women of higher-status background.

Age at Marriage and Educational Achievement. When we limit our attention to those who have been married less than 6 years, we do not find a consistent relation between age at marriage and education. There is a high correlation for women of high parental status (partial $r = .49$), but for high-status men there is no relation (partial $r = .02$), and in the two lower-status groups people who marry young actually have more education than those who marry later (partial $r = -.10$ for men and $-.21$ for women). We cannot be sure why this is so,[3] but the important point is that in three of the subgroups we will be looking at, those who marry young do not have an educational deficiency. Educational handicaps will not explain the other findings, except perhaps for women from higher-status backgrounds.

3 When we include marriages of longer duration the correlations become quite different. For lower-status males partial $r = -.10$, and for lower-status females, .09. For the two higher-status groups $r = .12$ and .43.

Age at Marriage and Income. Though among the recently married men those who marry young generally do not have less education, we would still expect them to have less income because they are younger and therefore have less seniority on their jobs. The data support this expectation. The partial correlation between age at marriage and personal income is .18 for males. In general, then, early marriage and low income do go together for "newlywed" black men. However, on further investigation it was found that this is true only for higher-status males. For those of lower-status background the partial r is .06; for higher-status men it is .22.

This, of course, speaks only to the respondent's own income. If high-status males who marry young are more likely to live with relatives or to have working wives, it could very well be that their total family income is equal to or greater than that of men who marry later. As it turns out that is not the case. The correlation for family income and age at marriage is also .22 (for lower-status males the partial r is .01). In the high-status group if those who marry young are more likely to live with relatives, the latter do not contribute enough to bring the total income up to that of persons who marry later. Marriage at a young age is associated with economic problems for those of higher-status background.

Age at Marriage and Kin Relations. We have just seen that if living with relatives is more common among those who marry young, it is not a sufficient answer to their economic problems. The question still remains, however, are they more likely to live with relatives than are people who marry late? Does their situation lead them back to the parental home?

The relationship between age at marriage and living with other relatives is trivial: partial $r = .05$ in the predicted direction for males and .02 for females. When the parental SES subgroups are looked at separately, we find that the relationship is stronger for lower-status males; partial $r = .21$. In the other three groups it continues to be low.

In general, then, contrary to the literature on white families, blacks who marry young are no more likely to live with relatives than are blacks who marry later. For lower-status males this is not so. Those who marry young are more likely to double up. But economic need does not explain this tendency, for in the lower-status group, age at marriage is not related to income.

We cannot determine directly how much other aid the respondents receive from relatives, but they were asked how many of their own relatives they could count on to help in an emergency, and this will at least tell us if the perception of the situation differs by age at marriage. And, if those who have received aid are more likely to expect aid, it will also give some hints as to the actual situation. In all subgroups the correlation is negative: those who marry young mention more relatives. For males, however, the correlation is higher than it is for females. For the men, partial $r = -.30$ for the lower parental SES and $-.25$ for the higher. For the women, partial $r = -.12$ and $-.04$. It seems that the extra aid received by young couples comes mainly from the man's family.

Again, the aid pattern does not follow the pattern of economic need. Men who marry young usually believe their relatives are more available in times of emergency, but only in the higher-status groups are they less well-off than men who married later.

In some cases kin do seem to be more helpful if the couple was young at the time of marriage. This seems to be particularly true for aid from his family to a young husband. If he is of lower status, he is more likely to live with relatives; and regardless of status, if he married young he perceives that he has more relatives who will help in an emergency. Economic need does not seem to hold the key to any of these relations, however.

Age at Marriage and Companionship. The description of the young married man suggested that he remains tied to persons other than his wife for much of his recreational activity. According to this view he is not ready for "wedding bells to break up that old gang" of his.

The data suggest that this picture is correct. The respondents were given a list of mainly recreational activities [4] and were asked if they had done any of them in the past few weeks. For each "yes," they

4 The activities are: went to a movie, attended a sporting event, ate out in a restaurant, took a drive or walk for pleasure, had a drink in a bar or tavern, played cards, visited friends in their home, had a long conversation about something interesting, fixed something around the house.

were asked if they had done it with or without their spouses. From the responses we constructed two measures which we call the companionship and spousal integration indices. The former is the number of activities in which the spouses jointly participated, and the second is the ratio of joint activities to total activities. For males, the partial correlation between age at marriage and companionship is .10 and for spousal integration partial $r = .13$. Men who marry young do fewer things with their wives, and their social activity is more separated from that of their wives. There does seem to be a weaning problem. Furthermore, this is not limited to men of lower-status background. The partial correlation is higher in this group (.22) then it is in the higher-status group (.11), but in both groups there is a difference. For women there is no consistent relation between age at marriage and these measures of husband-wife interaction.

Age at Marriage and Visiting Patterns. The data do not support the notion that women who marry at an early age are lacking for social contacts. In the lower SES group, those who married young report more frequent visits from friends and relatives (partial $r = -.21$), and for lower-status women, those who married young are more likely to report that they visited friends within the last few weeks. For higher-status women there is no relation between age at marriage and visiting. There is also an indication that newly married young wives are less dependent upon their husbands for social contacts. There is a strong correlation between age at marriage and the likelihood that a wife visited friends without her husband (partial $r = -.34$ for both PrSES groups). There is less companionship in young marriages, but the women are hardly isolated and tied to the home.

At the start of this analysis the question was posed, are there danger signs to be seen in the first years of early marriages? The answer is clearly yes, and the signs are similar in nature to those which have been described for youthful white marriages. At the same time that we say this, we must also stress that some parts of the description do not hold for blacks, and that the patterns are of different strength in the various subgroups. There are a number of exceptions, but the associations seem to be greater for higher-status persons, and perhaps particularly for higher-status women.

Age at Marriage and Satisfaction. Theory would tell us that much of what we have discovered indicates that in their early days, youthful marriages are less satisfying; but to conclude the case we must show more directly that this is so. The evidence bearing on this point is presented in Table 3.2. People who marry young have higher levels of frustration,[5] and they are less likely to say that their best times are with their spouses. The females are less likely to say they would marry again if they had their lives to live over again, and the males among them consider themselves less adequate as parents and spouses. Within the parental SES subgroups there is additional variation: particularly

Table 3.2.   Partial Correlations between Age at Marriage and Measures of Satisfaction; Parental SES and Years since Marriage Constant (First Marriages of Less than Six Years' Duration)

	Frustration Score	Would You Marry Again? *	Best Time With Spouse? *	Evaluation of Self As Spouse *	Evaluation of Self As Parent *
Total sample	−.13	.11	.21	.06	.11
Men	−.20	.05	.17	.15	.18
Women	−.10	.16	.24	−.05	.08
Low PrSES men	−.19	.04	.13	.06	.06
High PrSES men	−.21	.18	.16	.22	.31
Low PrSES women	−.06	.07	.23	−.06	.31
High PrSES women	−.12	.19	.24	−.06	−.19

* For all variables other than the frustration score a positive relationship means that those who married at an older age show greater satisfaction or a higher evaluation.

for males, the relation is stronger in the high SES group. In general, however, early marriages not only have higher instability; those which survive seem less satisfying.

One final step remains. We now know that youthful marriages are less satisfying, and we have seen that age at marriage is related to cer-

5 The measure of frustration and unhappiness is a factor-analysis scale composed of the following items: "Sometimes I get so frustrated I could break things;" "Sometimes I would like to get even with white people for all they have done to the Negro"; "Very often when I try to get ahead, something or somebody stops me"; "People like me don't have a very good chance to be really successful in life"; "Taking all things together, how would you say things are these days? Would you say you are very happy, pretty happy, or not too happy?"; a scale composed of several items which relate to the degree that the respondent believes his fate is beyond his control; and, "This country would be better off if there were not so many foreigners here."

tain danger signs. These latter factors have a logical relation to a lack of satisfaction, but we have not actually shown that they represent the intervening variables between age at marriage and satisfaction. And we have not determined how much of the correlation between age at marriage and satisfaction they can explain. We now have to run partial correlations between age at marriage and the satisfaction items with the danger signs controlled.

In Table 3.3 we consider, for the total sample and for males and females separately, the second-order partials of Table 3.2 which exceed .09. Those lower than this are omitted, for if the relationships between age at marriage and the satisfaction items are trivial to begin with, it makes no sense to ask if the supposed intervening variables are the cause of the relation. Next to each of the relevant second-order partials we present the "best" fifth-order partial. That is, of the seven danger signs, we took three at a time and added them to the second-order partials. The figures in the table represent the correlation which was associated with the combination which lowered the second-order partial most. In other words, the differences between the pairs of columns suggest the maximum explanatory power of the danger signs taken three at a time.[6]

As may be seen in Table 3.3, the factors we have isolated do not account for the bulk of the relationship between age at marriage and satisfaction. Only one of the correlations approaches zero after three additional controls are added to parental SES and number of years since marriage. On the other hand, there are indications that these factors are not totally irrelevant. In each case there is some reduction and sometimes it is quite substantial. We would conclude that these so-called danger signs are among the intervening variables between age at marriage and satisfaction. But at the same time we would also note that most of the relevant factors remain to be discovered.[7]

On a statistical level the reason for this is simple. Though the danger signs do have the assumed relations to the satisfaction items, the correlations generally are not strong, and the correlations between

6 The reductions are often less if all seven danger signs are included at one time. This is due to the fact that sometimes a danger sign increases the correlation rather than reducing it.

7 Evidence not presented here indicates that the greatest reductions are for the high PrSES women. Of course, this is not surprising, since they showed the greatest correlation between age at marriage and the danger signs.

Table 3.3. Second-Order and "Best" Fifth-Order Partial Correlations between Age at Marriage and Measures of Satisfaction * (First Marriages of Less than Six Years' Duration)

	Frustration Score		Would You Marry Again? †		Best Time With Spouse? †		Evaluation of Self As Spouse †		Evaluation of Self As Parent †	
	2nd Order	Best 5th Order	2nd Order	Best 5th Order	2nd Order	Best 5th Order	2nd Order	Best 5th Order	2nd Order	Best 5th Order
Total sample ‡	−.13	−.08	.11	.08	.21	.19			.11	.09
Men	−.20	−.17	.16	.11	.17	.13	.15	.10	.18	.11
Women	−.10	−.02			.24	.22				

* For the second-order partial, years married and parental SES are controlled. For the fifth order, three from the following list are added: family income, number of relatives could call on, type of household, number of visitors, number of children, companionship index, education.

† For all variables other than the frustration score a positive relationship means that those who married at an older age show greater satisfaction or a higher evaluation.

‡ A blank indicates that the second-order partial was less than .10.

age at marriage and the danger signs are also weak. The product of these two correlations gives an estimate of the amount of reduction produced by a single control factor, and the product of two small numbers is a very small number. Furthermore, the total reduction caused by all the factors is not the sum of each's contribution, for there is intercorrelation among the explanatory factors themselves.

On a more substantive level, we have simply not been able to measure all the relevant factors, and some of those we can measure are measured only roughly. Nonetheless, the data suggest that the answer does lie in the direction we have taken.

Extended Families, Premarital Conception, Age at Marriage, and Satisfaction. Now that we have studied the general relationship between age at mariage and satisfaction, we may go back and test two additional elements in the picture of the young couple. This description suggests that things are worst when there has been a premarital conception and when the couple lives with relations. The implication is that most young marriages are difficult, but that they are most difficult under these conditions. We now want to see if the correlation between age at marriage and satisfaction is greater when the couple lives in an extended household, and when there has been a premaritally conceived child.

The correlations between age at marriage and the satisfaction items are, with a few exceptions, stronger when the respondents live in an extended household (see Table 3.4). When we look at subgroups the N's get small, but the pattern seems to hold for both sexes. In general, the presence of other relatives worsens a bad situation for the young couples.

It will be recalled that we cannot be sure in many cases whether or not there had been a premarital conception, but for the present purposes we can combine the "certain," "probable," and "possible" into a single category which has an unambiguous meaning. These people, in contrast to the others, had to cope with a child early in marriage.

The data for women are the relevant ones, for in many instances the men's premaritally conceived children did not live with them. The women's data only partially support the idea that the effect of age at

Table 3.4. Partial Correlations between Age at Marriage and Measures of Satisfaction for Respondents in Nuclear and Extended Families; Parental SES and Years since Marriage Constant (First Marriages of Less than Six Years' Duration)

	Frustration Score		Would You Marry Again? *		Best Time With Spouse? *		Evaluation of Self As Spouse *		Evaluation of Self As Parent *	
	Nuclear	Extended	Nuclear	Extended	Nuclear	Extended	Nuclear	Extended	Nuclear	Extended
Total sample	−.11	−.35	.07	.36	.21	.28	.06	.09	.08	.29
Men	−.16	−.46 †	−.01	.37	.18	.10	.14	.21	.11	.66
Women	−.11	−.15 †	.17	.24	.24	.46	−.04	.12	.10	−.09

* For all variables other than the frustration score a positive relationship means that those who married at an older age show greater satisfaction or a higher evaluation.

† For the extended family group the N's are 42 for the men and 46 for the women.

Table 3.5. Partial Correlations between Age at Marriage and Measures of Satisfaction for Respondents Who Had Children Early in Marriage and for Those Who Did Not; Parental SES and Years since Marriage Constant (First Marriages of Less than Six Years' Duration)

	Frustration Score		Would You Marry Again? *		Best Time With Spouse? *		Evaluation of Self As Spouse *		Evaluation of Self As Parent *	
	Early Child	No Early Child	Early Child	No Early Child	Early Child	No Early Child	Early Child	No Early Child	Early Child	No Early Child
Total sample	−.15	−.03	.14	.03	.21	.17	.00	.21	.10	.12
Men	−.24	−.14	.01	.15	.18	.17	.02	.39	.10	—†
Women	−.13	.12	.28	−.17	.18	.16	−.05	−.08	.13	—

* For all variables other than the frustration score a positive relationship means that those who married at an older age show greater satisfaction or a higher evaluation.

† The N is too small to permit calculation of a meaningful statistic.

marriage is maximized when there are children present to "compli-cate" the early adjustments. The data for the frustration score and "Would you marry again?" are consistent with the prediction; in fact the correlation is in the expected direction only when the children come early (partial $r = -.13$ and .28). For the other two variables with an adequate N the correlations are about the same whether there are children or not. The proper conclusion is uncertain, though the two variables that are probably the best measures suggest the matter is rele-vant.

the general effects of age at marriage

Up to this point, our basic concern has been with the critics' claim that early marriages are less stable. This has led us to look into the early years of marriages, and has diverted us from a longer-range view. The question still remains, is age at marriage correlated with outcome vari-ables when we include marriages of much longer duration?

In addition to satisfying our curiosity about the generalizability of our previous findings, the answer to this question will cast some indi-rect light on the question of selection versus situation. If age at mar-riage is still related to variables such as income after many years of marriage, or if the correlation between age at marriage and fertility increases in the later years, this would suggest that at least some of the previous findings were due to the traits of those who marry young rather than to the fact that they were young when they married. Youth-fulness is something that one grows out of, but the traits that lead one to early marriage may be carried throughout life. If the explanation of our previous findings is youthfulness, the correlations should be higher in the early years than in general. If they are not higher, either there has been historical change—as time has passed, age at marriage has become less relevant—or the cause is to be found in the characteristics of those who marry young. We would favor the latter interpretation. It would seem, if anything, that age at marriage has become progres-sively more important rather than less.

In regard to fertility the data suggest that selection does play a part. For marriages of less than 6 years' duration, the partial r between fertility and age at marriage is .00 for males of lower-status back-ground, − .08 for high-status males, .16 for low-status women; and − .49 for high-status women. For all marriages, the correlations are − .06 for low-status males, − .17 for high-status males; − .10 for low-status women. The relation becomes less negative only for high-status women (partial $r = -.27$). In three of the subgroups, some of the extra fertility of those who marry early comes after their youth.

The usual explanations of the high fertility of young marriages suggest youthful ignorance, lack of planning, greater fecundity, and longer "exposure to risk." None of these is consistent with our data. If any of the first three was the explanation, the differences would reach their maximum in the early years and then remain stable or decline.[8] This happens only for high-status women, who show a decline over time in what was originally a very high correlation. The findings in the other groups are consistent with a selection explanation. People who marry young either want more children or are less able to control their family size. It's not their youth per se, for those who marry early are most distinctive when they have passed their youth. The usual explanation may hold for higher-status women, but not for the other groups.

In regard to personal income, the partial correlations for males in the first 5 years are .05 for those of lower-status background and .21 for those of higher status. For males in the sample as a whole, the comparable figures are .07 and .25. The gap between early and late marriages does not decline. This again suggests that selection accounts for at least part of the findings.

This cannot be pursued too far, however, for the method does not apply to some of the factors, and we cannot be certain of the conclusions where it does apply. Nonetheless, it is important to see that in the long run, the correlation with these two key variables does not disappear, and it becomes likely that selection is playing a part, as Bernard (1966a) and others have suggested. The selection factors, however, are not the usual social variables which are put forth; we tested these and they proved not to be relevant. The relevant factors must be value, personality, and ability variables we cannot measure.

8 Exposure to risk is irrelevant here since number of years since marriage is controlled.

conclusion

According to our data, the critics are right when they tell us that the prognosis for black marriages is poor if they are youthful marriages. We have seen that such marriages are more likely to be broken, and in the early years those which survive are characterized by less satisfaction, less companionship, etc. We also know that the effects tend to be greater in the higher-status groups. This is in sharp contrast to Bernard's (1966a) view, which suggests that age at marriage is most important when it is associated with a lower-status background.

Our data do not tell us, however, if anything would be gained by attempts to delay marriages. For one thing, this might be rather difficult to accomplish, since blacks already have an average age at marriage which is not particularly low. But if it could be done, it is not clear what the consequences would be. It is quite possible that it is not so much early marriage that is the problem, but rather the people who marry early. We tested some 5 factors which have been suggested as possible associated biases and none of them proved to be relevant, but we know there are a number of value, personality, and ability factors we could not control that are potentially relevant. Also, some of the findings fit in with a selection hypothesis. For example, early marriages are not more fertile because they involve youthful people. Some of the "extra" children come when the couple is no longer youthful.

At the same time, we have not presented data which put into question the assertion that part of the answer is simply that young people are less ready for marriage. We believe, but cannot prove, that it is a bit of both. For all people the likelihood of trouble increases as age of marriage decreases, but those who do marry young are even less suited for early marriage than the average young person. What it adds up to is that a delay in marriage will probably help only a little. And for lower-status males, the group which is supposedly most affected, it would not help at all.

Furthermore, even if early age at marriage had a strong causal effect upon outcome, youthful black marriages could not be blamed for black-white differences in outcome, since there is no difference between the races in age at marriage. The critics' charge on this count cannot be accepted.

chapter four

the effects
of
family size

Sociological studies of the relation between group size and group func-
tioning have shown that a group's organizational problems increase at
a rapid rate with increasing size. Each added person means increased
complexity, and this adds to the likelihood of conflict, chaos, and
disintegration. In the face of these dangers, large groups resort to the
mechanisms of formal organization: centralized leadership, established
rules, formal division of labor, restraint and unemotionality in interaction, etc.

These principles have been applied to the family in rather divergent ways. One group of writers emphasizes the problems caused
by large size, and another admires the skill with which large families
cope with them. The latter view, which can be called the ''cheaper by
the dozen'' position, sees the proverbial ''big happy family.'' The picture is one of love and companionship associated with a discipline, an
organization, and a willingness to sacrifice for the good of the group
which are not to be seen in the typical small family. Large families
may meet adversity, but they will usually conquer all. James Bossard
(Bossard and Boll, 1955, 1956a, 1956b; Bossard and Sanger, 1952;
Bossard, 1954) was a major proponent of this traditional view. Though
he sees problems in large families, the general thrust of his work is favorable toward them. He summarizes the characteristics of the large
family in these terms:

Under the sheer weight of numbers there is often not the concentrated care of
the large family child, nor the solicitous anxiety over him, nor the officious
oversight, nor the pervasive possessiveness, that are the more common lot of
the small family child. [Bossard and Boll, 1956a: 310]

Large family living makes for an early acceptance of the realities of life. [Ibid.]

Inherent in every fact and impression one gets from the study of the large family is its emphasis on the group rather than the individual. . . . Children in large families play together. . . . the children work together. . . . One must stay in line. . . . Problems must be solved and crises have to be met by sticking together. . . . Decisions must be made on a group, i.e., family basis. [Ibid.: 311]

In stark contrast to this is a "revisionist" image which sees chaos rather than organization, regimentation rather than cooperation, conflict rather than companionship, a losing struggle for survival rather than the triumph of a well disciplined army. The raggedly clothed mother wearily standing by the stove surrounded by drippy-nosed, unwanted children sums it up; but more specifically:

Research and theory suggest that autocratic and authoritarian child rearing structures are more common to large than small families. . . . Parents who have larger numbers of children living at home tend to prevent their adolescents from making their own decisions. [Schooler, 1972: 252]

We observe the complexity of maintaining order in a family with three or more children. [Ibid.: 254]

The scores revealed a tendency for more small-family children and fewer large-family children to view their families as highly cooperative. [Templeton, 1962: 56]

The number of relationships and experiences which may occur within the family setting multiply rapidly as family size increases. It is thus likely that conflicting demands, conflicting loyalties, conflicting interests, and conflicting goals will also increase. With the greater likelihood of such conflict, parents are apt to turn to more inflexible, authoritarian forms of control to maintain some order [Ibid.: 57]

There is some question concerning which image is predominant currently, but the revisionist view is the one which the critics have in mind when they discuss the large black family. Hylan Lewis (1955: 103) suggests, for example, that one of the common experiences of the black child is to find "himself in a large or extended family situation . . . competing with a number of siblings and relatives for care and desired responses." To this Bernard (1966a: 131) adds the comment,

"Actually, they may be competing not only for care and response but, in the lowest income levels, for sheer survival."

These problems are assumed to be only the beginning. In the long run, the rigors of living in a large family produce educational and economic problems. Scanzoni's (1971: 46) position is qualified but the point is clear. "The combined effects of limited economic resources, plus limited parental (often only maternal) attention to numerous children could have a deleterious effect on later performances of certain children from large households both in the occupational and conjugal spheres." He then goes on to cite data which show an inverse relation between family size and education.

Thus we can construct a rather full specification of the charge. The long-term effects of large families are to lower education and income. The short-term effects, which cause the long-term problems, are lack of response and care caused by economic problems, authoritarianism, conflict, and the various other ills that large groups are heir to.

This is as far as the indictment goes, but the matter will be pursued further. The two views predict opposite effects, but both lead us to expect that family size would be related to a number of personality traits: gregariousness, cooperativeness, frustration tolerance, assertiveness, etc. These possibilities are worthy of attention and we will return to them after we consider the validity of the critics' charges.[1]

number of siblings and education

The data leave no doubt that there is a negative association between number of siblings and the level of education achieved. Regardless of sex and parental SES, respondents from small families have more education. The Pearson correlations * are generally of the order $-.20$, except for women of lower-status background, who show a relation of $-.12$. In most subgroups there is about 1 year's difference in education between those who had 2 or fewer siblings and those who had 6 or more.

1 In order to remove ambiguities, the data on the effects of parental family size are limited to respondents who lived with both their real parents until they were at least 16.

Further investigation suggests that the relation is not spurious. Controlling for age and parental SES by partial correlations has practically no effect on the relation. The data also indicate that the educational handicap associated with being part of a large family is present regardless of the respondent's birth-order position. It is true that the correlation between family size and education is greater for oldest children than for middle and youngest children ($r = -.30, -.20, -.17$), but further analysis revealed that the difference is due entirely to the females of lower-status background. In this group, oldest children have a strong disadvantage if they come from a large family ($r = -.37$), but a youngest girl actually has an educational advantage if she is in a large family ($r = .40$). In all other cases educational achievement is low in large families regardless of birth-order position.

However, the size of the relation is variable, depending on region and size of community. Large families are more of a handicap to those born in the North and in urban areas. This is, of course, what the critics would suggest, and it leads us to ask if the association is, as they would also suggest, at a maximum for young, lower-status males. The answer is a clear yes. Large families have maximum effects among males of lower-status background who are now between 21 and 28 ($r = -.37$) and 29 and 36 ($r = -.32$). The gap between small and large families is about 1½ years.

In general, then, this first charge is completely supported. It is true that people from large families generally do not go as far in school, and the men most affected by family size are those who are young and of lower-status background.

Furthermore, the relationship is, in part, a direct result of the family responsibilities which fall upon the children in the large family. The respondents were asked whether and for how long they had had to miss school to help out at home or on the farm. When the responses to this variable were partialed out, the relationship between family size and education was somewhat reduced. For males, for example, the correlation was reduced from $-.25$ to $-.18$. Clearly this variable does not account for the facts we have reported, but it does contribute. To put it another way, if respondents from large families did not miss school as often as they did, the educational gap between them and the respondents from small families would be somewhat reduced.

number of siblings and adult income

The finding that large families act as a brake on education is of interest in and of itself, and it gives added credibility to the critics' claim that people from large families are less successful economically. It does not, however, ensure that that claim is correct, for the correlation between education and income is rather small. It turns out that for the males in the sample the correlation between family size and income is only $-.07$. Those who had 2 or fewer siblings have an average income of $6,231, and those who had 6 or more siblings have an income of $5,553.[2]

Further investigation shows, however, that dealing with the total sample hides relationships of considerable importance. In several segments of the population there is a substantial correlation between family size and income. Of greatest significance is the situation of the young men. For those under 29, coming from a large family is a considerable handicap, whether they are Southern or Northern born, low or high status in background. The correlations range from $-.19$ to $-.38$. The gap between large and small families is $1,500 or more. Furthermore, in this young group the differences in income are largely independent of differential education. Among older men, the relation between family size and income is either positive or practically zero.

Thus, childhood in a large family is not universally associated with reduced income, but it is for the young men in the sample. Why this association is not seen for older men is not clear. It may be a historical change. It could be that it is only in recent years that a large family has begun to represent a handicap. Or it may be that the handicap is only temporary. Perhaps when the young men in this sample are somewhat older, those from large families will catch up or exceed those from smaller families. At any rate, we do know that the handicap is not the lower level of education associated with a large-family background. For the young men, those from large families would have had lower incomes even if they had equal education.

The charge against the large family seems valid. In general, com-

2 We are using income here as a further index of achievement. The income of women is not considered because for married women the relation between personal income and achievement is ambiguous.

ing from a large family is associated with lower income and education, though the difference is not great in the former case. Furthermore, the associations tend to be strongest for the young lower-status males that the critics have in mind. The difference in income is, however, not due to the educational differences. Income differences would exist even in the absence of education differences, but they would be reduced in some groups.

number of siblings and personality

Frustration and Unhappiness. We would expect that parental family size might be related to adult personality, for the structure of a family influences experiences and these experiences shape personality. In fact, most writers on this subject, regardless of the image they have of the large family, start from the basic assumption that family size is a key structural feature.

According to the "cheaper by the dozen" view, adults from large families should be less frustrated and unhappy. They should feel less hampered, because their early experiences should have taught them to put up with frustration. The essence of the image is the idea that people in large families learn to accept limitations and to face crises. As Bossard (Bossard and Boll, 1956a: 310–11) put it, "Being reared in a large family makes for an early and a continuing adjustment to the changing vicissitudes of a realistic world. . . . The large family member learns . . . to take minor disturbances in stride: it is almost as if one developed an immunity against them." The opposing view would see too much frustration too early and a trained incapacity to cope. Thus, the product of a large family would suffer more from the normal frustrations experienced by all.

When we look at all respondents from unbroken homes, we do not see much support for either point of view. The data favor the idea that persons from large families are more frustrated and unhappy, but the correlation between family size and the frustration score is a trivial .06.

Dealing with men and women separately does not change very much. The correlations remain extremely low; .03 for males and .08

for females. However, when we look at each parental SES group separately, a major difference appears. Family size and frustration are strongly related in the group which comes from a higher-status background ($r = .31$ for men and $.38$ for women), although there is little relation in the other parental SES group. Furthermore, this is not merely a function of differences in income or education. Controlling education and respondent's or family's income does not destroy the correlation for higher-status people. It seems clear that the Bossard view is not consistent with the facts. The large family does not produce "frustration-proof" people. At the same time, the opposing view appears to be valid only under certain circumstances.

This finding is of particular interest in view of the fact that high-status people from large families are more likely to say "A person should deprive himself of having a good time in life to make sure he is saving to get ahead." For both males and females the partials are .12. The greater unhappiness of those from higher-status large families is not due to a lesser willingness to delay gratification. It must be that they are less well prepared to cope with frustration or that they have much more to cope with. Our guess would be that both contribute to the finding.

Before we go on special note should be taken of the statistical interaction * in these findings, for it has occurred before and it will recur. We often find that the association between a family variable and a dependent variable is greater among higher-status persons than it is among people of lower status.

If we assume that deprivation in childhood leads to frustration, the interaction makes sense. There are many sources of deprivation in the lower-status group. If a person does not "get it" because he has a large number of siblings, he will get it from something else; the advantages that go with a small family are not sufficient to overweigh the other forces. People of higher status are less subject to these other forces, and they are likely to avoid deprivation unless something like a very large family causes it.

This interpretation is supported by the fact that lower-status people are more frustrated than people from higher-status backgrounds—if family size is not too large. If the family is large, parental SES is not related to frustration. Or we can look at it this way: there is a strong correlation between family size and this trait in the higher SES group because of the unusual responses of those who are of high-status background and from a small family. People of higher status who are from large families resemble everybody else.

In more general terms, certain family traits lead to certain outcomes, but these same effects can be produced by other factors. For lower-status people, these factors are commonly present, so that outcome is similar whether or not the family trait is present. For people of higher-status background these other factors are not so common, so the person who "escapes" the family factor will show a different outcome than the person who does not.

Assertiveness. The cheaper by the dozen view would also suggest that people from large families would be low in assertiveness. At an early age such people would learn to be undemanding and self-sacrificing. They would not demand their rights, but would take what they were given as their contribution to cooperation and harmony.

The view which sees a lack of order in the large family has more complex implications. It would certainly suggest that some members of large families would become highly assertive in a situation where resources were limited and one had to fight for what he could get. At the same time, in such a situation some people would have to curb their assertiveness more than would be necessary in a small family. Males and first-borns, for example, can lord it over their weaker siblings unless there are enough of the latter to form a coalition. This would suggest a negative correlation between family size and assertiveness for men. For women we would expect family size to be less relevant since even in small families the assertiveness of females is often restricted. The Bossard view would not make these distinctions. It would predict a consistent negative correlation between family size and assertiveness.

The relation in the sample taken as a whole is very weak: only −.06; [3] but when males and females are considered separately the cor-

---

3 The assertiveness score is a factor-analytic scale composed of the following items: (1) When you hear about a Negro being discriminated against, does it usually bother you? When it does bother you, do you feel angry or do you usually feel sad and depressed about it? (2) Sometimes I feel I would like to get even with white people for all they have done to the Negro. (3) Did anything happen in the last month or so to make you angry? If not, do you remember the last time something happened to make you angry?

relation we predicted is found for males. In this group the association between family size and assertiveness is $-.15$; for females it is .03. Furthermore, in both parental SES groups the correlation for the men is the same. Large families tend to depress the assertiveness of males, but family size is irrelevant for women.

The revisionist view also gains support when we look at the association within birth-order position categories. For males who are the oldest in their families the correlation, with education held constant, is $-.23$; for those who are middle children, $-.10$; and for those who are youngest $-.06$. Thus the greatest effect of large families is on males who are the first-born in the family. They are much less assertive than first-born males who grew up in small families.[4]

Sociability. Bossard spoke directly to the effect of large-family living upon sociability and gregariousness. He believed that people from large families develop a desire to be surrounded by other people. "One comes to accept the constant presence of other persons. Persons reared in large families make better occupational adjustments when working in large groups" (Bossard and Boll, 1956a: 319). The implications of the contrary view are equally clear. People who grew up in chaotic large families should develop a desire to escape people.

The data, in this instance, do not give much support to either point of view. For the total sample there is an extremely weak relation, partial $r = .07$, which suggests that people from large families have visitors in their home more frequently. This proves, however, to be not entirely consistent. For higher-status men the relation is reversed (partial $r = -.05$) and in the other 3 groups it is of variable magnitude. For lower-status males it is .15 and for females .06 and .11. Furthermore, when there is a difference it is probably due to the fact that people from large families have more kin available for visiting. The data do not show that people from large families are more likely to receive visits from friends.

Along the same lines, people from large-family backgrounds report a larger number of people in answer to the question which asked how

---

Though two of the items refer directly to interracial interaction, we believe that the underlying factor is a more general predisposition to assertiveness or aggressiveness.

4 Higher-status women from large families who are the youngest in their family are more assertive than those from small families (partial $r = .31$).

many adults they could count on for help in an emergency (Pearson $r = .11$). Again, however, this seems to be a function of the larger number of relatives available. The Pearson correlation between number of siblings and number of one's own relatives is .16. The correlation with friends is .01, and with in-laws .06.

In general, then, neither point of view is supported. People from large families do not attempt to escape human association and support. In fact, they seem a little more involved with people than those from small families. This cannot, however, be taken as clear support for Bossard's view, for the differences are small and seem to be partially a result of kin availability. We see no evidence that the products of large families are characterized by particular attitudes regarding sociability.

It seems clear from these data that family size does have some long-range effects upon achievement and personality. The differences are not large and they are sometimes limited to particular segments of the population, but they are not to be denied. There is support for our general notion that structural features, such as size, are relevant. Furthermore, the claims of the critics seem to be valid. People from large families do get less education, and the males among them have lower income. This seems to be particularly true of the group the critics focus on; the young men from lower-status backgrounds. The associations do not seem to be spurious, and therefore they have to be explained in terms of characteristics of the large family. In the next section we will begin a search for this explanation.

The data lead us to reject the view of the large family set forth by Bossard. Those from large families do less well economically and educationally, though large families are supposed to be a good preparation for life; and his view does not correctly predict the personality correlates of family size. People from large families are not happier and less frustrated, even when the income difference is controlled. They are not consistently less assertive than small-family products, and they are not notable for their sociability.

These data seem more consistent with the view which sees the large family as a place of disorganization, but not all the predictions based upon this image proved to be correct either. Before we accept it we would want more direct evidence of its validity.

The next step becomes clear. In order to explain the long-range effects of family size we must determine the short-run effects, and when we have done that we will have a stronger basis for choosing between the two images of the large family. We will first consider the situation of the mother, as she is considered to be of central importance. Many of the outcomes we have described are supposedly a result of the heavy burdens she carries. Is her lot really so hard? Let us consider first some data from the respondent's family of origin.

short-term effects of family size

The Burdens of Mothers. The index of maternal control (see pp. 18–19) it will be remembered, refers to the situation in the respondent's childhood home. It is composed of responses to questions concerning decision making, control of family money, and the disciplining of children. Clearly this is an index of power, but it also tells us something about which parent had the greater responsibility and involvement. High maternal control in a large family implies the mother was carrying a large burden.

The general trend of the data is clear. Large families have lower maternal control scores. The fathers of large families were more involved than other fathers in the activities of the family. The correlations are small, however, less than .10 in each SES group. There is some indication that lower-status males are less likely to be totally uninvolved if they have a large family. The shift is, however, not to the opposite extreme of husband control, but rather to the middle category.

When we control for region of birth, we find that there is no relation between family size and maternal control among Northern-born respondents. Most of the original correlation is attributable to higher-status Southern families. If the respondent was brought up in a large family in the North, it seems likely that his or her mother did not get aid commensurate with her extra burden.

We obtained further information on this matter by considering whether the respondent's mother usually worked outside the home. If mothers with large families had to hold down outside jobs, we would have additional evidence that they were overburdened. The data show that women with large families, if they were higher SES, were less likely to hold jobs (partial $r = -.06$ and $-.23$ for lower and higher SES groups). But even in the complete families we are considering here, large numbers of women with 6 or more children held outside jobs most of the time: 45 percent of the lower-status mothers with large families held jobs, and in the higher-status groups the proportion is over one-fourth.

There is one saving grace. When women worked, their husbands became more involved in the activities of the household as the number of children increased. If the mother didn't work, number of children was not related to male involvement. This was again, however, mainly a Southern pattern. In the North number of children shows little relation to male involvement regardless of whether the wife worked or not. In general, in the generation of the respondents' parents, the mother of a large family carried a heavy load if she worked outside the home, as many did.

We have no more relevant information about the respondents' parental families, but we can go further if we turn our attention to the respondents' own families. By comparing respondents who vary in the number of children they have, we will be able to check out several of the supposed short-run effects of large families.

Insofar as our interest is descriptive, this shift of generation is no problem. Data from the present generation are at least as good as those from the previous one. However, we also want to use these data to explain our previous findings on the effects of growing up in a large family. Here the ice gets thinner, for under these conditions we cannot use the direct method of partial correlations to test the adequacy of our interpretations. We would have to control for events in the parental home, whereas what we know directly are events in the respondent's own marriage. Thus our explanation will have to be purely verbal, and must stand on its plausibility rather than on direct evidence that a particular variable is an intervening variable.*

Moreover, we have to assume that the correlates of a large family are the same in the parental and present generations, for in our explanations we will use the latter to judge the former. In some cases this may be debatable. For some material, however, there is no other way short of a long-term longitudinal study. For example, if we wanted to study the postulated causal chain, large families cause parental dissatisfaction and this, in turn, causes adult personality traits, we would have to follow a family through two generations if we were to get direct, valid data on each element.

If we keep in mind what is being done, the problems will not be too great. This can be partially demonstrated by showing that we would have reached the same conclusion regarding the relation between family size and maternal employment if we had used the respondents' experience rather than those of the parents. The data show that things have not changed very much. It is still true for women at all educational levels that the larger the family, the less the likelihood that the mother works (partial r for the total married sample is $-.14$, with age, education, and parental SES controlled). At the same time, many women with large families do work. Almost one-third of the women with 6 or more children work, and for women with a grammar-school education the figure rises to 45 percent.

It is, of course, true that the mother of a large family who holds an outside job is not necessarily overburdened. She may be able to shift many of her household responsibilities to her older children, to her husband, or to other adults if her household is not a nuclear one. There is no indication in our data of the extent to which children take over the mother's duties. We know, of course, that they may, at least in the lower class (Schultz, 1969). On the other hand, we also know that many working women with large families lack help from other adults, since they live in nuclear households. We cannot be sure, but it seems likely that for many women a large family means heavy home responsibilities and an outside job. The only conclusion that can be drawn is that black women with large families have been and continue to be very much overburdened.

Family Size and Economic Problems. All the descriptions of the large family seem to accept the notion that such families face greater economic problems. Even Bossard (Bossard and Boll, 1956a: 116) states that "economic pressure is the overshadowing problem in most large families." Nonetheless, we know very little about the dimensions of the problem, particularly for blacks. It seems appropriate, therefore, to look into the matter.

Large families do have more economic problems. The correlation between family size and family income is $-.18$. There is a consistent trend running from about $8,000 per year for childless families to

$6,150 per year for those with 6 or more children. Those who probably have the greatest family expenses have the least income.

The fact that income is low in large families is all we have to know for purposes of explaining long-term effects of family size, but for understanding it is necessary to know if this is a spurious correlation or whether number of children acts as a causal factor. Both possibilities are plausible. A large number of children reduces the likelihood that the mother will work, and it can lock a father into a low-paying job. On the other hand, low incomes and large families may both be effects of third variables, such as low education, early age at marriage, etc.

The evidence shows the relation to be partially spurious. When a partial correlation is computed holding constant age at marriage, number of years since marriage, number of marriages, education, and parental SES, the association drops by a third, from $-.18$ to $-.12$. This is due mostly to the effect of education and somewhat less to age at marriage. These factors are correlated with income and number of children, and therefore they strengthen the relation between income and number of children.

Assuming that there are no other associated biases, to say that the relationship proves to be partially spurious is the same as saying that there is some causal connection. We do not have data which will permit an empirical description of the causal path, but we can rule out one logical possibility. The connection is not due to the fact that the mothers of large families are less likely to work. If this were the reason, the correlation between family size and family income should be less when the mother works than it is in general. This is not the case. When we limit the sample to those families with working mothers, the partial correlation is $-.11$, about the same as it was for the whole sample. It must simply be that people who have large families have less earning power, even when education and so forth are equivalent.

Parental Values Regarding Children. The idea that parents of large families emphasize conformity in their child-rearing is reached by at least two lines of reasoning. First, parents of large families are more likely to be of lower status, and lower-status people are generally less permissive regardless of family size (Kohn, 1969). Second, the general view that large groups require leadership, established rules, and "toeing of the line" leads one to predict a greater stress on conformity as a reaction to the dictates of the situation. Thus we will again have to discover whether there is a relationship and if so whether it is spurious.

In testing the idea we will not deal with actual child-rearing practices, but rather with the values parents hold. This is the approach followed with great success by Kohn and Pearlin (Kohn, 1969, 1959; Pearlin, n.d.; Pearlin and Kohn, 1966). Our measure of parental values resembles theirs in that the respondents had to choose from among a number of desirable traits those which they valued most. As Kohn states (1969: 19), "It tells us little to know merely that a parent values honesty for his child; the critical question is whether he values honesty more or less than self-control, or obedience, or some other valued characteristic." In our study the respondents were given a list of seven items descriptive of children, and they were asked to choose the two things "you have found nicest about little children."

The items on the list were:

1. When they listen to what you tell them to do.
2. When they are polite and well-behaved.
3. When they are clean and neat.
4. When they hug and kiss you.
5. When they learn to do something by themselves.
6. Playing with them.
7. When someone else tells you how smart the child is.

The first two seemed to relate to submissive or conforming behavior, and they correlated with the other variables in a similar manner. They were combined into a simple score which indicates whether the respondent chose neither, one, or both of them.

Though the relationships are not strong, the mothers and fathers of large families are more likely to choose the conformity items ($r = .12$ for men and .17 for women). The relationship does not seem to be spurious, for when we control for five variables (number of years since marriage, family income, education, number of marriages, and age at marriage), the relationship remains practically unchanged for men (partial $r = .10$) and is lowered, but not eliminated, for women (partial $r = .10$). In the case of women, education is the effective control factor. Further investigation showed that the association for women is largely from the higher-status women. For them partial $r = .18$; for lower-status women it is .05. The reason for this seems to be that lower-status women "don't need" many children to lead them into an emphasis on conformity. They generally emphasize conformity regardless of family size. With the possible exception of this group, however, additional children do increase the emphasis on conformity.

Family Size and Satisfaction. The picture the data have been painting does show that large families do have some extra burdens, but for men the evidence does not show that number of offspring affects satisfaction. In both SES groups family size is not related to frustration and unhappiness score, willingness to remarry, or ratings of self as a mate and parent. For lower-status females the picture is pretty much the same as it is for males in general. None of the items is related to number of children.

Higher-status women show a different pattern, however. With five variables held constant (number of years since marriage, family income, education, number of marriages, and parental SES), family size is importantly correlated with several key variables. High-status mothers of large families have higher scores on the frustration and unhappiness scale (partial $r = .21$), they are less likely to say they would remarry if they had their lives to live over again (partial $r = -.23$), they rate themselves a little lower as parents (partial $r = -.10$), they rate themselves lower on a scale which asks them to rate the quality of their lives (partial $r = -.09$). The only item on which they equal those with small families is the evaluation of themselves as spouses.

It is rather surprising that family size has no appreciable effect on the father's satisfaction. We were prepared for the effect to be greater for mothers despite data from white samples to the contrary (Nye, et al., 1970); after all, size of family has more day-to-day effect on mothers. We did not think, however, that men would "escape" in this matter. On the other hand, we were quite prepared for the SES interaction among the women. This finding is further support for the principle that family variables are of only modest relevance when the social situation is stacked against a person. For lower-status women the extra burden of additional children and the associated economic problems do not add a noticeable difference to the already high levels of dissatisfaction. Higher-status females, on the other hand, are more satisfied with life unless they have many children. Given their situation, they are likely to be the ones to say, "But for the children, things might have been different."

This kind of reasoning led us to believe that perhaps Christensen (1968: 28) was right when he suggested: "more important . . . than just how many children and how long between them is how successful the couple becomes in controlling number and spacing according to their desires, or also in adjusting their desires to conform with reality, or some of both—but, in any event, reducing the discrepancy between desire and occurrence." Generalized dissatisfaction does not come from having many children, but from having more than are wanted.

The interview schedule included, in a section far removed from the questions about number of children, items which asked, "If you could live your life over again, would you have children? If Yes: How many?" By comparing responses to these questions with the actual number of children, we get an indirect, and therefore probably more valid, measure of the respondent's satisfaction with the number of children he or she has.

As Christensen's remarks lead us to expect, this measure of "excess fertility" relates to general and marital satisfaction more strongly than does number of children. As may be seen in Table 4.1, excess fertility is related to frustration score and willingness to remarry when five variables are partialed out. We also see that people who have more children than they want tend to give a lower rating to the quality of their lives, but here the differences are small.

All of this says that the attitude variable is more important in its effects upon satisfaction, which may seem to indicate that structural features are not important. Further investigation suggests that such a conclusion is wrong. The correlation between number of children and excess fertility ranges from .60 to .70 in the various subgroups. Though number of children does not influence satisfaction, it is the antecedent of the variable which does. To exaggerate; people who feel they have too many children are less satisfied in general, but people don't feel they have too many children unless they have many. Structural features are relevant at least at one step removed.

The evidence on the short-run effects of family size do not give

Table 4.1. Zero-Order and Partial Correlations between Measure of Satisfaction with Number of Children and General Measures of Satisfaction; Parental SES, Education, Number of Years since Marriage, Marital Stability, and Family Income Constant (Currently Married Respondents)

	Frustration Score *		Would You Marry Again?		Evaluation of Self As Spouse		Evaluation of Self As Parent		Rating of Goodness of Life	
	Zero Order	5th Partial	Zero Order	5th Partial	Zero Order	5th Partial	Zero Order	5th Partial	Zero Order	5th Partial
Total sample	.21	.15	-.27	-.24	-.03	-.01	-.03	.00	-.07	-.06
Men	.15	.13	-.19	-.20	-.05	-.02	-.10	-.06	-.07	-.07
Women	.24	.13	-.30	-.24	-.02	.00	.00	.02	-.09	-.07
Low SES men	.15	.14	-.24	-.25	-.01	.00	-.07	-.06	-.05	-.03
High SES men	.08	.11	-.12	-.14	-.09	-.06	-.12	-.06	-.07	-.11
Low SES women	.13	.07	-.22	-.18	-.02	-.03	-.01	-.02	-.04	-.04
High SES women	.31	.27	-.37	-.35	-.01	.01	.06	.07	-.12	-.13

* Given the ways that the items are coded, we would expect a positive correlation for the frustration score and a negative correlation for the other items.

unequivocal support to the revisionist view of the large family. The mothers in such families are overburdened as predicted, but in only one of the subgroups, higher-status women, is there a relation between family size, per se, and various measures of parental satisfaction. Despite the problems many parents must find compensations in their large families.

On the other hand, these new data do not lead us to accept Bossard's view. The long-range effects were not what he would have predicted, and the short-run effects are by no means favorable to his view. He does, we think, underestimate the mother's burdens and exaggerate the extent to which there is a shifting of responsibilities and cooperation.

The data lead us to conclude that the view which is opposed to Bossard's is closer to the truth, though it does not quite hit it. There are certain tendencies in the large family which lead to heavy burdens, economic problems, etc. These tendencies are those suggested by the revisionist position, but that view has not developed sufficiently to completely encompass the complexity of the situation.

The question which remains is, do the short-term effects make sense of the long-term effects? We think so. Large families know greater poverty and this could contribute to the lessened education, income and happiness. In large families mothers carry heavy burdens, parents are more likely to value conformity, and parents are more dissatisfied, at least when they define their family as too large. All could contribute to the psychological differences we reported. They would seem to add up to a less happy and more restricted childhood which could lead to adults who are less happy and so forth.

conclusion

We find little support for Bossard's view that the large family provides an environment full of love, cooperation, balance, and sanity which, at the same time, prepares children for the realities of life. Adults from such families do not have the traits one would expect if Bossard's description were accurate, and the direct evidence on the nature of large families is only slightly more favorable.

At the same time, the recent revisionist view, though closer to the truth, is insufficiently developed. Our data suggest that it properly describes the tendencies of large families, but it does not adequately handle the complexities of the situation. It gives insufficient attention to the interaction between a structural feature and its context. Under some conditions the structural feature proves to have an important influence on a particular variable and under other conditions it does not. The revisionist view does not always provide a basis for handling this variation. But, it should be noted, the Bossard view is probably even less adequate on this score.

We do not have the key yet, but it seems, more often than not, that the better the person's general situation, the more important family size is. This leads us to the general idea that family variables are only one of the possible causes of certain undesirable outcomes. If these other causes are generally present in the environment the family variable will not be very predictive of outcomes. If the person does not get there by the family route he will get there by another. Family variables show high correlations only in environments in which the alternate routes are not commonly present.

All this be as it may, there are differences in long-term outcome. People from large families do not go as far in school. They have less income in the early years of their working lives, and they show some personality differences from people from smaller families. For example, in the higher-status group, people are more frustrated and unhappy if they come from a large family than if they come from a small one. The men in the sample are less assertive when they come from a large family. We believe that these can be understood as results of the short-term effects. Large families produce economic problems, conformity demands, etc., and these produce additional economic problems, unhappiness, and a lack of assertiveness.

In general, the critics seem to be right that the large family contributes to the problems of the black community, though they probably exaggerate the extent of the contribution. It certainly seems clear that if all black families were small, the economic situation of the next generation would not be markedly improved.

chapter five

the consequences
of
maternal control

The literature on the black family is replete with discussions of family dominance patterns, the next structural feature we will consider. Various authors tell us what the typical arrangements are and why they take these forms. In other sources we can find instruction on the economic consequences that maternal control has for males, or a consideration of the relationship between maternal control and maternal identification. Few aspects of the topic have not been the subject of an essay.

Despite the frequency with which such matters are discussed, it turns out that there are few data from black samples which bear upon the issues. The systematic empirical evidence is extremely limited in quantity and scope. Actually, most of it relates to the question of interracial differences in female power, and even this question has not been extensively studied, perhaps because "everyone knows the answers already" (see p. 18). It is our contention that actually little is known, and we hope to be able to fill in some of the gaps.

maternal control and parental admiration

In regard to one's own marriage, the question of who is to make the major decisions is likely to be viewed as an important one; but is the matter of any general significance? In the larger sense, does it make any difference who makes the decisions in the family?

The critics, of course, say that it does, but we will leave discussion of their views for later. We would note first that a number of theories suggest that the locus of family power does have consequences, particularly for the nature of the relationship between parent and child. Usually the main dependent variable is identification, the choice of a particular person as a role model, and the theories suggest that persons who control a situation are likely to be the objects of identification. This modeling is thought to have multiple sources. According to some theories it develops out of a desire to resemble the other because he or she has characteristics that one wishes to have. In other formulations it is a defensive identification. It occurs because of a desire to avoid punishments which will be received if there is a failure to "be as I am."

We do not have a measure of identification in the strict sense of that term, but we do have an index of parental preference: "When you were growing up, who did you admire or respect the most?" It is a simple matter to adapt the discussion of parental identification to this variable.[1] For in essence, admiration is the intervening variable in the first group of theories just described. The full process involved in this type of theory is clear: certain characteristics of a particular person, in this case his dominance, lead the child to admire that person, and in an attempt to be like the admired person the child is led to imitation (modeling).

Our hypothesis, therefore, is that offspring tend to admire the parent who was perceived to have "made the important decisions."

The data of Table 5.1 leave little room for doubt concerning the validity of the hypothesis.[2] Though mothers tend to garner the major share of admiration and respect in all cases, the extent to which mothers exceed fathers is strongly related to the control pattern the respondent perceived. In the total sample, in each parental SES group and for both sexes, mothers who made the important decisions were more likely to be admired than mothers who did not, and the differences tend to be large. The partial correlations range from .26 to .37 (see Table 5.1). The predictions of identification theory, as modified, are borne out.

This finding is sufficient to provide an answer to a central concern

1 The question does not require the respondent to choose one of his parents, but almost every respondent from an intact home did so.
2 The relevance of the control question to broken homes is not clear, so the data are limited to those who lived with both their real parents until they were 16.

Table 5.1. Percent Reporting They Admired Their Mothers Most by Responses to, "Who Made the Important Decisions in Your House?" by Parental SES and Sex (Respondents from Intact Homes)

Who Did You Admire? *	Total Sample		Lower PrSES		Higher PrSES	
	Mother Decided	Father Decided	Mother Decided	Father Decided	Mother Decided	Father Decided
	Men and Women					
Mother	84	54	82	53	86	54
Weighted N	835	766	435	356	399	406
Partial r †		.32		.31		.34
	Men					
Mother	85	57	81	57	89	56
Weighted N	368	381	170	185	198	192
Partial r †		.30		.26		.37
	Women					
Mother	83	51	83	49	83	53
Weighted N	467	385	265	171	201	214
Partial r †		.34		.36		.32

* Those who chose someone other than a parent, could not decide, or gave no answer are not included.

† Parental SES and age are controlled.

of this work. A family structural feature, maternal dominance in decision making, does influence other factors. We wish, however, to carry it further. Is this particular structure a key factor in parental identification or, as the theories in the field would suggest, is it only one of several "magnets" which attract identification? For example, Winch's (1962) theory of parental functionality suggests that we identify with the parent who makes the greater contribution to our welfare. Burton and Whiting's (1961) status-envy theory would suggest that the possession of any valued resource leads to heightened identification. Other theories would suggest we look at other kinds of power.

As before, these theories are directly transformable into theories we can test. The question becomes, what other routes, in addition to dominance in decision making, lead to admiration and respect in black families?

In view of previous findings, a logical next question is, does power over the child also lead to admiration and respect by the child, or is it only dominance over someone else which has the effect? In this case, does the major agent of punishment get more admiration and respect? The answer is in contrast to the previous material. Though there is a relationship, it is quite weak and it is not universal. It is clearly present for males (partial $r = .14$ and $.13$ in the two parental SES groups) but it is limited to females from lower-status backgrounds (partial $r = .12$). For high-status females there is no relation (partial $r = -.05$). In contrast to what the defensive-identification idea would suggest, it is only for some segments of the black community that power over an individual produces admiration from that individual. With one minor exception, however, being the punishing agent does not reduce admiration.

Even this statement glosses over some of the complications of the matter. Additional data show that the effects of making the decisions and of being the agent of punishment are entangled with each other. Making the decisions always increases the admiration garnered, regardless of whether one is the punishing agent or not. When decision-making power is controlled, the effect of punishing becomes unclear.

What it boils down to is that making decisions is the more significant variable. Its effect is large and consistent in all subgroups, and it is independent of who does the punishing. Punishing does not have a clear, independent effect.

Making the decisions and punishing refer to control over two categories of persons, spouses and children. What about control over resources? Does that affect the amount of admiration and respect received from offspring? Specifically in terms of the variables available to us, does the parent who "keeps track of the family money" get more respect from the children?

For both sexes, there is a relation between taking care of the finances and admiration, but it is much stronger in the case of males (partial $r = .19$) than it is for females ($.08$). Furthermore, for both sexes the relation is, in effect, limited to the higher parental SES (partial $r = .35$ for high-status males and $.10$ for high-status females). When we control for "who makes the decisions" the picture becomes complex. Both variables have an independent effect for males from higher-status backgrounds, but in all the other groups, only "Who made the decisions?" has a clear independent effect. Again it becomes clear that making decisions is the key factor.

Though control over decisions is most important, we have just suggested that the other control items may also have independent effects, at least in some subgroups. One wonders then if we can predict maternal and paternal admiration better from knowledge of the three control items just discussed than solely from knowledge of who made the decisions. Are the three control items cumulative in their effects? Using the index of maternal control we find that the associations are, in every subgroup, lower for this measure than they are for the single item of who made the decisions. The importance of decision making is again indicated.

The theories of identification say that either sex can gain admiration by exceeding the other in some desirable trait, and power is only one of several such traits. We will inquire next into the importance of power relative to other potential sources of admiration.

First, does a parent gain preference by exceeding the spouse in education? When we simply run "Who did you admire?" against the relative level of mother's and father's education, the data seem to answer that question with an unambiguous "yes." If the mother had a higher level of education, she is chosen as most admired by 71 percent of the respondents. If the parents' educational levels were within one year of each other, the woman is chosen by 68 percent of the respondents, and if the man had more education the woman is chosen in only 60 percent of the cases. The differences are, however, small (partial $r = .08$).

Furthermore, the matter is not that simple. In fact, these findings are quite misleading. Higher education leads to enhanced admiration *only* when it is associated with decision making. As may be seen in Table 5.2, when the two go together levels of admiration and respect are very high. But if a person, particularly a man, does not translate his educational advantage into decision making his children's respect for him declines. It is not enough to have desirable social characteristics. You must use them if you are to be admired.

Winch's (1962) and Scanzoni's (1971) work suggests, the more functional the parent, the greater will be the identification of the offspring with that parent. In ending this section, we will test related hypotheses dealing with parental admiration. On the assumption that working mothers are seen as making a greater contribution to the family than nonworking women, we would expect that working mothers would have a higher level of admiration and respect. Similarly, we would predict that men who have always been employed would thereby increase their admiration and respect.

The basic data do not completely support the hypotheses. There are only trivial effects associated with the working status of the mother and with father's unemployment (partial $r = .08, .09$). However, as is usually the case, this gross comparison hides important facts. The relation for both variables is larger in the higher-status groups. For these

Table 5.2.   Responses to "Who Did You Admire or Respect the Most?" by Responses to, "Who Made the Important Decisions in Your House" by Relative Level of Father's and Mother's Education (Respondents from Intact Homes)

Who Did You Admire? *	Father Had More Education	
	Father Decided	Mother Decided
Father	64%	5%
Weighted N	101	62
Gamma	.94	
	Mother Had More Education	
	Father Decided	Mother Decided
Mother	58%	87%
Weighted N	297	272
Gamma	.66	

* Those who chose someone other than a parent, could not decide, or gave no answer are not included.

groups the partials are .15 and .17 for mother working and father unemployed respectively. For the lower SES they are nil. It seems quite clear that working wives and unemployed fathers are more likely to be taken for granted in the lower-status group and therefore one does not gain or lose admiration by one's standing in this regard. Among higher-status blacks, however, both variables have an influence upon children's attitudes.

In the case of father unemployment, the relationship in the higher-status group is not affected by controlling for decision-making power. Unemployment in this group lowers esteem whether or not the man controls the decision-making apparatus. Decision making has a stronger effect, but employment status has at least an independent effect.

For mother working, on the other hand, the power arrangement again serves to give meaning to the behavior. If a high-status working wife is seen as the decision maker in the family she is given almost universal admiration ($\gamma = .77$). However, if the father makes the decisions, the higher-status working wife does not receive greater admiration than the nonworking wife. In fact, in the eyes of her daughters she has slightly less respect.

The pattern revealed in this section is clear. For these families the road to respect from their children is paved with decisions won from the spouse. As the theories of identification would suggest, other factors also contribute, but there seems little doubt that they are secondary to decision-making control as a source of admiration. Even when these other variables have a clear independent effect, the nature of that effect is generally influenced by the individual's standing in regard to decision making. The very meaning of these other variables seems to depend upon the power arrangement. What is an admirable trait in a powerful person may be defined as undesirable in one with less power.

Maternal Dominance and Personality. Many would suggest that maternal control has influences which go beyond those we have noted. Specifically, maternal control is often assumed to have important effects on the masculinity of male offspring.

The exact nature of these effects is a matter of dispute. According to some, the line runs: control leads to admiration, admiration leads to identification (modeling), and identification leads to similarity. If we accept the notion that males will provide different models, it would logically follow that a man who comes from a female-controlled home would be more "feminine" than one whose household was male controlled.

Others suggest, however, that this is an oversimplified view of the situation. They argue that it is likely that a man brought up in a female-centered home will at some point realize that his behavior is "sex-inappropriate," and in an attempt to prove to himself and others that he is a complete man he will react against his feminine inclinations and exhibit a pattern of "exaggerated masculinity." Thus, completely opposed behaviors are viewed as being consistent with the idea. (For a discussion of the related case of the male who grows up in a household in which there are no adult males see Hannerz [1969], and p. 98.)

We have no adequate measure of exaggerated masculinity,[3] but we can test the alternate hypothesis, if the reader will accept that feminine behavior is simply behavior more common among females. The women in our sample will serve to define feminine behavior by their responses to the items we will consider. Of course, the theoretical question is, do men from mother-controlled homes show behavior which resembles their mothers; but obviously we cannot get the mothers' responses. Responses from contemporary black women, though not without problems, will have to do. The test is a weak one, however, and must be viewed as a first approximation.

Since decision making has the strongest association with the assumed intervening variable, we will use the responses to the decision-making question as the basis for classifying families as mother or father controlled. The hypothesis is: black men who grew up in unbroken homes where the mother made the important decisions are closer to black women in behavior than are men who grew up in "male-controlled" homes.

Specifically, the hypothesis will be supported if (1) there is a difference between the men of the two groups and (2) those from female-dominated homes are either close to the females or between the females and the other male group. If there is no sex difference on the item it is, of course, irrelevant to the present concern. If males and females do not differ, the lessons available will be the same regardless of parental preference.

The first thing that became clear when we began to look into this matter was that sex was not importantly related to many of the variables. We started with a long list of questions which we thought would

---

3 To say that a group shows exaggerated masculinity implies that the masculine response is very common in the group and that it is particularly strong when it occurs. We can determine whether the former is true, but we have no evidence bearing upon the latter. Thus, we may have a basis for rejecting the exaggerated masculinity hypothesis, but we will not have a basis for accepting it.

be proper tests, but most of them turned out to be irrelevant because there were no differences between males and females.[4] This in itself is of importance. Even if the hypotheses prove to be correct, the finding would be of limited applicability. It often does not matter whether a person admires his mother or father because they provide similar models.

Several items relating to assertiveness and docility did show sex differences, but data from them (Table 5.3) do not favor the hypothesis. These 8 variables permit 16 tests with parental SES controlled, and even with a rather generous definition, 7 or 8 at most can be counted as providing support.[5] An additional 4 variables, church attendance, attitude toward the death penalty, trustfulness, and attitude toward affection from children, also showed sex differences, and they provide additional tests. The support from these was even less strong than from the assertiveness items; only 2 of 8 comparisons are consistent with the prediction. It must be concluded that men from female-dominated homes are not more likely to show feminine traits.

There are several possible reasons for the failure of the hypothesis. It might simply be that the exaggerated masculinity [6] hypothesis is correct, or on the other hand the parents might not be important socializing agents for these behaviors. They may be learned from peers. Attempts at modeling may be unsuccessful, perhaps because some of these matters are not communicated from parent to child. Or modeling may not be the key mechanism.

It could also be that our independent variable is too far removed from the dependent variables. The immediate cause for the assumed similarity is identification, the "cause" of identification is admiration, and you have to go back another step before you come to the independent variable we used, maternal control. We know that maternal control is related to admiration, and we assume that admiration leads to modeling, but these associations are weak, and therefore there is considerable "slippage" at each point. Given the inadequacies of mea-

4 For example, the sexes did not differ in regard to several measures of anxiety regarding interracial interaction, and on items dealing with willingness to defer gratification, optimism, external-internal control, etc.

5 See, for example, item 1 for higher PrSES and item 3 for lower PrSES.

6 This does not seem to be the case, for there were only 5 instances in which the feminine response was less common among men from mother-dominated homes than it was among those from father-dominated families.

Table 5.3. Percentages Giving Specified Responses to Various Items by Respondents' Sex and Sex of the Major Decision Maker in the Family of Orientation, Controlled by Parental SES (Respondents from Intact Homes)

| | Lower PrSES | | | Higher PrSES | | |
| | | Men | | | Men | |
	Women	Mother Decided	Father Decided	Women	Mother Decided	Father Decided
1. Do you feel mad or sad when you hear about discrimination? *						
(Sad)	57	41	38	54	50	40
2. Do you ever feel you would like to get even with whites?						
(No)	73	61	59	64	62	69
3. Do you remember the last time you got angry?						
(No)	35	38	53	27	41	36
4. Have you ever been in a real fight as an adult?						
(No)	80	57	72	82	71	71
5. Would you buy a house in a white neighborhood if there might be trouble?						
(No or depends)	63	53	57	50	54	43
6. Are you careful not to make a bad impression on whites?						
(Frequently or sometimes)	53	53	40	44	49	40
7. Interviewer's rating of respondent's cooperativeness.						
(Very cooperative)	74	81	72	81	82	74
8. Reaction to a nasty white: avoidist, educative, aggressive.						
(Avoidist)	47	55	34	48	51	51
9. What do you find nicest about little children?						
(When they hug and kiss you)	14	9	4	12	13	12
10. Frequency of church attendance.						
(Once a week or more)	37	26	24	32	18	32
11. The death sentence for murder should be abolished.						
(Agree)	57	48	56	50	55	61
12. Most people can be trusted.						
(Agree)	28	37	39	37	34	34

* The items are paraphrased.

surement and the presence of other causal factors, it may be expecting too much to assume that the original hypothesis would receive strong support.

In an attempt to clarify the situation, we repeated our investigation starting a little closer to the dependent variable. We related parental admiration to the 12 behavioral items and obtained 15 positive results from 24 tests rather than the 9 or 10 obtained before (Table 5.4). Furthermore, several of the positive results were more substantial than those obtained when maternal dominance was used as the independent variable. Thus, maternal admiration has some relation to sex-linked traits but maternal control does not, probably because its tie to admiration is not sufficiently strong. We might also add that none of this proves that modeling is the key mechanism. It may simply be that the conscious teachings of mothers and fathers differ somewhat and we

Table 5.4.   Percentages Giving Specified Responses to Various Items by Respondents' Sex and Mother or Father Preference, Controlled by Parental SES (Respondents from Intact Homes)

	Lower PrSES			Higher PrSES		
		Men			Men	
	Women	Preferred Mother	Preferred Father	Women	Preferred Mother	Preferred Father
1. Do you feel mad or sad when you hear about discrimination? *						
(Sad)	57	46	35	54	44	36
2. Do you ever feel you would like to get even with whites?						
(No)	73	64	52	64	58	70
3. Do you remember the last time you got angry?						
(No)	35	49	50	27	38	38
4. Have you ever been in a real fight as an adult?						
(No)	80	67	70	82	64	75
5. Would you buy a house in a white neighborhood if there might be trouble?						
(No or depends)	63	58	60	50	49	30
6. Are you careful not to make a bad impression on whites?						
(Frequently or sometimes)	53	51	68	44	46	65
7. Interviewer's rating of respondent's cooperativeness.						
(Very cooperative)	74	78	65	81	82	73
8. Reaction to a nasty white: avoidist, educative, aggressive.						
(Avoidist)	47	47	43	48	56	41
9. What do you find nicest about little children?						
(When they hug and kiss you)	14	6	3	12	16	3
10. Frequency of church attendance.						
(Once a week or more)	37	25	20	32	24	16
11. The death sentence for murder should be abolished.						
(Agree)	57	55	64	50	57	66
12. Most people can be trusted.						
(Agree)	28	38	50	37	32	41

* The items are paraphrased.

accept the teaching of the admired parent; or, most probably, the mechanism is a combination of imitation and conscious teaching. All we can say with assurance is that admiration for the mother does have a small relation to a son's behavior.[7]

Before a final conclusion can be reached, an additional point must be considered. Students of identification almost invariably are concerned with the identification of males and the effects that they have upon male behavior. Almost no attention is paid to the situation of women, though the theory would seem equally applicable to them. In a male-dominated home women are, we have already seen, more likely to admire their fathers than are women who grew up in a home in which their mothers made the decisions. The relationship is about as strong as it is for men. And if the theory is correct, women who prefer their fathers should demonstrate more masculine behavior.

The evidence indicates almost no connection between paternal control in the parental home and masculine behavior in adult women. Only 6 of the 24 comparisons we made support the idea. When paternal admiration is used, there is at most one additional bit of supporting evidence. It must be concluded that neither father control nor admiration of the father leads women to masculine behavior.

In general, we would conclude that patterns of parental control and admiration are not important determinants of sex-linked behaviors. In no case is control by the opposite-sex parent associated with behavior in the offspring which is typical of the opposite sex. For males, admiration does show some relation, but it is not strong. Furthermore, it is not replicated for women, and they are equally relevant for the test of the theory.

Maternal Dominance and the Respondent's Marriage. Even though maternal control has little effect on sex-linked behavior, it may still be related to other behavior. In fact, it seems quite logical that the pattern of dominance in the family would be related to the occurrence, timing, and outcome of the son's marriage. Maternal control is related

---

7 There is, of course, another possibility. We are assuming that admiration for mother when growing up is the causal factor. It could be that men with certain traits are more willing to admit that they admired their mothers more than their fathers, or such men may be more likely to claim that that was the case whether it was or not.

to maternal admiration, and it has been suggested that males who are closely tied to their mothers make slower courtship progress (Johnson, 1963; Winch, 1943).

It would also seem likely that a strong tie between mother and son would have an influence upon the marriage, though it is not clear whether in sum this would be a positive or negative one. A continued tie to the mother might be a point of contention between husband and wife, or it might suggest that the husband will have less trouble "getting along" with his wife. It is not even necessary to consider the intervening variable of identification to tie maternal control to characteristics of the respondent's marriage. The dominance patterns in the family of origin probably have a direct effect upon the offsprings' role concepts and their evaluation of marriage as an institution.

The data support the hypothesis that men from mother-dominated unbroken homes are less likely to marry. Taking all age groups together, among lower-status men 17 percent of those from mother-dominated homes have never married as opposed to 11 percent of those from father-dominated homes (partial $r = .09$). For men of higher-status background the difference is considerably greater; the percentages are 30 and 12 (partial $r = .17$).

It seems, however, that these findings are not due to the intervening effect of the admiration variable, for there is no clear relation between parental admiration and marriage rate. It may simply be that marriage does not seem so attractive to men who have seen their fathers dominated by their mothers.

Men from mother-controlled homes show in addition, slightly higher broken-marriage rates, 30 percent as compared with 22 percent. (Pearson $r = .09$). When we control parental SES, education, age at marriage, and number of years since marriage the association remains about the same. However, further analysis reveals that the relation lacks consistency. For lower-status males the difference is 15 percentage points (partial $r = .14$). However there is an indication, based on small N's, that most of this is due to the men who marry before 20 (partial $r = .32$). For men who marry later the relationship is weak (partials $= .09, .11$). For men from higher-status background mother-dominance leads to stable marriages if they marry young (partial $r = -.34$) and the opposite is true if they marry at later ages. The partial is .11 both for men who marry between the ages of 21 and 24 and for those who marry after 24. Again, however, the N's are small, so caution is necessary.

It is clear that the pattern of dominance in the family of orientation does not have strong influence on characteristics of the male respondent's marriage. In general, maternal control is associated with a lessened likelihood of marriage and a higher rate of broken marriage. In the case of broken marriage, however, there is a reversal of the relation in one subgroup, and for both variables there are subgroups where the association is trivial. Furthermore, there does not seem to be any pattern to the variation. We would tentatively conclude that maternal dominance has a small effect on marriage rate, but no effect on broken-marriage rate except under special circumstances.

the critics v. the black family

So far, maternal control in unbroken homes has not proven to be a very powerful causal factor, but it still remains for us to test the major charges against it. Though it frequently takes a back seat to the broken home as the villain of the piece, the so-called matriarchal structure of the black family has been charged with similar and almost equally serious "crimes." Moynihan, et al. (1965: 29) state it forcefully: "In essence, the Negro community has been forced into a matriarchal structure which, because it is so out of line with the rest of the American society, seriously retards the progress of the group as a whole, and imposes a crushing burden on the Negro male and, in consequence, on a great many Negro women as well."

For the dubious, the critics provide a number of reasons why one would expect a matriarchal structure to have bad effects in the long run. Moynihan himself says that there is nothing wrong with female dominance, per se; it is just that, "it is clearly a disadvantage for a minority group to be operating on one principle, while the great majority of the population, and the one with the most advantages to begin with, is operating on another" (Moynihan, et al. 1965: 29). He then quotes others to the effect that female dominance leads to the favoring of

daughters, increasing bitterness on the part of husbands, female transmission of the culture, inadequate socialization for work, etc. These in
turn lead to the "tangle of pathology."

The existing literature provides no data bearing upon the question.
The "evidence" presented in this section of the Moynihan report is almost entirely beside the point, and no one else seems to have systematically studied the long-range effects of childhood in a female-
dominated stable home. Our data do not touch on all aspects of the
tangle of pathology, but they are quite sufficient to test the claim
regarding achievement. Here we will use the index of maternal control
since it comes closest to the concept the critics use.

In general we may say that maternal dominance does not have the
effects attributed to it. For example, education level achieved is unrelated to maternal control. Men from the most female-dominated families have an average of 10.6 years of education. Those from the male-
dominated families average 10.8 years. Furthermore, the high school
grades of men from various family types are almost identical.

The respondent's income does show some variation when parental
SES is controlled, but one has to be very selective if he wishes to use
this fact as evidence against "matriarchal" families. If the respondent
comes from a higher-SES family and his mother dominated in none of
the three areas, his income is about $700 higher than that of men in
the other three categories ($r = -.06$; see Table 5.5). But if his background was lower status, he does somewhat better the more dominant
his mother was. The range is somewhat less than in the higher-status
group, but the trend is more consistent ($r = .07$). When age, education, and parental SES are controlled by means of partial correlation
there are no important changes; the partials are $-.05$ and $.09$.

It seems, then, that there is some slight relation between parental
power arrangements and achievement, but the critics' view of it is inaccurate. Among lower-status men, if it matters at all it seems better
for achievement if there is female control.

It seems strange that this would not have been expected. We are
frequently told that lower-status women are more achevement-oriented
than their husbands, and it would seem logical that it would be preferable for them to be dominant in the family so that they would be more
influential in their sons' socialization. But the idea that it is bad for
black families to be female dominated is very strongly entrenched.

Table 5.5.   Mean Income of Males by Maternal Control Score by Parental SES (Respondents from Intact Homes Who Are Not Full-Time Students)

	Maternal Control Score	Mean Income	Weighted N
Total sample	0	$6,132	212
	1	5,519	271
	2	5,992	314
	3	5,846	205
	Pearson $r = -.01$ Partial $r* = .01$		
Lower PrSES	0	$5,656	96
	1	5,514	157
	2	5,877	150
	3	6,022	93
	Pearson $r = .07$ Partial $r* = .09$		
Higher PrSES	0	$6,438	112
	1	5,526	114
	2	6,098	164
	3	5,701	112
	Pearson $r = -.06$ Partial $r* = -.05$		

* Parental SES, education, and age are controlled.

The depth of this acceptance is indicated by Bernard's (1966a: 123–24) comment, "It is interesting that at the lowest socio-economic levels, the wife-dominant family was associated in the Straus study with the highest level of achievement orientation [among white boys]. This type is common among Negroes, as Blood and Wolfe have reported, but because the Negro wife is dominant not by choice but by default, it is doubtful that the same relationships would be obtained in a sample of Negro boys."

conclusion

While the sex of the decision maker in the family of origin does have some correlation with other variables, it does not seem to have the significance which has been attributed to it. It has a major influence on which parent will be admired, but the relation between parental admiration and other variables is not very strong, so that road leads nowhere.

Maternal control produces admiration, and maternal admiration has a slight influence on the few personality and behavioral items which have a sex link in this sample. The connections are, however, generally tenuous, and therefore knowledge of the sex of the dominant parent tells us little about the personality of males. For women it tells even less.

The problem may be that control does not always lead to admiration, and admiration does not always lead to attempts at modeling. When modeling is attempted it is not always successful.

More than this, modeling may be less important than direct teaching, and the dominant parent may not be the main teaching agent. Even if he or she is, there is no assurance that the lesson will be "Be like me." Parents tailor their lessons to the sex of the child, and though a man's view of what a boy should be may not be the same as a woman's, her view is not going to be that he should be like her. All things taken together, it is hardly surprising that the associations were so weak.

Maternal control in the family of origin does seem to reduce the attractiveness of marriage for the male offspring, and this connection is simply explained. People form their view of marriage from their observation of other marriages—particularly their parents'. A maternally dominated family would give marriage a "bad name" in the eyes of many men. It is not clear whether men from female-dominated homes fail more often in marriage. There appears to be a tendency in that direction, but the trend is not consistent across subgroups.

Finally, maternally controlled homes do not necessarily lead to lowered achievement, as the critics suggest. In the lower-status group, the one that most interests them, the effect is just the opposite. Here, maternal dominance leads to *slightly* higher income for sons—a finding which is not surprising in view of the reputed higher achievement orientation of black lower-status women.

In general, the evidence shows that the effects of one aspect of the "black matriarchy" have been exaggerated. We will turn later to the other, and supposedly key element, the female-headed home; but next let us consider another aspect of the internal workings of the family; the degree of husband-wife companionship.

chapter six

patterns of interaction
with
spouse and kin

One of the many variations on an old saw suggests that the family
that plays together stays together, and in this we find the key to the
charge against the family which lacks husband-wife companionship,
the family which shows conjugal role segregation. Rainwater (1970:
156) states, ''This pattern of conjugal role segregation accurately char-
acterizes the marital relations of Pruitt-Igoe husbands and wives. It
highlights as particularly problematic the issues of loyalty, intimacy
and stability.'' As he sees it, conjugal role segregation leads to scarce
resources being invested outside the family, and it may also cause jeal-
ousy, embarrassment, and conflict, particularly if it is associated with
sexual infidelity.

Though Rainwater speaks of marital stability, we will have to
revise the charge before testing it, as we can measure degree of segregation only for existing marriages. We can relate indices of marital
and general satisfaction to integration, and this seems an adequate way
to test the basic idea lying behind the assertion.

As will be remembered, we have two indices of the extent of joint
activity. These are the number of different activities engaged in with
spouse—the companionship index—and the measure of spousal integration, the ratio of ''with-spouse'' activities to total activities
engaged in. The latter seems closer to the concept used by Rainwater
and others, and therefore we will use it here. It should be noted, however, that the two indices are highly correlated ($r = .80$). The results to
be reported would have been about the same if the companionship
index had been used. Nonetheless, for conceptual clarity the reader
must keep in mind that we are dealing with a ratio and not the absolute
number of activities. A person can score high on spousal integration

even if he or she does little with the spouse. In such a case, all that is required is that activities with outsiders also be limited.[1]

As is shown in Table 6.1, in the total sample high conjugal integration is related to low frustration and to favorable responses to an index of marital satisfaction, the question on whether the respondent would marry if he had his life to live over again. The Pearson r's are small, .16 and .10, but these figures may be somewhat misleading. There appears to be some curvilinearity to the relationship. Satisfaction increases as integration increases, but it falls off somewhat at the

Table 6.1.   Zero-Order and 4th Order Partial Correlations between Index of Conjugal Integration and Measures of Satisfaction; Parental SES, Respondent's Age, Length of Present Marriage and Age at First Marriage Constant

	Frustration Score		Would You Marry Again?	
	Zero Order	4th Partial	Zero Order	4th Partial
Total sample *	−.16	−.14	.10	.08
Men	−.08	−.07	.07	.06
Women	−.21	−.20	.12	.10
Low SES men	−.01	−.02	.00	.00
High SES men	−.12	−.14	.15	.15
Low SES women	−.17	−.16	.10	.09
High SES women	−.25	−.25	.11	.10

* Given the way that the items are coded, the expectation is that the frustration score would show a negative correlation and the measure of marital satisfaction a positive relation.

top of the integration scale. From low to high integration the percentages of respondents who said they would marry again are: 63, 71, 75, 81, 72. The corresponding frustration scores are 1.57, .10, −.08, −2.14, −.71. Very high levels of togetherness reduce satisfaction somewhat.

Furthermore, the relations are not spurious; they hold up when parental SES, respondent's SES, length of present marriage, and age at marriage are partialed out. The strength of the relation varies, however, among the different subgroups. The correlations are somewhat higher for the women than the men, but this is due to the fact that the correlation is effectively zero for lower-status males. For high-status

1 If the respondent reported that he engaged in none of the activities on the list, the case was omitted in analyses which use spousal integration.

males, the correlation is about .15. There is, then, no question for 3 of the subgroups that conjugal segregation is associated with lessened satisfaction.

The reason for the variation is not certain, but it may be related to differential stress placed on the value of joint conjugal activities. Women and higher-status men probably give a central place to joint activities in their conception of a good marriage. Therefore, if they do not have such activities they feel cheated and their satisfaction is reduced. For lower-status men the matter may be of less significance, and failure to achieve the norm less disturbing.

All this assumes, of course, that joint activities are the independent factors, as the charge suggests, but we cannot be sure of that. It is also reasonable to suggest that the correlations obtained are due to the fact that people tend to associate with those they like. Satisfaction may be cause and integration the effect. Or, the relation may be reciprocal: we engage in joint activities when we are satisfied with our relations with the other, and interaction with the other increases our satisfaction.

In circumstances such as this where the time order is not clear conceptually, it is difficult to sort out cause and effect. Our findings suggest however, that conjugal integration does have some causal effect. If satisfaction produced the interaction, the correlations should be higher for males, and particularly for lower-status males, since they probably have greater control over the extent of shared activities relative to nonconjugal activities. The correlations are, however, lower in these groups. Also, if satisfaction produced integration we would expect the highest satisfaction to be associated with the greatest interaction, and this is not so.

Of course, the issue is not settled by these considerations, but they do seem to say that interaction has some causal significance, while at the same time they do not deny the possibility of a reciprocal relation. On this basis, we would accept the validity of the general charge that conjugal role segregation is productive of dissatisfaction; but at the same time, we would emphasize that the relationship is probably reciprocal and that the generalization does not hold for the lower-status male.

Having seen that the extent of conjugal role segregation is related to satisfaction, we will now look at each activity separately to see if any are of particular importance. Do some activities influence satisfaction more than others? Are there any which have a negative relation to satisfaction?

For the separate items, it seems appropriate to switch to a measure comparable to the companionship index. On this measure one category includes those who engaged in the activity with their spouses; the other category includes both those who did not engage in the activity at all and those who did it, but not with their spouses.

The data are too complex to present here, but a few of the highlights may be noted. First, it is clear that there is no item which has a consistent negative relation to the satisfaction variables. In most cases a report that the respondent engaged in a specific joint activity is associated with less frustration and a greater willingness to marry. In the several SES and sex subgroups only 14 of 72 correlations are negative, and only 3 of these exceed $-.10$. (The highest is $-.13$.) Furthermore, 8 of the negative correlations are found in the lower-status male subgroup—a group which we know does not fit the generalization. There is no evidence that joint participation in certain activities is generally counterproductive for satisfaction.

Second, there is no particular activity which has an outstandingly strong relation to both satisfaction variables in all subgroups. A few of the items show Pearsons of .20 or higher—the highest is .26—but the existence of a high correlation for one subgroup does not necessarily suggest that this will be the case for other subgroups. The most consistent item is the one having to do with conversation. In all subgroups people who reported they had recently had a long conversation with their spouses about something interesting show a moderately strong tendency to report satisfaction. None of the other items show much consistency. The implication is that for different groups different kinds of activities are most relevant for satisfaction. In general, however, we would suggest that the extent of integration permits better prediction than the character of the activity.

Role Segregation and Self-Evaluation. The critics' interest in patterns of spousal integration is limited to its relation to marital stability and conflict, but there is an additional matter we ought to look into. Earlier we interpreted our data as indicating that 3 of the 4 subgroups desired role integration. Now we turn to a closely related question, do blacks consider the achievement of role integration a measure of their worth as a spouse? Is there a positive correlation between spousal integration and evaluation of self as spouse?

The data show only a very small relationship. For the total sample partial $r = .06$, with parental SES, respondent's SES, length of present marriage, and age at marriage controlled. For males, regardless of social status, there is a slight tendency for higher spousal integration to be associated with higher self-evaluation (partial $r = .08$ for higher-status men and .12 for those of lower SES). For higher-status women the correlation is .16, but for lower-status women it is reversed (partial $r = -.07$). For them, the less the conjugal integration the higher the self-evaluation.

It would seem that the relationship between integration and self-evaluation is weak. The details of the relation are complex and puzzling, but in general it seems that many people who do not achieve integration do not think any the worse of themselves. This would suggest that the norm favoring integration is weak, at least in some groups. The argument would run: if the norm were strong, a person who did not achieve integration would be negatively evaluated by himself and others, and this would lead to a low evaluation of "self as spouse." Since degree of integration is weakly tied to self-evaluation, the norm must be weak.

For the separate items the correlations are lower than they were when satisfaction items were the dependent variables. The highest is .16 and only 6 of the 36 are .10 or above.

the extended household

The general consensus tends to be that some kin interaction is desirable, but there is, after all, a limit. In the opinion of many that limit is passed when an extended household is set up. As Parsons (1942:616) puts it, "It is of course common for other relatives to share a household with the conjugal family, but this scarcely ever occurs without some important elements of strain."

Parsons had in mind the middle-class white family when he wrote this, but similar views have been expressed with regard to black families. Bernard (1966a: 130) suggests that multigenerational households produce crowding and "disturbing effects on the family," and Scanzoni (1971: 134–35) states "the independently based conjugal unit is seemingly the family form best suited to move about and to be flexible enough to take advantage of whatever economic opportunities arise."

Of course, the multigenerational household does have some defenders, but the majority seem to accept the negative view. What is needed in any case is some systematic data; for as Udry (1974: 290) said in writing about white families, "There is really no definitive evidence that shared living arrangements are more productive of stress than separate arrangements. Evidently, American values in support of separate households are so strong that even social scientists have not thought it worthwhile to demonstrate the benefits."

If the charges are correct, people in extended households should have higher levels of frustration and unhappiness as measured by our frustration index. In fact, if the effect is as strong as it is sometimes made out to be, those who are living in extended households might be more likely to say they would not marry again if they had the chance to do it all over again.

The data indicate, to begin with, that currently married people living in extended-family households are only a little more frustrated. The correlation is .06 with parental SES, SES, age at marriage, and number of years since marriage held constant. This difference must be considered trivial. Furthermore, the relation is consistently small. The "effect" upon males and females is about the same, and the correlations are not much higher in any age group. They reach their maximum in the youngest age group, .08 for males, .11 for females.

The data on willingness to marry are similar. The relation in the total sample and for males and females separately is trivial. When we look at each age group separately we find the expected relation only for the younger respondents. They are less certain they would marry if they live in an extended household (partial $r = .16$ for young males, $-.08$ for those 29–36, and $-.09$ for the oldest group). Among the females the relationship are .07 for the youngest, .14 for those in the middle, and .00 for those 37–45). In general, we must conclude that the relation between multigenerational living and satisfaction is weak and inconsistent.

There is a possibility, however, that we are missing something.

The people in the extended-household group are of two kinds, those who live with their own relatives and those who are living with in-laws. Though many would suggest that the two situations are equally bad, others would make a distinction between them. In addition we have lumped together those who live with their parents, those who live with their married children, and those who live with ''other relatives.'' Each of these might have a different relationship to satisfaction. It seems wise to determine if the small differences we have found are due to the grossness of the categories we have used up to this point.

It seems beyond question that this is not the case. When we compare those who lived with their parents [2] with those who lived in a nuclear household we get about the same results as when we compare those who lived with their parents-in-law with the nuclear group. For frustration scores all the correlations hover around zero. The responses to the question regarding willingness to marry do not show much more of a relation. Those who live with their parents do not differ in any consistent way from those who live in a nuclear household, and males who live with their in-laws are actually somewhat more willing to remarry (partial $r = -.09$).

All in all, we would conclude that living in an extended household has at most, a minor effect upon the satisfaction of married blacks. This is not to say that there are no strains associated with extended-family living. To quote Udry again (1974: 291), ''Tensions are inherent in *any* living arrangement. The legitimate question which has not been answered is 'are there significantly more tensions present in living together arrangements over separate households?' '' The answer we would provide for this black sample is that these tensions are not significantly greater.

The Multigeneration Household and Self-Evaluation. It is not possible to formulate general hypotheses about the relationship between residence in a multigenerational household and self-evaluation, for much depends on who is living with whom and the aspect of self-evaluation involved. However, if we start from the assumption that

2 Most of the respondents in extended households were living with their parents or in-laws. The other possibilities occurred too rarely to permit separate analysis.

such households are defined as abnormal and undesirable, more specific hypotheses are possible. For example, a married man who lives in an extended-family household should have a low evaluation of himself as a spouse, since he is "failing" to provide his wife with an independent home. However, if his in-laws are living with him we would expect a high evaluation of self as spouse since he is helping his wife's family. If he has taken in his parents, this should increase his self-evaluation in regard to his performance as a son. For a woman we would expect similar effects, but they will probably be smaller for she will get less credit or blame, since it is usually assumed that she has less control over the situation.

The data give almost no support to the idea that living with their parents is viewed by men as evidence that they have failed in their duty as a spouse. The correlation is in the right direction; it shows such men rate themselves lower as spouses, but the partial r is only .06. For women it is in the opposite direction ($-.07$). Furthermore, men who are the main wage earners and report that their parents-in-law live with them are not appreciably more likely to rate themselves higher as a spouse than those in nuclear households (partial $r = -.04$). The partial for women is $-.02$. In general we would conclude that people's opinion of their value as spouses is not influenced by the presence or absence of parents or in-laws in the home.

Another indication that this is not a crucial matter emerges when we look at people's evaluations of themselves as offspring. Men who are main wage earners rate themselves higher as sons if their parents live with them, but the partial r is again minute (.03). For women, the correlation is equally low.

It is clear then that multigenerational households do not have the negative effects which have been attributed to them. They do not seem productive of greater problems; those who live in them are not more dissatisfied than others, and their effects upon self-evaluation are minor. This is another aspect of the black family which does not have the negative consequences that have been attributed to it. And at the same time that we acquit the black family in this matter, we also bring into question more general notions that the sharing of a household with other relatives "scarcely ever occurs without some important elements of strain."

the income of multi-generational households

Before we end our consideration of the extended family, there is one final issue to examine: the relation between family composition and financial well-being.

It is often assumed that men in extended families earn less, either because the extended family is a barrier to advancement (Scanzoni, 1971) or because men who have low earning power retreat into extended households. Our data, however give no support to the idea. Married men who are main wage earners earn about the same whether they live in a nuclear family or in a extended household. The gap is $160 per year in favor of the nuclear-family residents (Pearson $r = .02$). Further investigation by means of multiple classification analysis * indicates that this difference would be a little larger if the groups did not differ on other factors, but even with education, age at marriage, present age, and parental SES controlled, the difference is only $294. A difference of this size is unimportant, and cannot be taken as support for the point of view that extended families are a brake on advancement or a refuge for failures.

Respondents' income does not, however, tell the whole story. Part of the point of living in an extended family is that it makes earning more than one paycheck easier, either because it frees the wife to work (see Ladner, 1971) or because it permits the pooling of the incomes of more than one family. If the strategy is effective, the *total family income* of men in extended families may be greater than that of those in nuclear households.

The data show that this is the case. In both groups family income exceeds personal income; even in nuclear homes many wives work. The increase is, however, much greater for those in multigenerational households. Men in such households report that their family income is, on the average, $1,561 more than that of men in nuclear households. The Pearson r between family income and family composition is .14. Partialing out age, etc. by multiple classification analysis has little effect; the gap is reduced to $1,325 (partial $r = .13$). The relationship is clearly not spurious.

It would seem, then, that there are economic advantages associated with extended families, but the issue is still not settled. Extended households are larger, and the added income may not be commensurate with the added expenses. This is difficult to determine. We can calculate the per-capita income for the two family types, but it is clear that this gives us only hints about economic well-being. A family with a higher total income may be better off in a real sense even if its per-capita income is less. Housing expenses, for example, do not increase proportionately with increasing numbers. At the same time, there does come a point when a per-capita-income difference becomes relevant.

The data show that on a per capita basis the nuclear families have an apparent advantage. The gap is $391 per year (Pearson $r = -.08$), and with other variables controlled it increases to $439 (partial $r = -.09$).

A difference of $400 per person is considerable, and though we cannot be sure, we would suggest that the apparent economic advantage of the extended family is washed away by the necessity of stretching income further. This view is bolstered by the fact that the monthly debt payments of the nuclear-family residents are $10 less, and 28 percent have no debts or could pay them off. The comparable percentage for extended-family residents is 19.

relations with kin

Earlier in this chapter we suggested that the common belief was that too extensive contact with relatives is destructive of satisfaction, but the absence of contact is also undesirable. By now we have discovered that the first part of the statement is untrue if one accepts the multigenerational household as an index of too extensive contact with kin. We now turn to the second part. Does isolation from kin lead to negative consequences?

The respondents were asked how often they received visits in their homes and then were asked, "Who usually comes over?" About one-third of the married respondents who were not living with relatives mentioned only friends in response to this question. For our purposes, they are the group which is socially isolated from kin.

When the isolated group is compared with respondents who receive visits from kin, we find no difference in degree of frustration and unhappiness. The correlation is $-.01$ for the total sample. In fact, for lower- and higher-status women and for lower-status men, the small differences are in the other direction (partial r's range from .04 to .07). The hypothesis is supported only for high-status males (partial $r = -.12$). In general, social isolation from kin does not have negative effects on satisfaction.

Though most studies of kin relations focus on contact patterns, an equally appropriate measure is the extent to which kin can be called on to help in an emergency. The view we are considering would suggest that people who have few relatives they can count on would be less satisfied, since they would lack a certain degree of security.

In regard to the respondent's own relatives the data show what we have come to expect: there is no clear-cut relation between the variables. In only one subgroup, high-status females, is there even a small relation between number of relatives who would help and the frustration score (partial $r = .11$). The data on in-laws are, however, surprising. In 3 subgroups, potential aid from in-laws is associated with satisfaction. Partial r equals .20 for lower-status males and about .10 for each of the women's groups. For higher-status males there is no relation.

Taking the data as a whole, we would suggest that this last finding not be taken too literally. It does not seem likely that it is just the promise of extra aid that is the effective factor. If it were, there should be at least an equal relation with the "own relatives" variable. We think the correlation reflects the general quality of the interaction with in-laws. We suspect that responses to this question tell us little about the quality of relations with own relatives. More than four-fifths of the respondents said some relatives would help and most people named several (mean = 3.0). There is strong obligation for relatives to aid each other, and this holds even if there is tension in the relation. The norm is not strong for in-laws, however. Many named none. A person who reports several of his in-laws would help is saying, essentially, that there is a good relation with the in-laws, and it is this more general aspect of the relation, we think, which is operating to influence satisfaction.

At any rate, even with this possible exception, the data do not support the view that isolation from kin has an important effect on satisfaction.

conclusion

There seems to be little doubt that patterns of kin interaction do not have a major influence on the satisfaction of blacks. People who live in extended households are not significantly less satisfied than those who live in nuclear homes and this holds for several different kinds of multigenerational homes. On the other side of the coin, those who do not receive visits from their relatives and those who could call on few of them in an emergency do not seem to suffer for it. In general, there is little evidence to support the charge that these patterns of kin relation produce frustration and unhappiness.

In addition, household composition does not seem to raise or decrease self-evaluation. Men who live in a nuclear household do not think they are better husbands for it, and men whose parents live with them do not think they are better sons for it. Similar findings emerge for women.

We are not prepared to state that household composition is totally irrelevant, though the distinction does not seem to be a crucial one in quantitative terms. Multigenerational households produce some tensions, but they also produce compensations, and nuclear families have their own tensions. Taking in a parent may increase the likelihood of conflict, but it also provides a built-in baby-sitter, and other advantages. The ''problem'' probably is that none of these tendencies predominates.

Conjugal role segregation does not influence self-evaluation strongly, but it is clearly associated with general and marital dissatisfaction. However, even these correlations are not large, and quite importantly the association is effectively zero for lower-status men. Togetherness is not always associated with satisfaction. In fact, even when the degree of satisfaction tends to increase as conjugal integration increases, there is a limit. In the total sample the degree of satisfaction declines when the top of the integration scale is reached.

Furthermore, there is a problem of time order here. The critics' charge suggests that segregation produces dissatisfaction, but a case can be made for a reciprocal relation or a reversal of the postulated causal line. Our data suggest that there is some causal significance to the degree of segregation, but we suspect it works the other way too. The relation is probably reciprocal. If this is so, the *causal effects* of segregation are less than the correlations would suggest. This would mean they are quite low.

The jury is still out on the question, but we suggest that the verdict will be that conjugal role segregation does produce dissatisfaction, but only for those persons who are socialized to desire togetherness in marriage. This group clearly includes black women and higher-status black males. It may not include lower-status men.

chapter seven

the long-range effects
of the
broken home

Without at all denying the importance of the charges we have considered to this point, we may fairly suggest that in the view of many critics of the black family, the case stands or falls on the accusations made against the broken home. This is the trait which is most often the focus of attention, the one which is supposed to have the strongest effects, and the one whose "guilt" is most taken for granted.

We will start with a number of charges having to do with the attitudinal, value, and behavioral consequences of broken homes. Though these are not the key accusations, they are logically prior.

the relation of the "female-only" home to attitudes

Female Households and Feminine Response. When we tested the idea that the sex of the dominant parent in an intact family influences the behavior of the offspring our results were essentially negative. Males who grew up in a mother-dominated home did not show the predicted feminine traits, and women raised in father-controlled homes were not masculine. Similar predictions are made about men from "female-only" homes, and we turn first to a consideration of them.

The line of reasoning is exactly analogous to the one used for female-dominated homes. Hannerz (1969: 118–19), who does not accept the view, states it succinctly.

A boy growing up in a household where the father is more or less absent comes to suffer confusion over his sexual identity. First of all, the person with whom the boy ought to identify is missing, so the boy has no appropriate model for his sex role. . . . The adult who is available, the mother, is inappropriate as a role model for him; if he starts to identify with her, he will sooner or later find out that he has made a mistake. This misidentification with mother could lead the young male to become more feminine. Some commentators on black family structure do indeed cite examples of men out of matrifocal families of orientation inclined toward feminine behavior. . . . Many more writers, however, see as the final consequence of this early misidentification and confusion a compulsively masculine reaction. . . .

As we noted before, we have no adequate measure of exaggerated masculinity, but we can determine if men from female-homes are more likely to give "feminine responses." We do this by comparing the responses of women with those of two categories of men: those from female households and those who experienced a broken home and then were brought up in a household which contained adults of both sexes. We will not include those from unbroken homes in order to avoid confusing the effects of sex composition with those of family stability.

The results of these comparisons do not show any clear pattern (see Table 7.1). In general, differences are small and their direction is not consistent. Perhaps 7 of the 24 comparisons show men from female households to be similar to the women and different from the men from both-sex homes. (See, for example, item 1 and item 5 for lower-status respondents.) At least as many show the opposite pattern, i.e., there is a small gap between the responses of the women and the men from two-sex families, while the men from the female households diverge even more in the same direction (for example, number 10, which shows men from female homes are least religiously observant).

The data do not support the predictions, but before we reject the critics' claim we must consider the possibility that these results are influenced by the fact that some of the broken homes occurred rather late in life. The ideas underlying the hypothesis would suggest that a home broken at 15 or 16 would not have much effect. We checked this by limiting the "female-only" group to those whose families broke up before they were 10, and found no reason to change the conclusion. Usually the responses were about the same as the total "female-only" group, and when there was a difference the change showed no consistent pattern. We do not see feminine behavior among the products of the female household.

Table 7.1. Percentages Giving Specified Responses to Items by Respondent's Sex and Sex Composition of Broken Home by Parental SES

| | Lower Parental SES | | | Higher Parental SES | | |
| | | Men | | | Men | |
	Women	Female-Only Home	Both Sexes in Home	Women	Female-Only Home	Both Sexes in Home
1. Do you feel mad or sad when you hear about discrimination? *						
(Sad)	55	56	36	53	45	31
2. Do you ever feel you would like to get even with whites?						
(No)	70	79	69	69	64	58
3. Do you remember the last time you got angry?						
(No)	30	42	29	27	38	25
4. Have you ever been in a real fight as an adult?						
(No)	78	50	48	81	60	52
5. Would you buy a house in a white neighborhood if there might be trouble?						
(No or depends)	61	49	39	54	44	51
6. Are you careful not to make a bad impression on whites?						
Frequently or sometimes)	48	36	58	44	42	51
7. Interviewer's rating of respondent's cooperativeness.						
(Very cooperative	76	79	82	84	79	87
8. Reaction to a nasty white: avoidist, educative, aggressive.						
(Avoidist)	52	66	56	45	60	51
9. What do you find nicest about little children?						
When they hug and kiss you)	11	12	5	12	6	15
10. Frequency of church attendance.						
(Once a week or more)	34	15	26	34	16	21
11. The death penalty for murder should be abolished.						
(Agree)	53	50	53	47	58	58
12. Most people can be trusted						
(Agree)	28	36	33	34	28	25

* The items are paraphrased.

The reason for this lack of effect is again succinctly presented by Hannerz (1969), and paraphrasing him, we would suggest that the usual view of male development in the black-female household requires modification. The problem of the fatherless boy is finding someone from whom to learn masculinity. This is, however, not unique to him. The presence of a father does not ensure that the youth will wish to model himself after him. But let that pass. Does the fatherless boy lack an available male model? We would agree with Hannerz that the answer is usually no. There are older siblings, the boy friends of sisters and mother, and most significantly there are innumerable men and boys outside the home.

It is characteristic of many ghetto dwellers, in particular of that segment of the community where matrifocality occurs most frequently, that they participate intensively in the social life of the street, and they start to do so at an early age. And when young boys start taking part in street life they are exposed to a great number of males even if there is little by way of an adult male presence at home. [Hannerz, 1969: 125]

In addition, there is the assumption that the effect of the mother is to teach feminine values. This seems dubious. For one thing, the mother in the female-headed black family may not have as "smothering" a relation with her son as is the case in some of the studies of white samples which are used to support the mother-modeling theory. But even more importantly, we would join Hannerz in responding, "of course she can," to the question, "Cannot the mother in her domestic behavior, get her distinction between her own sex category and that of her son across to him, and thereby contribute to having him choose other models?" (ibid.: 123). In fact we would drop his qualifying "to some extent." When we add the fact that the mothers make distinctions between their children in choosing what to expect of them and what to teach them, it hardly comes as a surprise that our results were as they were.

Female Households, Delay of Gratification, Trouble, etc. This does not cover all the psychological charges against the female household. Some authors suggest that improper sex-role socialization is not the only problem faced by a boy from such a home. The situation is said to be conducive to general maladjustment. Pettigrew (1964: 17) speaks, for example, of "a hunger for immediate gratification among fatherless children" and suggests that "Children manifesting this trait also tend to be less accurate in judging time, less socially responsible, less oriented toward achievement and more prone to delinquency." He also states that mother-raised boys, "Concerned about their sexual identity assert their masculinity through person directed violence" (ibid.: 22).

We cannot fully test these assertions with our data but we do have some relevant items. We see first of all in Table 7.2 that men who grew up in female households are not less willing to delay gratification than men who grew up in two-sex broken homes. Though the differences are not large, in both parental SES groups those from female households are *less* likely to disagree that "a person should deprive himself of having a good time in life to make sure he is saving to get ahead"; and in the higher SES group they are less likely to say on an open-ended question that they would spend a $400 bonus rather than putting it in the bank.

Table 7.2.   Partial Correlations * between Living Arrangement after Disruption of Parental Home (Female-Only v. Both Sexes) and Attitudinal and Behavioral Items by Parental SES (Male Respondents Only)

	Lower PrSES	Higher PrSES
1. A person should deprive himself to make sure he is saving to get ahead.† (Disagree)		
	−.14 ‡	−.08
2. What would you do with the money if you got a $400 bonus or inheritance? (Spend it rather than save it)		
	.10	−.17
3. Have you ever been arrested? (Yes)		
	.02	.13
4. Have you ever been in a real fight as an adult? (Yes)		
	−.02	−.05
5. Do you remember the last time you got angry? (Yes)		
	−.13	−.17
6. Do you ever get so frustrated you could break things? (Yes)		
	−.06	−.07
7. Do you ever feel you would like to get even with whites? (Yes)		
	−.13	−.03
8. Reaction to a nasty white. (Educative or aggressive)		
	−.08	−.13
9. Would you buy a house in a white neighborhood if there might be trouble? (Yes)		
	−.12	.08
10. Are you careful not to make a bad impression on whites? (Never)		
	.31	.07
11. Interviewer's rating of the respondent's cooperativeness. (Less than very cooperative)		
	.00	.12

* Age, number of years since marriage, respondent's SES and parental SES are held constant.
† The items are paraphrased.
‡ A positive relation means that the response given in the parentheses is associated with being from a female-only household.

This does not necessarily say, however, that the general thrust of Pettigrew's point is incorrect. The product of a female household might still have more trouble and problems even if he does not have difficulty delaying gratification. The data, in fact, show that those from higher-status female households are more likely to report that they have been arrested, but in neither PrSES group are they more likely to have been in a real fight. These data give no basis for accepting the assertion that those from female homes are generally more trouble prone. This group also does not show hostility or a lack of self-control. They are less likely to say they want to get even with whites, and less likely to report anger or extreme reactions to frustration. And, finally, they are not clearly more assertive than men from two-sex broken homes. The data are not consistent with the picture drawn by Pettigrew.

Stable Homes and Female-Headed Homes. Given the lack of difference between the two forms of broken home, our question now becomes, does the female household differ in its psychological consequences from the unbroken home? The answer is a muted no. The broken-home group does not show inability to delay gratification, and though 12 of the other 18 comparisons show differences in the predicted direction, only 4 of the partials are even .10 or above. Those from unbroken homes are less likely to have been arrested or in a fight, all the correlations being .09 or above, but that is the only clear difference.

On these variables female households do not have negative effects as compared with intact or both-sex broken homes. We will delay until later a consideration of why the effects are not greater.

broken homes and income

The second aspect of the charge contends that growing up in a broken home leads to lessened achievement for males. Our next task is to determine if it is true that "Negro children without fathers flounder and fail. Not always to be sure" (Moynihan, et al., 1965: 35).

The best existing evidence bearing upon the question comes from a study by Duncan and Duncan (1969). Utilizing data from a 1962 Census Bureau current population survey, they found that the occupational-level scores of black men from female-headed homes were *slightly* lower than those of men from intact homes. Duncan and Duncan also found that men who came from intact homes entered the work force later and moved further from the level of their first jobs. They also had on the average 10.1 years of formal education, as compared to 8.5 for those who lived in female-headed households. All in all, then, there is evidence to indicate that the achievement of men from nonbroken homes is somewhat greater. At the same time, it should be stressed that the extra burden carried by the product of a female-headed household is not particularly great in the Duncans' study.

Duncan and Duncan limit their consideration to a comparison of those who lived with both parents most of the time until they reached age 16 with those who grew up in a female-headed home, for these are the only categories which have sufficient numbers in their sample. This is the key comparison, which many of the critics have in mind even when they do not specify it, but it does blur an important distinction. They are not actually investigating the effects of having experienced a broken home, for many of those who had this experience grew up in a male-headed home because the mother remarried or lived with relatives.

We will attempt to present a more complete picture by first contrasting those who lived with both their real parents and those who did not. Then we will divide the second category into a female-headed group and a group in which adults of both sexes were present after the break. This will permit us to separate out the effect of the broken home from the effect of the sex composition of the household. We will also depart from the Duncans' study by using income differences, since they are more sensitive as a measure of differential achievement than are differences in occupational level.

The data show first of all that men from unbroken homes earn $576 more than those from broken homes: $5,903 as compared with $5,327 (partial $r = .12$). However, the men from female-headed households are not the ones who are making the smallest salaries. The really low income comes from those who lived in two-sex households after the break. They earned $874 less on the average than those from unbroken homes. The gap between those from intact homes and those from female-headed homes was $425 (see Table 7.3). We also found that the relationship is not spurious. The gaps do decrease somewhat when we control for parental SES and age by means of multiple classification analysis, but the bulk of the difference remains. It would seem that income is affected by the experience of a broken home and by the sex-composition of the postbreak home. When we deal with the parental SES groups separately, we find that the relationships are more complex than this. For those of lower-status background the difference between those from intact homes and those from all broken homes is $398. For those from higher-status backgrounds the difference is $702. The difference between the two types of broken homes is also much greater in the higher parental SES groups. But the ordering in both cases is: men from stable homes, men from female-headed homes, and men from two-sex households who did not live with both real parents. The gaps are clear in all cases and they are reduced only slightly when parental SES and age are controlled (Table 7.3).

Obviously the charge against the broken home has some validity. Our data and Duncan and Duncan's (1969) do show differences in achievement associated with broken homes. However the critics seem to have the details wrong. First, the effect of the broken home is less in the lower-status group than it is in the higher, though the critics are most concerned about the impact of broken homes on lower-status males. In fact, the gap is rather small for lower-status males. Second, those from female-headed households do better than those from homes which had adults of both sexes present after the break, although the female-headed home is supposed to be more destructive of achievement. Finally, it should be noted that despite the existence of these important differences, the low income of the black community cannot be attributed to parental marital disruption. If all the black men came from unbroken homes, their average income in 1966 would have been $5,903. This is not much more than the actual income of the men in the sample, which is $5,685. Even if all black parents remained together, their sons would have low income. The broken home is not the key to black poverty.

All this notwithstanding, the fact is that there is a difference in income associated with parental marital stability, and this fact demands explanation. We turn next to that task.

One of the major hypotheses to be found in theories which attempt

Table 7.3. Effects of Living Arrangement after Disruption of Parental Home (Female Only v. Both Sexes) upon Men's Income by Parental SES, Expressed in Deviations in Dollars from Mean Income of Men from Intact Homes

	Total Sample			Lower PrSES			Higher SES		
		Broken Home			Broken Home			Broken Home	
	Mean of Intact Home	Both Sexes	Female Only	Mean of Intact Home	Both Sexes	Female Only	Mean of Intact Home	Both Sexes	Female Only
Zero Order	$5,903	−$874	−$425	$5,752	−$483	−$307	$6,024	−$1,190	−$569
Partials: controlling for:									
Parental SES		−$878	−$408		−$500	−$406		−$1,182	−$638
PrSES, age		−$802	−$307		−$425	−$240		−$1,138	−$588
PrSES, age, education		−$813	−$372		−$649	−$300		−$882	−$763
PrSES, age, education, plus 12 attitude and behavioral items *		−$767	−$196		−$437	−$27		−$984	−$667

* The items are those used in Table 7.2 and number of jobs held in the last five years.

to tie broken homes to later achievement suggests that educational differences represent the major intervening variable. The idea is that the economic and other problems associated with a broken home make for school difficulties. The child may be required to work while he is in school or help out at home. This may decrease the time he can devote to his schoolwork and it may increase his rate of absenteeism. The problems of a broken home might also require that he take a full-time job earlier, and this would increase the likelihood of his becoming a dropout. Similarly, the lessened parental supervision which is supposedly associated with a broken home is thought to decrease his attention to school, and this may hurry his leaving. Several routes lead to the hypothesis that people from broken homes have less education, and from this flows the prediction of lessened job opportunities and poor income.

Our data are totally inconsistent with these notions. The education of people from broken homes is not less than that of those from intact homes. In fact, more often than not it is higher. Thus when we control for education in Table 7.3 the difference in income increases rather than decreasing in all but one case. Generally, if there were no educational differences the gap between intact homes and both kinds of broken homes would be greater than it is. Men from higher-status both-sex families are an exception to this generalization, but even for them education explains little of the difference.

An alternative explanation starts from an assumption that the events associated with the break and the postbreak situation cause values and behaviors which are antithetical to achievement. A list of all the conditions which have been laid at the door of the broken home is not necessary here; we have already considered many of them. Suffice it to say that if broken homes led to only a few of the conditions attributed to them, the achievement levels of men from such homes probably would be lowered, for such characteristics are hardly likely to endear one to the boss.

Our data do not touch on the more extreme of these assumed consequences of broken homes, but the attitude and behavioral items we used before do have relevance. Their relation to broken homes is not strong or consistent, but in combination they could explain at least part of the income difference. To test for this possibility we used multiple classification analysis to relate family type and income, with parental

SES, age, education, and 12 additional variables held constant.[1] This permitted us to determine what the income differences between the family types would be *if* each family type showed the same distribution on the factors being controlled.

As usual, a simple answer does not emerge from the data, but it is possible to reach some tentative conclusions. For men from lower-SES backgrounds, it does seem in Table 7.3 that part of the differences in income among the three family types can be attributed to differences in the control factors. When the 12 variables are added to education, age, and parental SES, the income difference declines by $212 for "both sexes" and by $273 for female-only households. This washes out the gap between intact and female households. The implication is clear; if the family types did not differ on these items, the income differences would be smaller. These variables are, for this group, intervening variables between family type and income.

Other features of the situation seem consistent with the notion that for lower-status men personal traits are involved in the lower incomes of persons from broken homes. For one thing, among the youngest men those from unbroken homes have somewhat lower incomes. Men from intact homes don't start with an advantage, but they apparently get better salary increases. This would fit in with the picture we have of these men. They are not better qualified, but they get along better on the job.

For higher-status respondents the situation is quite different. The addition of the 12 variables has little effect on the income differentials. Some of the variables increase the gap by a few dollars and others decrease it by a small amount, but none has a significant effect. Furthermore, in contrast to the lower-status respondents, the young men from intact homes have a salary advantage over those from broken homes.

It is clear that the dynamics of the relation between family type and income are different depending upon the social status of the respondents' family; but with the available data we cannot be very specific about the nature of the difference. The personality differences which are important in the lower-status group are not relevant for higher-status males, and education differences have some slight relevance for

1 The variables used are those which appear in Table 7.2 plus number of jobs held in the last five years.

higher-status males and none for those of lower-status background. We suspect the key lies in personality for the lower-status males and in preparation for those of higher-status background.

All this aside, we would reiterate that the critics are right when they charge that broken homes have a depressing effect on income. At the same time, we must stress the small size of the difference for lower-status males and the superiority of the female-headed home over the broken home which has adults of both sexes in it. Neither of these points is recognized by the critics, and they both seem essential to an understanding of the situation.

the transmission of marital disruption

Another major charge against the black family might be called the "tradition of instability" idea, the suggestion that marital instability in this generation is the legacy of broken homes in previous generations. Frequently the line is drawn back to slavery, but our concern is with the variant which looks back just one generation. In this case, it is postulated that the instability of contemporary black marriages is related in some way to the fact that many blacks grew up in broken homes.

For example, Pettigrew concludes from a study which compares black men who grew up in fatherless households with men whose fathers were present that "the most critical distinction involves marriage; the first group was more likely to be divorced or separated" (Pettigrew, 1964: 20). Bernard, in turn, takes note of this study and states, with some subsequent qualification, that "Men socialized without fathers reveal a marked inability to maintain a marital relationship" (Bernard, 1966a: 125). A similar position is reflected in Rohrer and Edmonson's (1960: 190) explanation of why a particular group of blacks has a stable family life. They state, "both by precept and by example our 'family members' were taught by their parents to prize the values of stable family life above other goals, and they in turn are well-embarked on transmitting these same values to their children."

In part, the theoretical underpinnings of this charge are exactly the same as those supporting the previous one. Broken homes are supposedly important sources of personal and social maladjustment, and these qualities lead to a high rate of marital instability.

In the present case, however, additional effects are postulated. Pettigrew (1964: 17–21) points to problems of sex identification and sex-role learning among children from broken homes, and it is only a short step from this to the suggestion that such children fail to learn adequate versions of the husband and wife roles. This might work two ways: the interaction prior to the break in the parental marriage may teach ''inappropriate'' spousal roles, or a role model may be absent after the break. In either case, the child who grows up in a broken home may not have the opportunity to learn how to be a ''good spouse.''

Another path could be through income. Broken homes we know lead to reduced income, and this may be a source of marital difficulties. Many authors, of course, suggest that economic problems are a major contributing factor to marital instability among blacks.

The view that parental family disruption generates instability in the next generation may be plausible, but few data from blacks bear upon the point. Studies by Duncan and Duncan (1969) and Pettigrew (1964) do, however, provide directly relevant systematic data. Duncan and Duncan found that parental family instability and *current* marital status are not related. The study by Pettigrew (1964) did show differences in the marital stability of matched samples of working-class black males whose parental homes differed, but the samples numbered only about 20 in each group. Given the paucity of studies, their contradictory results, and their limitations, further investigation of this topic seems indicated. We propose to test the transmission-of-instability idea in detail. Do broken homes run in certain black family lines? If so, is there a causal connection? If so, do the usual explanations square with the facts?

The data presented in Table 7.4 show only a weak relation between disruption of the parental home and instability of the respondent's marriage.[2] For both sexes, those from broken parental homes

2 A respondent is classified as having had an unstable marriage if he or she has ever been divorced or is currently separated. For the calculation of the correlations we use number of marriages broken through conflict as the dependent variable. This is, however, practically a dichotomy, for only 3 percent of the sample had experienced more than one broken marriage.

are somewhat more likely to experience divorce or separation in their own marriages ($r = .08$), but when we consider the emphasis often put on breaks in the parental family, the association is hardly striking. Though there is probably a relationship between these variables, it is clearly a trivial one.

However, this analysis is a weak test of the charge with which we are concerned. The assumption is that there is a causal connection between marital disruption in the two generations, and these data barely touch upon that assumption. Even the small association found may be

Table 7.4.   Respondents' Marital History by Stability of Parental Home by Sex

| | Percentage Ever Divorced or Now Separated | | |
Stability of Parental Home	Males	Females	Total
Unbroken Home	25	36	31
Broken Home	34	42	39
Weighted N	1,492	1,995	3,487
$r12$ *	.08	.08	.08
$r12.3$	.08	.08	.08
$r12.4$	.08	.08	.09
$r12.34$	.08	.08	.09
$r12.5$	.06	.06	.06
$r12.345$	.07	.08	.07

* $r12$ is the Pearson correlation between variables 1 and 2; $r12.3$ is the partial correlation between 1 and 2 with 3 held constant.

1 = Number of marriages broken through divorce or separation.
2 = Stability of parental home (unbroken = 0, broken = 1).
3 = Parental SES (lowest = 0, highest = 9).
4 = Number of years since first marriage.
5 = Age at first marriage.

spurious; but on the other hand, we may be underrating the importance of breaks in the parental marriage because a third variable is acting as a suppressor or because the relationship is limited to a particular subgroup. Even if none of these is true, the effect may be indirect, through some intervening variable not implied in the theory.

Finally, as we have noted before, negative responses to the question on whether the respondent lived with both real parents until age 16, though frequently used, leave something to be desired as a measure of the independent variable even when we eliminate those who are in this category because they left home. The charge suggests that certain consequences are likely to follow from a broken home, but it is clearly assumed that certain kinds of broken homes are more likely to have these consequences than are others. The variable we have used contains within one category a variety of situations—homes broken for varying reasons, followed by a variety of postbreak living arrangements, occurring at different times in the respondent's lives. If we are to completely test the idea and the reasoning behind it, we must try to separate out these varying conditions. We want to be certain that the weak relationship reported above is not due to a dilution effect caused

Table 7.5. Respondents' Marital History by Stability of Parental Home by Sex and Parental SES

| | Percentage Ever Divorced or Now Separated | | | | | |
| | Low Parental SES | | | High Parental SES | | |
Stability of Parental Home	Males	Females	Total	Males	Females	Total
Unbroken Home	28	38	34	12	30	22
Broken Home	36	40	39	29	45	38
Weighted N	1,146	1,528	2,674	320	408	728
$r12$ *	.06	.05	.06	.22	.16	.18
$r12.4$	.06	.06	.06	.22	.17	.16
$r12.5$	.04	.04	.04	.21	.12	.12
$r12.45$	.05	.05	.05	.21	.14	.13

* $r12$ is the Pearson correlation between variables 1 and 2; $r12.4$ is the partial correlation between 1 and 2 with 4 held constant.

1 = Number of marriages broken through divorce or separation.
2 = Stability of parental home (unbroken = 0, broken = 1).
4 = Number of years since first marriage.
5 = Age at first marriage.

by particular kinds of broken homes which are not expected to have a strong effect upon the respondents' marital stability. We turn now to a test of these various possibilities.

To test for spuriousness, we controlled for number of years married and parental SES, as these seemed to be logical possibilities. The results using partial correlations indicate, however, that these are not associated biases. In every case the partials are about the same as the zero-order correlations (Table 7.4). However, the partial correlations hide an important finding which is revealed when tabular control is used (Table 7.5). In the higher-status group there is a clear relation between a broken home and respondent's marital instability ($r = .22$ for men and .16 for women). The small relationship for the sample as a whole is due to the fact that in the lower-status group the correlations are of trivial size.[3] The existence of this interaction is by now so familiar that it causes little surprise. We would merely note that the focus on the lower class in discussions of the inheritance of family instability is apparently a misplaced emphasis.

Though the relationship is not spurious, it is still possible that the transmission-of-instability idea is inaccurate even for those of high-status background. According to this view the main intervening variables are traits of the individual respondents, but it is possible that broken homes have their effect upon later marital stability because they influence some aspect of the marriage: for example, the age at which it is contracted. If this were so, the idea would require important modification though, of course, it would not lead us to reject the general conclusion that broken parental homes contribute to later marital instability.

To test this possibility we controlled for age at marriage and found in every subgroup that it had little effect upon the zero-order correlations. We conclude that age at marriage is not a significant intervening variable.

Of course, there are other variables which might be associated biases or intervening variables; but as far as we can go, it does seem that the transmission-of-instability idea holds for respondents of high-status background but not for those from lower-status homes. The next step is to set up more specific categorizations in an attempt to determine if the pattern is general or whether certain types of broken homes differ in their effects from other kinds.

For the sample as a whole there is no consistent relation between

3 In this section the dividing line between the two parental SES groups is set somewhat higher than in the rest of the book. This is done to make these materials reasonably consistent with a previous publication on this subject (Heiss, 1972). Also, if we had used the lower cutting point we would have hidden some of the differences between the SES groups. The correlation for higher-status males would have been .11 and for women it would have been .10. It seems from this and from direct evidence that the correlation between instability in the two generations is substantial only toward the top of the black social-status scale. We should also note that the data presented here differ slightly from those in the article referred to. This is due to the fact that a different rule was used for the elimination of cases which had missing data on one or more, but not all, of the variables involved in the calculation of a partial correlation. The effect of this change is generally trivial.

the age at which the break in the parental family occurred and respondent's marital instability. However, with parental SES held constant the picture changes. As before, there is no relationship for people of lower-status background, but in the higher-status group we find a relation for the women. The younger the respondent when the parents' marriage was ended, the greater the likelihood of a break in her marriage. The partial r, with age at marriage and number of years since marriage controlled, is .38.

We now ask, is it the broken home, per se, or a particular postbreak living arrangement which has the effect? Judging from the concern with the female household we would expect persons brought up in such homes to show greater marital instability, but recalling previous data we would be prepared to find the opposite. The data say, however, that it does not matter very much. For both men and women with lower-status backgrounds and for men of higher-status background the association approaches zero. For women of higher-status background there is a weak relation, partial $r = .08$, which indicates that it is better to live in a household that contains only women. Including two-sex households in the original comparison did not dilute the relation.

Though we have disposed of the notion that female households are breeding grounds for later marital instability among blacks, this does not necessarily mean that postbreak family arrangements are irrelevant. We have shown only that the "both sexes versus female" distinction is unimportant. The data indicate, however, that this gross classification does not hide any difference of note. When the "both sexes" category of the previous variable is divided into two parts— reconstituted families in which the remaining parent remarried, and expanded families in which the respondent, with or without one of his parents, joined another family group—no important differences emerge. The highest correlation is only .12, and the directions are not consistent.

Our final task is to investigate the relationship between the cause of the break in the parental home and the outcome of the respondent's marriage. One gets the feeling when reading the literature on the black family that many authors equate the broken home with the home broken by conflict, as though that were the only kind. This is obviously not the case. In fact, almost half the broken homes were broken by death. It seems quite important to determine whether the cause of the break is related to the dependent variable.

The data indicate, first, that there is no relationship in the total sample between cause of break in parental marriage and respondent's marital instability. However, particularly in the higher parental SES group, men who come from a home broken by death are more likely to have a broken marriage than men whose parents are divorced or separated (partial $r = .07$ for lower SES and .18 for higher). For females the data show no clear pattern.

In summary, then, our findings indicate that a break in the parental home affects marital stability primarily among those of higher-status background, and in this group a break at an early age has more effect, but only for women. The composition of the household after the break is irrelevant. There are only small differences between those whose parental home was broken by conflict and those who experienced a home broken by death.

All in all, the correlations indicate that the variables we are considering explain little of the variance in marital instability. Most of the factors which affect marital stability among blacks remain to be discovered. In the light of this, the next question seems to be, why are the relationships discovered so weak, in general? When this question has been answered we will attempt to explain why certain of the associations are stronger.

In general, the hypothesis that parental family instability is an important cause of marital disruption in the following generation suffers from the problems shared by all hypotheses predicting marital outcome from the premarital characteristics and experiences of individuals. Marriage is a relationship and a process, and its outcome is determined not only by the characteristics each individual brings to it but also by the relationship between the traits of the married pair and by the details of the situation in which they interact. While the characteristics of individuals are of some relevance, and while they are perhaps predictive of some of the relevant postmarital factors, to deal with a single premarital trait of individuals means that one is using extremely limited information. Such a focus ensures that only a small part of the variance will be explained. Furthermore, this problem is compounded when one uses a characteristic which is only indirectly relevant, i.e., one which influences marital instability by its influence on some inter-

vening variable. It should be remembered that marital prediction studies of whites which use instruments composed of large numbers of factors which are primarily of this type have never explained more than
25 percent of the variance in marital outcome.

More specifically, we believe that parental marital disruption is so
weakly tied to respondent's marital instability because it is weakly
correlated with the intervening variables: adjustment problems, inadequate spousal role conceptions, and income. These are, in turn, weak
predictors of marital success and failure.

This is all rather different from the assured contentions about the
effects of broken homes we quoted earlier. Therefore, we should go
off on a slight tangent at this point and provide the previously prom-
ised explanation of why broken homes do not have the strong effects
they are reputed to have.

The postulates that a broken parental home leads to poor adjustment and low income are based upon several assumptions which on
close scrutiny appear rather weak. For one thing, it is assumed that
breakup of the parental home is traumatic and productive of psychological upset. Though this is often the case, it is clear that black
children face many traumas, regardless of the nature of their homes.
The difference between broken and unbroken families may be minimal
in many cases. In fact, a parental breakup may come as welcome relief
in cases where there is constant battling. There is, of course, limited
evidence from whites that the children of broken homes are better ad-
justed than those living in conflict-ridden homes (Nye, 1957). Also we
should not overlook the fact that many black women without spouses
and many remarried women manage to provide good homes for their
children. The evidence on the effects of broken homes cannot be denied, but it is more complex and not as strong as is generally assumed
(see, for example, Rosenberg, 1965).

The postulated relationship between parental family disruption and
learning of the spouse role can also be questioned. The following assumptions seem to be involved: (1) The presence of both parents indicates that adequate models will be presented. (2) The major, if not
the sole, source of role learning is the family. Others—relatives, substitute parents, and members of the surrounding community—have
little relevance. (3) Not only is the major learning done within the
family, but the only adequate teacher is the occupant of the role.

Specifically, it is apparently assumed that a mother or stepfather cannot teach her son to be a "good" husband, and she or they cannot teach her daughter what to expect from, and how to adjust to, a man. (4) If a role model is presented, it will be learned. (5) The relevant socialization takes a long time to accomplish.

Though there is probably some element of truth in most of these assumptions, they are at best weak tendencies. The breakup of a family does not ensure inadequate role learning, and stability does not ensure adequate learning. Particularly dubious, in terms of the general good showing of the female households, is the notion that the mother and/or the general community cannot provide the necessary instruction for males.

Our data do not permit an adequate test of this explanation, for we have no measures of role conceptions and only a few weak indices of personal difficulties.[4] However, the materials we do have are of some interest. For the total sample, which showed little correlation between parental marital history and respondent's marital stability, the correlations between parental marital history and the assumed intervening variables are quite weak. None reaches .10, and several are not in the expected direction. This finding is clearly consistent with our speculations.

We saw earlier that the correlation between marital disruption in the two generations is stronger for higher-status people. Does this mean that under some circumstances the standard explanation is valid, even if it is not in general? In a previous work (Heiss, 1972) we speculated that this was the case. We thought that particularly the first link would be stronger in the higher SES group. As we suggested previously, we believe that the lower-status child is faced with innumerable difficulties. If he or she escapes the problem of a broken home, there are several other aspects of life which can lead to the same outcome. For higher-status respondents the cards are not so strongly stacked, and if the parents stay together the child has a reasonable chance in life. In addition, we thought that in general the family is more central for the higher-status group, and thus children are more affected "for good or evil," by what goes on there. All this would suggest that the link between parental instability and the inter-

4 We cannot test the postulated path through income, for we only have information on current income.

vening variables would be stronger for those who come from the higher-status group.

One way of testing the idea is to hold constant these assumed intervening variables and see what happens to the correlation between the marital histories of the two generations. If our explanation is valid there should be a reduction in the correlation.

For higher-status males this does happen. The beta * between marital disruption in the two generations is .21 with number of years since marriage and age at marriage controlled. When we add the 12 other variables it is reduced to .12. Given the weakness of our measurement, a reduction of over one-third is rather impressive.

For higher-status women, however, there is no reduction. The beta with two variables controlled is .16, and with the additional factors held constant it is still .16. Furthermore, when we look more carefully at the situation for the higher-status males, we discover added complications. We find on further analysis that some of the correlations between parental marital disruption and the intervening variables are not in the expected direction. For example, respondents from broken homes were less likely to say they wanted to get even with whites. (partial $r = -.18$) This variable contributes to the reduction in the original correlation, only because the relationship between "wanting to get even" and respondent's marital stability is also in the "wrong" direction.

Given all this, we are loathe to reach a definite conclusion. The data we have presented cannot be taken as support for the assumed causal chain. However, we do not wish to reject the hypothesis, for we have been unable to test it adequately. Our test of the postulate that parental marital disruption leads to personality problems is weak, and we have no data bearing upon the assumed chain which involves spousal role conceptions and income as the intervening variables. A conclusion must await further research, but the data currently available do not support the standard explanation or our earlier speculations.

The critics' charge regarding the transmission of marital disruption receives slight support. In some cases there is a connection, but again, the relationship is not found in the segments of society which they focus on and it is not at the level of magnitude they imagine.

conclusion

A fairly clear picture emerges concerning the long-range effects of broken homes in the black community. Growing up in a broken home has a depressing effect on income, and it somewhat increases the likelihood that the respondent's own marriage will be broken. However, neither of these effects is large or universal. Most notable is the fact that if the respondent is from a lower-status background the effects are very small. Furthermore, the female household is not the main culprit, as has generally been contended. Men from female households earn more than men from broken homes which contained adults of both sexes after the break, and people from female households have at least as good a marital record as those in the other category.

The attitudinal and behavioral differences which are reputed to be specifically associated with the female-only variety of broken home were not found. When compared to men from both-sex broken homes, the responses of men who were brought up by women were not more feminine, nor did they differ in other ways. The products of broken homes did differ from men from intact homes, but the differences were not major and many were not in the predicted direction. Finally, the personality differences we have been able to locate do not adequately explain the association which exists in the higher-status group between marital disruption in the parental and respondent's generation.

chapter eight

mothers
   without
spouses

The empirical literature on the effects of broken homes is largely concerned with the effects upon the children. The other actors in the
domestic drama have been much discussed but little researched.
Goode's students would no longer report to him, as they did when he
was starting his *After Divorce* (1956), that there was only one research
study of postdivorce adjustment; but the bibliography they would produce would still be rather short, particularly in the section dealing with
black marriages. Despite this lack of empirical research, or perhaps
because of it, a small controversy has grown up concerning the situation of the divorced black woman, and it is to this matter that we next
turn our attention.

   The standard view is largely an extension of the results of Goode's
(1956) study. In brief summary, he found in his research on a largely
white sample that women suffer a certain degree of trauma during the
process of becoming divorced, and that their postdivorce situation
leaves much to be desired There are serious economic problems and
difficulties of social adjustment which may be described as a fifth-
wheel syndrome. There is no place in society for the divorced mother,
and her role is not institutionalized. She has no clear-cut guidelines for
behavior, and the others with whom she interacts do not quite know
what is expected of them. What do her parents owe her; and what does
she owe to her former in-laws, the grandparents of her children? As
long as she remains unmarried problems of this kind will continue to
dog her. In Goode's view the only really viable solution to the problem is remarriage, and this is the route that most women follow.
Twenty-six months after the divorce, over half the women had already
remarried, and he suggests that 94 percent of women divorced at age
30 ultimately remarry.

It is not absolutely clear whether white or black divorcees are more likely to remarry. Goode found that blacks remarried somewhat more quickly, but after a couple of years the rates were fairly close: 59 percent of the black mothers had remarried in comparison to 53 percent of the whites. Census data which include nonmothers and older persons indicate, on the other hand, that nonwhite remarriage rates run about 7 or 8 points less than those of whites (Carter and Glick, 1970: 239).

This, however, is not the key issue. It does not matter much whether the remarriage rates go in one direction or the other. Since more black women experience divorce and separation, unless the divorced have high remarriage rates there are going to be many more mothers without spouses in the black community. In our sample only 27 percent of the mothers who have had a broken marriage are currently married, which means that a third of all mothers do not have spouses. If the only family which "works" in this society is the husband-wife family, a large number of black women are in trouble.

However, a number of students of the black family have denied the "necessity" of a husband-wife household. Some suggest that the female-headed home is as functional as the alternatives which are realistically open to the lower-class blacks. Others see it as somewhat less desirable than a complete nuclear family, but would argue that its deficiencies are relatively minor. Others would merely assert that a female-headed household need not necessarily be a problem-laden one, etc. Robert Staples (1971: 7) puts it thus:

Such characteristics as divorce, illegitimacy, and female headed households are not necessarily dysfunctional except in the context of western, middle-class, white values. . . . Those who argue from a class position ignore the uniqueness of black culture whereby such traits as female-headed households, out-of-wedlock births, etc., can be integrated positively into the dynamics of family patterns.

Billingsley (1968: 156–57) is a little more specific when he suggests that there actually may be economic advantage in the single-parent family. Given high rates of unemployment for men and the nature of welfare laws,

Many low income Negro families are often forced to choose between a father in the house and money in the home, and many make the pragmatic choice for money. This behavior is generally viewed as dysfunctional and a sign of the disorganization of Negro family life. It is, on the contrary, quite functional, indicative both of the ability of low income Negro families to survive and of their concern for the welfare of their children. Stability, then, sometimes may be a means toward viability, but sometimes it may be an obstacle.

The issue, then, is clearly joined. Is it true as charged that the instability of black marriages causes great problems for many black women, or is the status of husbandless mother functional in the black community?

The comparisons we will present will be more complex than a simple spouse-present–spouse-absent classification, for that is too gross to be informative. For one thing, the spouse-absent category includes both mothers who are truly on their own and women who have been reabsorbed into a larger household, typically that of the mother or parents. The life situations of these two categories of mothers without spouses would be quite different, and our data should be permitted to reflect this. In the tables which follow, two categories of mothers without spouses will be presented—those who live with other adults and those who live alone with their children.[1]

The category, "spouse present," is also too heterogeneous for our purposes. Most of the mothers in that category have never had a broken marriage, and they should be separated from those who have. Thus we will present a fourfold classification: (1) currently married, no previous marriage; (2) currently married, previous marriage; (3) no spouse present, other adults in the home; (4) no spouse or other relatives present ("solo" mothers). This will permit us to pinpoint the effects associated with a broken marriage and those attributable to remarriage and household composition.

presence of spouse and economic well-being

In view of Goode's (1956) findings it seems appropriate to start with a consideration of the respondents' economic history and present situa-

---

1 About 5 percent of the mothers in the sample report they were never married. They are included in the analysis of this chapter. Almost 90 percent of the women who had had a broken first marriage were separated or divored rather than widowed.

tion. The first variable, the index of economic difficulties, is composed of responses to three items. The interview schedule read,

Next, I have a few questions about good and bad things that happen to people. Please tell me whether or not each of them has happened to you. . . . (E) Have you ever gone hungry for a period of time? . . . (H) Have you ever had to move from a house or apartment because you couldn't pay the rent or mortgage? (I) Have you ever had your lights, gas, or phone turned off?

These items are combined into a simple score which indicates the number of these events experienced by the respondent.

The evidence of Table 8.1 may appear, at first glance, somewhat surprising. True the "solo mothers" are most likely to have experienced one or more of these events, but the remarried respondents have not done much better, and those who have no spouses but are living with other adults have done at least as well as those who have never experienced a broken marriage.

Why this is so becomes clear when it is recalled that these questions refer to the respondent's economic history, not necessarily to

Table 8.1. Economic Characteristics of Mothers by Marital History and Education

	Marital History	Percent Had An Economic Disaster *	Mean Family Income	Percent Could Not Pay Off Debts
Total sample	Married once	39	$6,611	71
	Remarried	50	7,144	63
	No spouse, lives with relatives	33	7,308	63
	"Solo" mother	64	3,814	66
Less than four years of high school	Married once	50	$5,892	73
	Remarried	62	5,938	76
	No spouse, lives with relatives	41	4,994	63
	"Solo" mother	68	3,489	61
Four years of high school or more	Married once	28	$7,300	68
	Remarried	34	8,810	44
	No spouse, lives with relatives	27	9,328	62
	"Solo" mother	54	4,445	75

* A respondent is classified as having had an economic disaster if she reports: she has gone hungry for a period of time, she has had to move because she couldn't pay the rent, or she has had her gas, lights, or phone turned off.

their present situation. What seems to be the case is that the chances of economic disaster are increased when a mother is on her own for a period of time. A spouse or some other adult in the household can prevent this occurrence. Thus the "once-married" women are not likely to experience economic crisis because they have always had the contribution of a man. On the assumption that the period between the marriage breakup and moving in with other adults is short, the relative immunity of the "other adult" group is also understandable. These women have usually had someone to help out.

Remarriages, however, don't occur overnight, and that explains the high lifetime incidence of economic crisis for the remarried. Some of them probably lived with other adults between marriages, but the large majority of women without spouses do not; so we believe that most of the remarried had a period of time when they were on their own. This, we believe, but of course cannot prove, was the time that many of them faced the economic problems they reported. The source of the problems of the women who are currently on their own is obvious.

Thus if the criterion is the avoidance of economic crisis, the mother who is on her own is seen to do less well. However, this is not to say that mothers without spouses have more economic problems. Some mothers without spouses, those who live with other adults, are less likely to experience crisis than those who remarried.

This is not, however, the whole picture. The presence or absence of economic crisis is a rather limited measure and the use of a lifetime incidence index does not tell us how things turn out ultimately. A person may have had a hard time in the past but may be doing very well at this point in time. The answer we want can be found in a comparison utilizing current family income.

The picture drawn by the data in the second section of Table 8.1 is striking. The family income of women who are living alone with their children is markedly below that of the other groups, and the remarried mothers are doing at least as well as the women who have remained with their first partners. In fact, the well-educated women who remarry seem to make a "better match" the second time.

The case of the mothers without spouses who live with other people is more complex. Clearly, they do better than women who are on their own, but their standing relative to the other two groups varies depending upon their education. If they are in the higher education category their incomes are higher than those in the other groups. If they have less education their incomes exceed only the solo mothers.

We do not have the data to prove it, but we believe this interaction exists because poorly educated women are more likely to live with their mothers, while more highly educated women are more likely to return to a complete parental home. The availability of a man's income in one case but not in the other would go a long way to explain the differences. It might also be that when there is a man present, usually the father, he is more likely to have high earning power if he has a well-educated daughter. The assumption here is that girls are more likely to finish high school and go to college if their fathers are relatively well-off.

The picture is, however, complicated by the finding that the less educated solo mothers are less likely than the married to say they could not pay all their debts off if they wanted to (Table 8.1). This seems strange, given their very low incomes, but a possible reason for this is suggested by the fact they have fewer debts than the others. They can pay off their debts because they owe less. And, we would guess, they have fewer debts because their very low incomes, and perhaps welfare rules, force them to forego buying a car or appliances on time. It may well be that what appears to be an indication of relative affluence is actually a reflection of greater deprivation.

In sum, the relationship between presence of spouse and economic situation is complex. It seems likely that the key question is, does the woman have to go it alone? If she does, she is likely to have economic problems. However, this is not to say that the only route to economic well-being is through remarriage. Living with other adults always helps, and under certain circumstances it may be economically preferable to remarriage. It should be noted, however, that though there is an alternative to remarriage which is economically adequate it is not frequently used. Only 30 percent of the mothers without spouses report that there are other adults in the home.

the social life of mothers without spouses

Goode's data indicate that though the typical divorcee does not lack social contacts, she does suffer from problems in regard to her social life. She is a single in a society which uses the couple as its basic unit of sociability, and thus she may miss opportunities for social interaction and get less satisfaction from the interaction she does have. In addition to this, there are other difficulties, including the problems which arise from the fact that the old friendship group is unlikely to provide desired opportunities for setting up new attachments with men.

Goode's study did not include a control group of never-divorced women, so we really know only the divorcees' perception of the changes over time. We can, however, make a direct comparison which will tell us if divorced women do have restricted social activity relative to other women.

The data we have on informal group involvement shows that the black woman without a spouse is no more of a social isolate than her married sister. Table 8.2 does not show a consistent relationship between marital status and interaction with friends. Among those with less education, the two currently married groups are more likely to report that they have visited friends in the last few weeks, but there is as much variation between these two groups as there is between them and the groups which are without a spouse present. Furthermore, this finding does not hold for more highly educated respondents, and it is not supported by the responses to the question concerning the number of friends one could call on in an emergency (Table 8.2).

The data on the number of relatives one could call on also show that the mothers who maintain their own households have at least equal access to their relatives. As might be expected, the spouseless mothers who live with other adults report the largest number of relatives they can call on (Table 8.2).

The mothers without spouses also engage in as many recreational and entertainment activities as the other women (see Table 8.2). In general, most women in this sample do not go to the movies or sports events very often, and few of them report that they play cards, or drink in bars. Eating in a restaurant is the activity most frequently mentioned. None of the marital-status groups is clearly distinguishable from the others in most of these activities. The differences are small and inconsistent. Only in regard to the item relating to having a drink in a bar is there a noticeable difference in both educational groups. The spouse-absent groups respond "yes" somewhat more often—particularly the group living with other adults. But this finding is not suf-

Table 8.2. Group Ties and Social Participation of Mothers by Marital History and Education

	Marital History	Percent Visited Friends	Mean Number of Friends Could Call on	Mean Number of Relatives Could Call on	Mean Number of Activities Engaged in	Mean Number Formal Groups Belongs to
Total sample	Married once	76	1.4	3.0	4.3	.62
	Remarried	81	1.6	2.5	4.5	.79
	No spouse, lives with relatives	80	1.7	4.4	4.8	.93
	"Solo" mother	65	1.4	2.9	4.1	.79
Less than four years of high school	Married once	72	1.3	2.7	3.8	.33
	Remarried	85	1.3	2.3	4.4	.53
	No spouse, lives with relatives	66	1.0	3.5	4.2	.36
	"Solo" mother	62	1.3	3.0	3.7	.34
Four years of high school or more	Married once	80	1.4	3.4	4.7	.96
	Remarried	76	2.0	2.7	4.7	1.15
	No spouse, lives with relatives	93	2.2	5.1	5.4	.88
	"Solo" mother	70	1.6	2.7	4.8	.72

ficient to overcome the general point that extent of recreational activities is unrelated to marital status.

Though it is getting somewhat afield of the other items, before we conclude this section it seems of value to look into the formal group ties of these women. Do the problems of raising a family without a husband cut into the community participation of these women?

The answer to this question seems to be no. The average number of formal association memberships does not appear to be associated with marital status. The formal group membership of these women is very low in general. If we exclude church and union membership, the average women who is less than a high-school graduate belongs to .36 groups; the average of the higher education group is .89. Being without a husband neither increases nor decreases these averages in any systematic way.

The answer to our original question about the social activities of the mother without a spouse is clear as far as we can take it. There is little relationship between marital status and interaction with family and kin, recreational activity, and formal group participation. We do not know anything about the attitudes of these women in this regard, but all the objective indices suggest that they do not suffer from important social disabilities. Neither their situation nor the attitudes of others toward them seems to act as a barrier to social lives equal to those of the married women.

attitudes toward marriage and men

One of the key findings of the Goode study was that the divorced women in his sample had undiminished faith in men and the institution of marriage. Their broken marriages were not bad enough to turn them off marriage, and their divorced status was not good enough to turn them on to the single state. Their typical attitude was that there was nothing wrong with love, men, or marriage—the problem was a particular man and a particular marriage. Remarriage seemed quite attractive. They had made a mistake once and they did not expect to make the same error again.

A clear-cut, consistent picture does not emerge for the women in

Table 8.3.   Mothers' Attitudes toward Men and Marriage by Marital History and Education

	Marital History	Percent Agree Most Men Make Good Husbands	Percent Agree Women's Best Time When Married	Percent Would Marry Again
Total sample	Married once	32	51	69
	Remarried	29	58	67
	No spouse, lives with relatives	28	35	75
	"Solo" mother	15	41	67
Less than four years of high school	Married once	30	46	59
	Remarried	34	61	58
	No spouse, lives with relatives	21	33	71
	"Solo" mother	13	39	67
Four years of high school or more	Married once	33	56	80
	Remarried	23	55	79
	No spouse, lives with relatives	35	37	78
	"Solo" mother	17	45	67

our study (see Table 8.3). No group is consistently more favorable or unfavorable. For example, lower-status solo mothers are least likely to agree that men make good husbands, but they are not the group least likely to say a woman's best time is when she is married, and they are more willing to marry than some of the others. Like Goode we find no support for the idea that women who have experienced a broken marriage have attitudes toward men and marriage which are very different from those of other women. In general, all the subgroups tend to show a rather jaundiced attitude toward these matters. All groups favor being married while at the same time they do not seem very happy about the state of marriage. Variations on this theme are not related to present or past marital status.

self-esteem, frustration, and marital status

All these data on the situation and attitudes of mothers without spouses are, we feel, of considerable interest and value, but when it comes down to it, the most relevant question is, what does it mean to a black woman to be in this status? Are such women as happy as other women? Is the status destructive of self-esteem?

In regard to the second of these questions, Parker and Kleiner's (1966) data from a study of black mothers in Philadelphia showed that mothers in intact families have self-esteem scores which are only very slightly higher than women without spouses, and our data tend to sup-

Table 8.4.   Miscellaneous Characteristics of Mothers by Marital History and Education

Marital History	Rating of Self as Mother *	Rating of Appeal to Opposite Sex *	Percent Agree Most Women Make Good Wives	Mean Frustration Score
Total sample				
Married once	29	11	46	− .04
Remarried	23	14	40	− .15
No spouse, lives with relatives	26	7	35	.97
"Solo" mother	30	8	37	2.32
Less than four years of high school				
Married once	27	13	42	1.61
Remarried	20	18	47	1.40
No spouse, lives with relatives	32	5	38	2.68
"Solo" mother	28	5	38	3.32
Four years of high school or more				
Married once	31	8	49	− 1.68
Remarried	28	9	30	− 2.29
No spouse, lives with relatives	21	9	33	− .59
"Solo" mother	34	13	35	.42

* Percentage rating self "above average."

port the notion that marital status has no important effect upon various elements of self-evaluation (see Table 8.4). Rating of self as a mother shows no trends, and for the group as a whole there is no relation between marital status and evaluation of one's attractiveness to members of the opposite sex. Among the lower-status women, those who have husbands, and particularly those who have remarried, rate themselves higher on attractiveness. None of the other self-evaluation questions show a relation to marital status, but better-educated women who have had a broken marriage are less likely to agree that most women make good wives—a response which may imply some degree of self-criticism. Among the less well educated this difference is not apparent.

It would appear that "failure" in a marriage and "failure" to find a new spouse do not lead these women to think less of themselves. This would suggest that others do not denigrate such women, and their marital problems do not represent failure in terms of their psychological framework.

This is not to say, however, that all is well with the unmarried mothers. There is little doubt when we look at our measure of frustration and unhappiness that those who remarry are better off. Certainly it is better to live with other adults (frustration score = .97) than to be on your own (score = 2.32), but neither of these compares with those who are remarried (score = −.15), or married once (score = −.04). The results with education controlled are comparable. Interestingly, the economic advantage of the better-educated unmarried mothers who live with other adults is not translated into greater satisfaction. In both educational groups the ordering from low to high frustration is: remarried, once married, unmarried who live with other adults, and mothers on their own.

The lesson of these data is clear. Regardless of the arrangement, it is not satisfying to be a mother without a spouse.

conclusion

Our data would suggest that black mothers without spouses are not heirs to all the ills of the world. They are not social isolates, they do not think poorly of themselves, and they are not disillusioned. By the same token, our findings suggest that the status of mother without spouse is not as functional as it has been painted by some. The woman without a spouse is likely to be in a disastrous economic situation unless she is living with other adults. Economically, a spouse is not necessary; some black mothers get along very well without one. But most of these women have the aid of other adults, someone to babysit and/or contribute income. The problem is that this kind of arrangement is relatively rare. It should also be stressed that "economically" is the key word in the previous sentences, for the frustration levels of both groups of unmarried mothers are substantially above those of the married. There may be an economic alternative to marriage, but in more general terms there appear to be no acceptable alternatives.

Aside from any long-range effects, it seems clear that broken marriages do cause suffering for many black women. The critics' charge is supported in this instance, though again not in all details.

chapter nine

a summation
and
decision

By now it is amply clear that a one- or two-word verdict is not possible in the case of the black family. We could not possibly catch the complexity of the situation in such a statement. Our conclusion will therefore resemble a judicial opinion more than a jury's decision.

It has been well established that the structure of black families is different from that of white families in a number of ways. Our data and/or those of other researchers show that black fertility and family size are higher than those of whites. Blacks are more likely to live in multigenerational households, and among those in nuclear households, blacks have fewer relatives they can call on. In addition, black marriages are more likely to be disrupted.

The data also suggest that these are not merely SES differences in disguise. When we control for SES the gaps do not disappear. Even if the races were the same on SES, there would be differences between them in regard to these family traits.

All this is as the critics suggest, and these data represent support for one aspect of their charges. But there is more to the story. Blacks and whites do not differ on age at marriage, and the evidence regarding maternal power is contradictory. The critics are wrong when they suggest that the contrast between black and white families is primarily a lower-SES phenomenon. In regard to fertility this is true—the differences are greatest among those who have the least education. But the racial gap is about the same in both SES groups for maternal dominance, marital stability, and kin aid.

The critics may also be somewhat off the mark when it comes to the size of the gap between blacks and whites. They contend that racial status is a major factor in family structure. "There is one truly great discontinuity in family structure in the United States at the present time: that between the white world in general and that of the Negro American'' (Moynihan, et al., 1965). In this sample the difference in fertility is less than 1 child per woman on the average, and it is about 2 on kin available for aid. There is an 18-point divergence in the incidence of extended households, and a 14-percent gap in the occurrence of female dominance. About 25 points separate the races in regard to rates of broken marriage.

Obviously, this has to be a matter of judgment, since there is no criterion for deciding how large a gap has to exist before it is major. Without attempting to play down the existence of important racial variation, we would contend that the critics give an exaggerated picture of its size. But we would also note that the black-white differences are greater than the SES differences within racial groups for kin aid, maternal dominance, and stability. Even if the differences between races are not major, on some variables they are larger than those associated with another key sociological variable.

One gets the clear impression from some of the literature on the black family that these traits are not only more common among blacks than among whites: it is often implied that they are the traits of the typical black family, or at least of the typical lower-status black family. This does not seem to be true. Sixty percent of the lower-status black women marry after age 18, and over 60 percent of the men marry after 21. Most black families are not female dominated. Even in the lower-status group, most blacks can call on several relatives, and a large majority live in nuclear households. Seventy-five percent of our respondents who have ever been married are now married, and 60 percent of the ever-married have had stable marriages. And, finally, though a majority of urban black children live in families of 6 or more members, less than 40 percent of urban black families have that many members. These traits do not describe the modal black family.

It seems, therefore, that the picture painted by the critics requires alteration in some significant details. At the same time, we should not lose sight of the fact that the gross outline of their position is correct.

All this does not get to the heart of the matter, however, for it is no ''crime'' to be different from the white family. Many, of course, would argue that the traits which are more common in black families are intrinsically less desirable, but generally the case is tied to the assertion that there are demonstrable negative effects associated with certain family forms. All that has been shown so far is that black families show a greater incidence of some family traits which are reputed to have undesirable consequences. We now turn to the key question, is the reputation a deserved one?

Age at marriage, which for recent years does not show racial variation, is clearly associated with marital stability and difficulties in the early years of marriage. This is particularly so for those who come from higher-status backgrounds. There is, however, some question as to whether age at marriage is causing these problems, or whether people who marry early are the kind of people who would have difficulty regardless of when they married. A definite answer to this question cannot be given, but indirect evidence suggests that selection does account for some of the variation. The selective factors are not, however, the social traits, such as education and parental SES, that are usually suggested. When those traits are controlled, the correlations with age at marriage remain unchanged.

The key point, however, is that the *effects* of age at marriage cannot be very great. The correlations are not large to begin with, and in fact, for lower-status men they are trivial. In those groups where there is an association, some of it should be attributed to selection. There isn't much left over. Age at marriage has an effect on later events, but it is probably not as great as has been suggested.

The data on the correlates of family size tend to support the critics' view that large families have consequences which may be labeled undesirable. People who were brought up in large families do not go as far in school, they have less income when they are starting out in the world, and they are generally more frustrated. The data also suggest that there are short-run effects. The mothers of large families carry heavier burdens, and there is an inverse relation between family size and family income.

On the other hand, only higher-status females show greater dissatisfaction when they are the parents of large families. However, in all groups people who have more children than they want are less satisfied. Since number of children is strongly related to satisfaction with number of children, family size may be viewed as an indirect cause of general satisfaction. All in all, the critics' charge is supported in general outline, but they exaggerate the strength of the effects and their variability by socioeconomic status.

Theory and data from whites suggest that the sex of the dominant person in the family has an influence on sex identification and through this upon personality and achievement. This is the source of the critics' claim that undesirable consequences flow from female dominance in black homes.

The data do not support these claims. It is true that the dominant parent is more likely to be chosen as the person who was admired and respected the most during the respondent's youth, but this is as far as it goes. Men who were brought up in female-controlled homes are not feminine in their behavior. They are less likely to marry and somewhat more likely to divorce, but the differences are small and inconsistent. Most importantly, there is no consistent indication that those from maternally dominated homes achieve less. In fact, if the respondent is from a lower-status background his income tends to be slightly greater if his mother was dominant.

Patterns of kin interaction do not have important effects. Living in a multigenerational home does not produce lessened satisfaction, nor does it affect self-evaluation. Also, people do not seem to suffer if they rarely see their relatives or if there are few relatives they can call on for help.

A lack of husband-wife activities (conjugal role segregation), is related to dissatisfaction in several subgroups, but not for lower-status men. And when there is a relation it is not certain that a lack of husband-wife interaction is the cause rather than the effect. The relation between role segregation and self-evaluation is not strong nor completely consistent. It appears that the norm of togetherness is not universally accepted in the black community, and its absence does not cause much in the way of dissatisfaction.

The key charge in the indictment is the one lodged against the broken home. Men from such homes are supposed to be poorer marital risks, to be less successful economically, and, if they lived in a home in which there was no adult male, they are supposed to grow up to be more "trouble-prone" and more feminine in behavior.

The data indicate that men from broken homes do not have more problems than those from stable homes, and the differences between female-only homes and both-sex broken homes are neither clear nor consistent. Men from intact families do earn somewhat more than those from broken homes, but it is not the female-only household which is the main culprit. In fact, men from such homes earn more on the average than those from two-sex broken homes. We would also note that the differences are generally larger for those who come from higher-status backgrounds.

A similar picture emerges for the transmission of marital instability. Those from disrupted homes have a somewhat lower marital success rate. The difference is largely to be found among respondents of higher-status background, and it is the fact of a broken home that is important rather than the details of the break or the postbreak situation.

In addition to these matters we inquired into the short-term effects of a broken marriage and found that mothers without spouses are in a precarious economic position unless they are in the relatively rare situation of having other adults in the household. In other respects—social life, informal group involvement, and formal group membership— marital status does not have much relevance. In addition, marital status is not clearly related to self-evaluation or to attitudes toward men and marriage. Currently unmarried mothers are, however, less satisfied than married mothers regardless of whether or not there are other adults in the home. We consider this to be a key finding and it strongly supports the position of the critics rather than that of those who contend that blacks have worked out an acceptable substitute for the husband-wife family.

The findings of this study provide mixed evidence on the validity of the second part of the critics' charges. Some of the "indicted" structures do incline people in the predicted direction, but the critics generally have the details wrong, and clearly none of the effects are as strong as they say they are. The full meaning of the data will not emerge, however, until we have the answer to the next question: as compared to other variables, how important are family traits in influencing outcomes?

how much is explained by family factors?

Family and Income. The most direct way to answer the question we have just posed is through a regression analysis. The beta weights which emerge from that procedure show the effect of one variable upon the dependent variable with all others in the equation held constant, and the multiple correlation coefficients * when squared tell us how much of the variation in the dependent variable is accounted for by any desired combination of independent variables. By varying the order in which the variables are entered we can get an indication of the relative importance of different kinds of variables. If one set of variables, let us call it set *B,* is entered after set *A,* and it increases the explained variance more than set *A* does when it is added to set *B,* then set *B* may be considered more important.

In Table 9.1 we use 4 family factors and 4 nonfamily factors as the

Table 9.1. Effects of Familial and Nonfamilial Variables upon Respondents' Income by Parental SES (Ever-Married Males Who Are Not Students)

| | | Beta Weights | |
Variable	Total Sample	Lower PrSES	Higher PrSES
Age	.25	.26	.21
Age at marriage	.03	−.05	.11
Number of siblings	.02	.00	.06
Maternal control score	.01	.07	−.03
Parental marriage unbroken *	.10	.08	.10
Parental SES	.00		
Education	.28	.26	.29
Urban birth	.04	.10	.00
R †	.37	.35	.41
R ²	.13	.12	.17

* For the nonnumerical variables, a positive beta means that the response indicated is associated with high income.
† Multiple correlation coefficient (see glossary).

independent variables and income as the dependent variable. The data show clearly that the variables we have do not explain very much of the variation in the male respondent's income. The 8 variables used account for only 13 percent of the variation in the total male sample; 87 percent remains unexplained. However, more to the point is the fact that the 4 family variables add about 1 percentage point to the variation accounted for by the nonfamily variables. On the other hand, education adds 7 points to the variation explained by the age and the family variables.

The nonfamily variables are clearly more important, though their strength is hardly impressive. It is not surprising to find that as age increases income goes up somewhat, and aside from that education is the only variable which has an independent effect on respondent's income. (A year's education is worth about $250 in income on the average.) The table shows that parental SES has no independent effect on income, which is a rather surprising finding. However, that datum is a bit misleading, for the social status of one's parents is not totally irrelevant. If PrSES is entered into the equation immediately after age, it has a beta weight of .08. This decreases to near zero only when education is entered. Thus it is better in regard to later income to come from a higher-status family, but this relation is due to the fact that men from higher-status backgrounds go further in school. The table also underplays the significance of urban birth. Before education is introduced, its beta reaches .09; but urban birth also works through its effect on education, and therefore in the final table it seems less important.

We see in the other sections of Table 9.1 that these variables "do slightly better" in the higher SES group. Adding the family variables to the equation after all the other variables are in increases the explained variance by 3 percentage points, and all the variables explain 17 percent of the variance in income. Both these figures are higher than they are in the total sample, but the improvement is trivial.

In the higher SES group, age at marriage and parental marital stability do have a small effect upon income, but they clearly are not as important as age and education, which have much larger betas. After age and the family variables have explained all the variance they can, education adds 7 percentage points to the explained variance. As noted above, family variables add 3 points if they are put in last. Family variables may be of greater significance here than in the total sample, but they are still not very important.

For men of lower-status background the family variables account for almost none of the variance. It is somewhat better to come from a stable home and one dominated by the mother, as we have seen before, but the real advantage for lower-status black males comes if they manage to obtain more education.

In general, it is amply clear that changes in black family structure would have little influence on the income of black men. The solution to the economic difficulties of blacks does not lie in changing these structural features of the family.

The Sources of Frustration. As has often been suggested, money isn't everything. We also want to know if family features influence the frustration level of blacks in a significant way.

The general answer for the sample as a whole (see Table 9.2) is that these variables have only a small effect upon the measure of frustration and unhappiness. Ten family variables and 4 nonfamily variables have a multiple correlation of .40 with frustration and unhappiness. They account for 16 percent of the variation. The nonfamily variables seem to have a slightly stronger effect, but here the difference is small. If they are put in last, the family variables add 4 points to the variation explained by the nonfamily variables. If the order is reversed the nonfamily variables add 7 points.

When we deal with the sex and parental SES groups separately, the results are basically the same in each group. For males and for lower-status females the total explained variance is 16 percent; for

Table 9.2.   Effects of Familial and Nonfamilial Variables upon Respondents' Frustration Scores by Sex and Parental SES (Ever-Married Respondents)

| | | Beta Weights | | | |
| | | Males | | Females | |
Variable	Total Sample	Lower PrSES	Higher PrSES	Lower PrSES	Higher PrSES
Maternal control score	.06	−.03	−.12	.12	.18
Number of siblings	.00	−.14	.05	−.02	−.09
Parental marriage unbroken *	−.03	−.02	−.08	.01	.04
Age at marriage	−.03	.01	−.08	−.05	−.04
Number of children	.02	−.01	.06	.07	−.01
Currently married	−.07	.02	−.16	−.12	−.04
Companionship score	−.14	−.05	−.06	−.15	−.18
Number of in-laws can count on	−.06	−.21	.02	−.03	−.06
Number of own relatives can count on	.01	.09	.00	.00	−.06
Lives in nuclear household	.03	.00	.01	−.02	−.04
Education	−.22	−.20	−.28	−.18	−.33
Born in urban area	.02	.02	−.06	.02	.04
Age	−.10	−.12	−.13	−.12	−.10
Family income	−.11	−.18	.07	−.14	−.07
R	.40	.40	.40	.40	.51
R^2	.16	.16	.16	.16	.26

* For the nonnumerical variables a positive beta means that the response indicated is associated with high frustration.

higher-status females it reaches .26. In general, neither the family nor the nonfamily variables seem to be clearly "superior." When the family variables are added to the nonfamily variables the gain in explained variance is generally about the same as when the nonfamily variables are introduced after the family variables have been entered into the equation.

We have, then, another indication that the critics have exaggerated the importance of family-structure variables. We would not argue that these variables have no relevance, for several of them have clear independent effect upon this dependent variable, and they are also related to others. Nonetheless, they explain very little of the variance. Most of the relevant factors remain undiscovered.

At the same time, supporters of the black family have clearly exaggerated the importance of some nonfamily variables. Education is clearly the most important variable we have. It has a beta of .18 or higher in all subgroups for both dependent variables. At the same time, the beta exceeds .30 only once, and thus we may conclude the effect of education is not overpowering. Age operates similarly at a lower level. Income influences satisfaction for persons of lower-status background, but it does not have a consistent influence for those of higher status. Urban background does not seem to have a general independent effect on income or satisfaction.

Family Variables and Black-White Income Differentials. A final component of the charges against the black family suggests that blacks would be less deprived relative to whites if their family characteristics were more like those of whites. Though we must consider the possibility, the assertion need not detain us overly long, for the answer to it is contained in what has gone before. If race has a weak or moderate association with family traits, and family variables have only a weak association with income, the income gap between the races could not be attributable to these family factors.

Family stability, in this generation and the previous one, does not, however, fit these premises; and it is therefore worthwhile to determine the extent to which the income gap would be reduced if the races were equivalent in marital stability. Looking at the respondents who have ever been married, we find a large difference in family income between whites and blacks. On the basis of grouped data we estimate that the difference between the mean incomes is about $1,894. When we limit the analysis to currently married persons, the means of both races increase, as would be expected since we are removing, among others, women without spouses. The change, however, is about equal for blacks and whites. Thus the gap between married respondents is $1,739, about the same as for all respondents.

This means that the racial income gap is not due to the differential number of "previously married" persons in the two groups. If everyone in the two racial groups were married, the income differential would be just about what it was in the total sample. This is not to say that eliminating broken marriages would have no effect on income. All it means is that it would not reduce the black-white differences. Whites would gain as much as blacks.

This perhaps seems somewhat strange. Divorced and separated women are more frequent in the black group, and one might think that if they were removed from consideration this group's income would increase more than if the relatively few unmarried white women were removed. According to this reasoning, there should be some narrowing of the difference between the races. The reason why this does not occur becomes clear when it is realized that the increase in group income is a function of the number of persons removed *and* the extent to which those who are removed deviate from those who are left. The "previously married" white women have very low family income relative to other white women; the gap is $4,587. Among blacks the difference is not so great: $1,954. Fewer white women are "lost" when we go from all ever-married respondents to currently married respondents, but the gain in income is much greater every time a white previously married woman is removed from the sample.

Parental marital instability shows a similar pattern. Earlier (see p. 105) we saw that if all black men came from unbroken homes, the average income of black men would increase very little. We may now add that if all people, black and white, came from unbroken homes, the gap between the races in family income would be only $327 less than it is. The differential distribution by race of intact parental homes has little to do with the lower income of blacks.

In general, it would seem that changes in the family characteristics of blacks would have little effect upon income differentials, and this is a final indication that the black family is not guilty as charged.

the theoretical significance of family structures

As we stated at the beginning, our interest in the black family goes beyond the narrow concerns of the critics' charges. The data we have permit us to make a contribution to family theory, for they allow us to test a number of specific theories, hypotheses, and generalized conceptions which have been offered by previous authors. We turn now to summary of the results bearing upon this second interest.

There is no theory relating to the consequences of early marriage, but the literature contains generalized descriptions of such marriages which are supposed to explain their high rates of instability. Much of our effort was devoted to considering whether these descriptions held for black marriages.

In general the early marriages in this sample are less satisfying and more fragile, but the data are only partially consistent with the hypothetical descriptions of early marriage which are found in the literature. Some of the associations are weak, and few are found in all subgroups. The usual descriptions of young couples seem oversimplified and exaggerated when applied to blacks.

A subsidiary interest in this area relates to the reasons behind the distinctive aspects of young marriages. Are youth inherently susceptible to such traits or are they a result of the fact that young couples represent a select group of young people? We do not have a final answer to this question, but at this point it seems that selection is involved. This is the only way we can account for the fact that the correlations between age at marriage and other variables are as high or higher in the later years of marriage as they are in the earlier. If the correlations were caused by youthfulness, they should decline with increasing age. If the source is certain traits associated with a tendency to marry early, the correlations could very well remain high or increase. This does not rule out the possibility that black youth as a group are less well prepared for marriage than are older black persons. We strongly suspect that this is so. All we have suggested is that this is not the whole story.

Our data also indicate that the selection factors are not the ones which are usually mentioned. We controlled for parental SES, stability of parental marriage, number of siblings, etc. and found that these factors did not account for differences between early and later marriages. The relevant factors will, we suggest, be found by an investigation of value, personality, and ability variables.

The theoretical concern of the chapter on family size is a little more sophisticated because it can be tied to the general sociological interest in the effects of group size. The materials are, however, similar to those we just surveyed. They also represent a test of the validity of a generalized description which is intended to make sense out of the correlates of a structural feature.

The data are not entirely consistent, but in general they do not support the view associated with James Bossard which sees in the large family an environment characterized by love, cooperation, self-sacrifice, etc. On the contrary, large families seem to suffer from conflict, authoritarianism, and limited resources. And the products of such families show some scars of their early experience. These findings are consistent with the general sociological perspective which suggests that as group size increases problems of organization and integration multiply. These problems lead to conflict, and the limitation of individuality occurs in an effort to reduce it.

In the chapter on parental dominance the major theoretical focus was on ideas which come from theories of parental identification. However, since we do not have a measure of identification these ideas were applied to the closely related variable, "parental admiration." The major postulate we tested states that people tend to admire, or to identify with, those who have characteristics which are valued.

The data give strong support to this general theoretical notion. The respondents tended to admire more the parent they perceived as more powerful: the parent who controlled decisions, the purse strings, and the children. They also tended to prefer the one who possessed other desirable traits: more education, greater functionality, etc. Moreover, we find that in this situation, at least, power over family decisions is far and away the most potent attractor of admiration. In fact, some of the other variables have varying effects, depending on the decision-making power of the person. For example, fathers who had more education than their wives were often admired if they made the decisions. If they did not make decisions they were rarely mentioned as the more admired parent.

A second major postulate of identity theory asserts that the sex of the preferred parent has an important influence upon various traits of adults. According to this view, men who admired their mothers most model themselves after her. Therefore, they develop feminine traits, or, according to an alternative interpretation, traits of exaggerated masculinity when they react against their growing femininity. And since maternal power is a key source of maternal admiration we also get the hypothesis, maternal dominance leads to femininity or exaggerated masculinity. A similar line of reasoning suggests that a woman who identifies with her father would be expected to be more masculine than other women, or ultrafeminine, but this connection is not often made. We cannot adequately measure exaggerated masculinity, but when we use the power-over-decision item for males, about 9 of 24 comparisons support the femininity hypothesis. This does not seem sufficiently strong to support the hypothesis. When we come closer to the dependent variable and use maternal admiration as the independent variable the success rate goes up somewhat: 15 of the 24 comparisons show more femininity for those who preferred their mothers. This is taken as weak support for the hypothesis. For women, however, there is no relation between father dominance or father admiration and masculinity. Our general conclusion is that parental power and admiration are not major determinants of sex-linked behavior.

We suggest that the hypothesis fails because imitation of a dominant parent is not the major mechanism of socialization. For one thing, dominance does not always lead to admiration, and admiration does not always lead to imitation—particularly of sex-linked traits. In such matters, children know that many behaviors of the opposite-sex parent are not appropriate for them, and if they are not aware of this their parents will make sure they soon learn it. When this is added to the fact that much of this learning takes place after childhood and outside the home, it is not surprising that our results were so weak. It seems clear that previous theorists have taken one aspect of socialization and grossly exaggerated its significance.

A similar theoretical problem is considered in the chapter on the broken home. Admiration for the mother is supposed to lead a man to model his behavior after his mother, and the absence of the father is assumed to have the same result. Father absence supposedly means the absence of a ''proper'' role model. The mother is not an acceptable substitute, and this starts the boy down the road to feminine behavior.

Some continue in this direction, others react and become super-masculine. In both instances, however, the basic mechanism is the use of an inappropriate role model. The data bearing upon this issue are even weaker than those we obtained with maternal admiration. Seven of the 24 comparisons show greater femininity among those from female-headed homes. These data do not give an acceptable level of support to the hypothesis.

The reasons that the hypothesis failed are similar in part to those which lie behind the failure of the maternal-dominance predictions. Parents can teach proper behavior to children who are not of the same sex as they are. We would note further that the physical absence of a father does not ensure the absence of a male socializing agent. Male siblings, peers from the street, etc., can and do serve in that role. This would be particularly true in the case of ghetto dwellers, where the young boy typically breaks his strings to his mother very early and engages in an intensive street life. Again it seems that the hypothesis is based upon an oversimplified view of the socialization process and it is not at all surprising that it is not supported.

In addition to its effects upon femininity, the broken home is postulated to be an important source of personal and social maladjustment. The general idea is that the breakup of a marriage is a traumatic experience for all involved, and the postbreak situation involves continuing difficulty: financial insecurity, lessened opportunities for parental supervision, overworked and dissatisfied mothers, lower levels of educational achievement, early demands for self-reliance, etc.

The evidence we used to test these ideas does not entirely support them. The broken home does have some correlates which may be considered undesirable, but by no means does it lead to all the consequences it has had attributed to it. The theory obviously needs additional refinement and extension. As a start in this direction, we would suggest that it must be recognized that the distinction between the good intact family and the bad broken home is too stark. A conception which took into account that some structurally intact homes can be "bad" and broken homes can be "good" would be closer to the truth. The balance may favor the intact home, but the gap is not so large as it is viewed to be. This idea is certainly not new, but it does not seem to have been integrated very well into the existing theories.

Second, this revised theory must realize that a single outcome may have various causes. A person who escapes a broken home can show the same trait we associate with a broken home because there is something else in the environment which can produce it. If there is a low or negative correlation between the other ''cause'' and a broken home, this would serve to reduce the gap between the broken and intact homes. Even if people from broken homes were more likely to experience these factors also, the gap would be reduced if the effects were not cumulative. This, we believe, is why the broken home seems to make more difference in the higher-status group. These other causes are not so common there. Thus, the person who does not experience a broken home will ''escape.'' For lower-status people there is no escape. If the broken home doesn't get you, something else will.

Finally, it seems that greater stress should be placed on the similarities between the female-headed home and the broken home that has adults of two sexes, for they are similar in their consequences. Perhaps we should stress more the experiences associated with a broken family per se, and the unlikelihood that a stepfather will fully replace a missing father. In fact, it may be more difficult to adjust, psychologically, to a stepfather than it is to adjust to the absence of a father—particularly in a community where many fathers are absent.

The theory which suggests that in our society there is inherent strain associated with extended-family households does not receive adequate support. The frustration scores of those living in extended households are only trivially higher than the scores of those in nuclear households. Extended households are associated with a lessened willingness to ''marry if you had it to do over again'' only for younger respondents, and the effects on relevant aspects of self-evaluation are trivial.

The next hypothesis tested stated that when spouses engage in joint activities (conjugal role integration), there will be greater satisfaction and higher evaluations of self as spouse. Conjugal role integration is said to be part of the definition of the spousal role. Failure to achieve it leads to dissatisfaction, because of a failure by the spouse to live up to expectations. Negative attitudes toward the self result, because of a failure to fulfill one's obligations to the other.

Though the hypothesis received some support it was weak and variable. The associations are higher for satisfaction than for self-evaluation. They are particularly low for lower-status males. Our guess is that the norm of togetherness is not strong in the sample, and it is particularly weak for lower-status males. We also see here an indication that people are quicker to blame the other than they are to blame themselves when a norm is broken.

Finally, we considered the hypothesis that contact with kin and the availability of aid from them was a source of security and satisfaction in a society which was becoming increasingly anonymous. This idea received no support. People who reported visits from relations did not differ in frustration score from those who did not, and there was no correlation between the latter variable and number of kin available for help in an emergency.

In general, our data give spotty support to the theories we have tested. Few of them are completely off the mark but all could benefit from revision and tightening.

are the dynamics of black families unique?

The theories we have been considering were worked out with white families in mind, and the basis for some of the critics' charges is an extension of materials from whites. Since neither the theories nor the charges are completely supported by data from black families, it might appear that the processes we have been studying do not have generality. However, this would not necessarily follow. The theories and charges may have their roots in materials about white families, but this is not equivalent to saying that they are actually descriptive of such families. In fact, some of the ideas have not really been tested, and others have not received consistent support. If we are to reach a conclusion on the extent to which black and white families are similar in their dynamics, one of the central concerns of this book, we need a replication of our study on a white sample.

As the reader already knows, we have data which will permit a limited replication. We cannot do a full restudy, even if the reader's patience would permit, for our data from whites are not as rich as those from black subjects, and our sample size is much smaller, so some of the more complicated comparisons are not possible due to inadequate sample size. Nonetheless, we can test some of the key findings, and we turn next to those.

Correlates of Family Size. The effect of family size upon the mother's employment turns out to be much weaker for whites than it was for blacks. For the latter there was a clear association between large families and a lack of outside employment (partial $r = -.14$). In these data, however, the association for whites is trivial (partial $r = -.04$). This is quite surprising and apparently contrary to evidence from other studies (in Nye and Hoffman, 1963: 13, 70, 224, 225). Though the previous studies do not present their material in the same way, it seems that the relation we found is unusually weak. At any rate, our concern is with black-white differences, and the data say clearly that the number of children has less effect on the employment of white women. Specifically, a majority of blacks work if they have few children. Those who have many children are less likely to work. Among whites, however, only 27 percent of those with 1 or 2 children work. Additional children do not decrease the figure at all.

In white families there is a negative relation between number of children and family income, just as there was in the black group, but it is considerably smaller in size ($r = -.08$ for whites and $-.18$ for blacks).

It soon turns out, however, that this is misleading. Among the whites there is a curvilinear relation involved. Childless couples have a mean income of $8,107, 1-child families earn $9,552 on the average, and 2-child families over $10,000. From this point, as expected, income declines with increasing family size. The reason for the curvilinearity became clear when we controlled for age. Among other variables, age is acting as a suppressor. If age were constant the relation would be on the order of $-.13$. (This is also the partial correlation for blacks.) The low income of those with fewer than 2 children is probably a function of their youth.

Our conclusion, then, is the same for both races. There is a negative relation between family size and income, and it is not to be explained away in terms of such variables as education and age. In both races those with the greatest burden have the least income.

Except for high-status females, the parents of large black families did not show differences in satisfaction when compared to parents of smaller families, despite the several problems they have. People who had more children than they wanted, however, were generally less satisfied.

For whites, number of children itself proved to be of considerable significance, particularly for males. Men who are fathers of larger families are somewhat less likely to say they would marry if they had their lives to live over (partial $r = -.09$); they rate themselves lower as spouses (partial $r = -.10$); they place themselves lower on a scale which measures "goodness of my life" (partial $r = -.15$); and they indicate greater feelings of frustration on 3 items (partial r's $= .17, .08,$ and $.11$). The only possibly inconsistent element is that they rate themselves more highly as fathers than do the men with small families (partial $r = .13$). On the four items which relate directly to satisfaction, the picture is the same for the women. It seems generally true that large families are associated with lessened satisfaction for whites.

Each of the three dependent variables we related to family size suggests a different conclusion. The relation between family size and income is about the same in the two races. In regard to maternal employment, family size has a greater effect for blacks than for whites. On the other hand, the satisfaction of whites is more tied to family size then is the satisfaction of blacks. We should emphasize, however, that in no case are the effects in opposite directions in the two groups. The differences are only differences of magnitude.

Parental Power and Admiration. The relationship between maternal power and maternal admiration is as strong for whites as it was for blacks. For both sons and daughters there is a strong relation between the response to "Who made the important decisions?" and the response to "Who did you admire most?" ($r = .59$ and $.60$). Furthermore, though the details are different, the data from whites lead us to conclude, as we did for blacks, that control over decisions was a key factor in determining who would be the object of the respondent's admiration. Responses to the questions, "Who punished you when you were young?" and "Who kept track of the family money?" are also related to parental admiration but less strongly and less consistently.

The data on the relationship between admiration and the relative education of mother and father are different for whites than for blacks.

For whites, a woman with more education than her husband garners added admiration, but a father with higher education than his spouse gets no advantage. For blacks the pattern is reversed; fathers gained more than mothers. This probably means that the general rule is that the person with an unexpected amount of education gets respect for it. In black families the expectation is probably that the woman will be better educated, for this is the case very often; so the man who has more education than his wife gets admiration for it. Among whites neither sex surpasses the other in education, but the expectation is that the wife will have less if their education is not equal. Hence the reversal.

Both groups also show a tendency to give low admiration to a person when he or she exceeds the spouse in education but does not make the decisions. However, the tendency is much weaker in regard to white fathers than it is for black ones. For mothers the relation is equally strong in both races. For whites, if a woman had more education than her husband and she also made the decisions, the chances are 83 in 100 that she will be mentioned as the admired person. If she did not make the decisions, despite her higher education she is chosen by about 55 percent of the respondents.

As with blacks, both "mother worked" and "father was unemployed" have an effect on admiration, though care is indicated by the fact that the sample of unemployed white fathers is only 10 in this test. In regard to the working-mother variable we find, just as before, it is only higher-status women who gain admiration by working. More than that, the advantage goes primarily to higher-status working women who made the decisions.

With a few exceptions, then, the road to admiration from children is the same for both blacks and whites. The theories we tested seem to hold for both blacks and whites.

Our discussion of the effects of maternal preference upon the adult characteristics of whites will have to be limited, for we do not have many of the variables that were used for blacks. Particularly unfortunate is the fact that we have only two of the personality items.

We do, however, have data on income, and this is of particular importance. It will be remembered that the data from blacks did not give support to the charge that female dominance in the parental home is a brake upon the achievement of the sons. In both parental SES groups the correlations were low, and, in fact, in the lower SES group it was "better" to come from a female-dominated home.

The data for whites are also in opposition to the charge. For whites of lower-status background the partial correlation between maternal dominance and respondent's family income [1] is .30, which indicates that those from maternally dominated homes have higher incomes. For higher-status males the correlation is in the same direction, but it is of trivial size. The patterns are not the same in both races, but both sets of data lead us to reject the charge against the female-controlled home.

In several of the subgroups, marital instability is unrelated to parental dominance, but when there is a difference it favors those from father-dominated homes in both races. Seventy-seven percent of black males from low-status father-dominated homes have had stable marriages. The comparable figure for men from mother-dominated homes is 62 percent. Similarly, 94 percent of the white men from high-status father-dominated homes have had no broken marriages. The percentage is 83 for those from mother-dominated homes.

Finally, we would note that in the area of marital behavior there are differences as well as similarities. Black men of higher status have high rates of nonmarriage if they come from mother-dominated homes (30 percent v. 12 percent). For high-status white men, those from female-dominated families have lower rates of nonmarriage (15 percent v. 25 percent). No comparison can be made for lower-status white respondents because one of the N's is too small.

Kin Aid and Satisfaction. For blacks, there is no general relation between the total number of kin who would help in an emergency and our measures of satisfaction, but we did find a relation in 3 subgroups when extent of aid from in-laws was correlated with the frustration score. For whites we have 3 of the items that were used in that measure, and they also fail to show a general relation to kin aid (partial r's $= .09$, $.00$, and $.05$). We do not, however, find the stronger relation for in-laws which appeared for blacks.

1 When this matter was considered in chapter 5 we used the respondent's income. The shift to family income is necessitated by the fact that we do not have respondent's income for the white respondents.

Parental Marital Stability. Black males from stable homes have family incomes considerably above those of men whose parents did not live together until they were at least 16 years old (partial $r = .15$). For whites the association is almost the same (partial $r = .18$). Duncan and Duncan (1969), using occupational level, show a stronger relation for whites than for blacks.

As we noted earlier, the critics are wrong about the details of the relationship, but nonetheless, this association is the strongest indication we have that black family structures may have negative consequences. It is important, therefore, to take careful note that a similar effect occurs for whites. The difference between blacks and whites lies in the incidence of broken homes, not in the effect of broken homes upon income.

The data for blacks showed, in addition, that there was a slight tendency for marital stability to be transmitted from one generation of blacks to the next. The correlation between parental marital stability and the respondent's marital stability is .08. Duncan and Duncan (1969) conclude that there is no association for white males, but they use respondent's current marital status as the dependent variable rather than whether or not the respondent has ever experienced a broken marriage. Thus, their data are not exactly comparable. Our materials say the relationship is considerably stronger for whites (partial $r = .17$) than for blacks. As with the blacks, the data for people of higher-status background are more supportive of the transmission idea. For higher-status white females the cross-generational correlation is .29; for those of lower-status background it is .13. For high-status males the partial r is .21, and for the lower-status males there is a reversal: partial $r = -.12$.

Correlates of Age at Marriage. Our data do not permit any further black-white comparisons, but we can go on by comparing our findings to data which are already in the literature. First we will look at the consequences of early marriage. We have already summarized this material in some detail, so we may be brief here. For both blacks and whites, those who marry young are characterized by lower marital stability, and in the early years of marriage, financial problems, lack of satisfaction, low levels of companionship, and high levels of parental aid. In both races the correlation between education and age at marriage is higher for women than for men. There are two aspects of the usual description of the youthful marriage which do not seem to hold for the black group. In the first few years of marriage, blacks who marry young are not more likely to live with relatives, and their fertility rates are not much higher than those who marry at a later age.

Psychological Effects of Parental Marital Instability. The data in the literature suggest that for white males there is some relationship between absence of a father and psychological traits. For blacks, however, we found no differences when we compared men brought up by women with men from broken homes which had adults of both sexes, through remarriage, etc. A comparison of men from stable homes with men from broken homes was equally unproductive.

Despite what we have just said, we are not completely certain that the effects of broken homes are, in fact, different in the two races. We lean toward that conclusion, but it should be noted that we cannot be sure the data in the two groups are actually contradictory. We do not have relevant data for whites, so the differences in our results and those of previous researchers could be due to differences in the measures used. It should also be noted that the previous studies usually use young people in their samples, and it may merely be that the effects they discover do not carry over into adulthood. Finally, previous findings are not entirely consistent or all that strong. We cannot be sure that the postulated effects are present among whites.

These considerations are certainly relevant and should be kept in mind, least we distort our findings. Nonetheless, we do not believe the differences can be explained away. We believe that the black and white data do truly differ, and we think that at least part of this difference is due to differences in the situations of blacks and whites. Not so much in the basics; a boy who is surrounded by women is more likely to show feminine traits than one who is not, regardless of race. But the application of this underlying idea is somewhat different in the two races. A female-headed home may have different implications in the different races. A white boy brought up in a fatherless home may be more likely to be "surrounded" by women in a psychological sense than would a black boy. We would suggest, then, that the lack of comparability is not due to a basic difference, but rather comes out of the fact that the index of the key condition is less valid in one case.

In general, the data from white and black samples show many similarities, but there are also differences. The associations are generally in the same direction, but they are frequently of different magnitude. There are one or two reversals, and sometimes there is a relation in one race and not in the other. One gets the general impression that family variables are working along the same principles in the two groups. However, at the same time the contexts do vary, and this leads to some lack of congruence. We conclude that family dynamics in the two races are similar—not identical. They are perhaps two variations on the same theme.

some general considerations

All the details and specifics aside, there are two striking features of our data. The associations in the total sample tend to be quite weak, but when we look at the several subgroups separately, we find that the relationships are frequently much higher in one or more of them. We will attempt to account for this below, and in the process of so doing we will be led into a general consideration of the nature of structural effects. Little of what follows is particularly new. The ideas are implicit in hundreds of studies, and they have been touched on at several points in this book. Our goal is to make them explicit, particularly for the students who may read this book.

First let us consider the general weakness of the relationships. Some of this is, of course, due to measurement error; but we believe that even with perfect measurement, the correlations and betas would be small. The reason is more basic than simple methodological problems.

Before we face the point at issue directly, we need a general discussion of the way in which structures operate. Starting at the most general level, we would suggest that structural features such as group size and composition influence human behavior because they influence interaction experiences. The point is quite simply that no person has ever been made wealthy, happy, or feminine by a structural arrangement he or she lived under. At best, these structural features are conducive to the occurrence of certain socialization experiences that teach the person behavior patterns, or that may affect his or her opportunities and possibilities. They have, however, little *direct* effect on behavior. To illustrate: growing up in a large family may lead to parental neglect, which may influence personality; or it may cause economic problems which increase the likelihood of the child's leaving school early, thus affecting his mobility. But family size cannot be viewed as an immediate antecedent of personality or level of achievement.

Of course, the fact that there are intervening variables between the antecedents and the dependent variables does not ensure that the associations will be weak. If the presence of the structural feature always led to the presence of the first intervening factor, and this always led to the second, and so forth down the line, there could be innumerable intervening variables and yet high correlations between antecedent and dependent variables. In this case, however, the association at each point is weak. That produces low correlations, for slippage occurs throughout the causal chain.

The reason for these weak associations is clear. The causal factors are actually complex, and we focus on only one aspect of them. When the structural feature occurs in the presence of the other necessary factors, the expected result occurs. In a particular context the effect is as predicted. But the necessary context is not always present, so the structural features at best increase the likelihood of the next link appearing.

Even this is oversimplified, for a structure may have different tendencies in different contexts. Thus the push of a structural feature is not always in the same direction, and the correlations are lowered by a canceling effect.

In addition to complex causation, there is also the problem of multiple causation. The single effect may have several different sources. If the conceptualization is not highly generalized, there will prove to be many causal routes to any particular outcome. A large family may increase the likelihood of economic problems, but so might many other characteristics of individual, family, and society. All these could perhaps be brought under a single rubric, but at the level we are accustomed to they are all different causes of the same effect. If this is correct, it would follow that the effects of a particular structure would not be clearly seen when the environment contained other causes of the effects in question.

We have already discussed the point in this chapter in regard to some of our specific findings, so it need not delay us long here. If there are numerous sources of a particular trait, knowledge that a person has missed one of them is not a very firm base for predicting that the trait will be absent. There will be many deviant cases, people who have the trait, even though they have not experienced the "cause" we are focusing on, because it developed from some alternative source. If, however, there is only one source, its absence assures the absence of the trait. In this oversimplified case there would be a low correlation in the first instance and a high one in the second.

The situations we have investigated fall into the first category, and when we add the two points made previously it becomes amply clear why structural features do not have a strong association with the dependent variables of this study.

All the above notwithstanding, the fact of the matter is that there is considerable variation in the strength of the relationships in the various subgroups. In some cases there is actually a reversal of the direction, but more often we find that a particular variable shows an effect only in certain segments of the population.

The reason for this is implied in what has gone before. When we deal with subgroups, we are limiting the context and decreasing the likelihood that the alternative causes are present. If the complex cause is the presence of a structure in a context of a close tie to the family, for example, women are perhaps more likely to have the additional element which is required than men are. And if poverty can cause the same effect as the family trait at issue, higher-status persons are going to show the effect only if they have the family trait, but many lower-status people will show the effect even when they lack the family experience.

If we are to improve our predictions, therefore, we must get closer to the dependent variables—we must cut down the number of intervening variables. This probably means that we should shift our attention from some of our traditional concerns to variables which are conceptually and temporally more proximate. We ought, for example, to give greater attention to adult experience and less to childhood. Also, some

variables which are usually accorded the status of unmeasured intervening variables might profitably become the antecedent or dependent
variables of our studies.

    We must also learn to limit our generalizations, for this will lead
us to more limited contexts for our studies and reduce the problems of
multiple causation. And, finally, we need more detailed definitions.
The relevant aspects of the context should be included in the definitions of our categories. The utility of this is clearly seen in the chapter
on the spouseless mother. If we had used the simple classification
scheme usually used in this area most of our findings would never
have emerged.

summary

The evidence considered so far tends to support the following conclusions:

    (1) The general outline of the critics' charges receive some support
from the data. The incidence of certain family traits is greater among
blacks, and, though there are important exceptions, these traits tend to
be associated with the consequent variables that the critics have said
they are associated with.

    (2) The associations are not caused by associated biases. They are
not spurious.

    Though the critics' charges have this degree of validity, it is essen-
tial that the following also be recognized:

    (3) The associations are at best moderate, and generally they are
quite small. In some instances the postulated relationships do not
exist. There seems little doubt that the critics present an exaggerated
picture of the importance of family traits as a cause of the problems of
black people. Changing family structure would have little influence on
income or on frustration and unhappiness.

    (4) Nonfamily variables such as age, education, and income are at
least equal to the family variables in their effects, but their effects are
not, as the defenders of the black family have suggested, appreciably
stronger.

    (5) In different subgroups, the effects of family factors are quite

variable in magnitude. Family variables, however, are not more important for lower-status persons, as the critics state. Variations in family factors explain more about the behavior of higher-status persons than they do of the lower-status respondents.

(6) The dynamics of black family life are not identical to those of the white family, but there are many similarities. The black family does not seem to operate in unique ways.

(7) Theories of the family which have been worked out with the white family in mind are supported by data from black families in several instances, though minor changes are sometimes required. This is the case in regard to theories bearing upon age at marriage, the consequences of family size, and the sources of parental identification. Much weaker support was found for a theory of the general consequences of broken homes, and little support was found for theories which relate maternal dominance and female-headed households to femininity among males.

Though the dynamics of white and black families are more similar than they are different, there are discrepancies, and these contribute to the failure of some of the hypotheses. This is not, however, the only reason our data do not support the theories. There is some doubt whether the theories are totally applicable to white families either. They frequently contain a germ of truth, but present an oversimplified picture.

Part Two

The Antecedents of
Black Family Structures

chapter ten

antecedents of age
    at marriage
and family size

Lengthy as our discussion has been, it has been essentially limited to
one side of the coin. With the exception of occasional references to the
sources of marital instability and dissatisfaction, we have totally ignored the antecedents of black family forms. This is inappropriate
whether one's major interest is practical or theoretical; and the re-
mainder of the book will be devoted to correcting the omission.

As before, each chapter will focus on specific theories which bear
upon the topic under consideration. Our major theoretical contribution
will be to provide additional data to test theories which have been put
forth with white families in mind. Our goal will be, again, to test the
generalizability of these theories and to answer the question, "Are the
dynamics of black and white families the same?"

In addition to this, much of the data of Part Two will relate to an
issue of great controversy in the field. In Chapter 2 we saw that certain
traits were more common among blacks. The question is, what are the
sources of these differences? Are they to be found in general social
and economic factors, or are they caused by antecedents within the
family itself?

This is one of those areas in which the debate is in part over who
said what and what they meant by it (see Adams, 1971: 126–27). We
would like to avoid becoming involved in that. The remarks that
follow are not to be taken as the position of any particular author.
They represent a synthesis of a variety of comments to be found in the
literature.

Those who look outside the family, and outside the black community, for the sources of black family structure generally play down the
structural distinctiveness of the black family, but they suggest that

white racism and the resulting poverty and deprivation are the causes of the differences that do exist. ''You can't have family stability when a man cannot get a job.'' ''Large families are always produced by poorly educated impoverished people.'' ''Men cannot exercise power in the home if they are denigrated outside of it.'' And so on.

As Adams (1971: 127) puts it, this view suggests that if you want to improve the situation of black families, ''stop discrimination against blacks, especially males, and the family will eventually stabilize.'' Any attempt to ''strengthen'' black family structure is doomed to failure unless there are changes in general social conditions.

The opposing point of view suggests that though the original sources of black family structures may be found in slavery or in general societal factors, things have become ''so bad'' that the system has become self-perpetuating. The family has bad effects on individuals: it makes for difficulties in relating to others and sets poor examples. Thus in the next generation the same family forms emerge. ''You can't have family stability if most people have been brought up in broken homes.'' ''People from larger families tend to have more children than people from small families, so it is not surprising that blacks from large rural families have high fertility.'' ''Men cannot exercise power in their families if everyone expects the women to be dominant because that is what they knew as children.'' And so on. This view leads to suggestions for massive national programs directed toward the establishment of a stable Negro family structure, and tends to direct attention away from programs aimed at basic social change.

Of course, the issue is generally presented too starkly. The two approaches are not mutually exclusive. In some instances the only difference seems to be at what point on the causal chain the analysis begins. Nonetheless, there is a real issue here, and it is one which is amenable to empirical resolution.

It is clear, then, that our data will bear upon a question of general practical relevance, but they will also relate to a theoretical question of some import. It is a truism of the structural approach that the form of an institution is a function of other aspects of the culture, within that institution and outside it. A particular structural trait has to mesh with other traits in the system. Generally, however, little is said beyond this. In addition to testing the basic idea, our data will provide some very preliminary answers, in a limited context, to such issues as the relative importance of traits in the same institution as compared with external traits, the conditions under which structural features exercise their greatest influence, etc.

age at marriage

Theory on the subject of age at marriage is not well developed, but it is possible to discern two approaches that are used to explain early marriages. The less used approach is a cultural one. It explains differences in age at marriage in terms of differences in societal definitions and norms. It suggests that the norms of some societies are more favorable to such marriages or, at least, that they do not set up as strong barriers to them. These explanations are usually used to explain differences between societies, but they are not limited to that. An author is using the cultural type of explanation when he suggests that youthful marriages are more common in a particular segment of a society because they are less frowned on there, or when he speaks of a bandwagon effect making them appear less deviant.

Most explanations of early marriage start, however, with the assumption that marriage at an early age is not normative in the society and then discuss the factors which lead the young couple to violate the norms.

The answer is usually found in personal or social disorganization. Early marriage is not viewed as a simple matter of falling in love and getting married. On the contrary, the authors generally see early marriage as an inappropriate means of solving some personal problems. People marry early to escape an intolerable home situation, to prove to the world that they are adults, because they are "forced" into it by a pregnancy, because of personality inadequacy, etc. When the focus is more macroscopic, early marriage is seen to be a result of some failure in the society—a failure of social control, "tensions created by urbanized living and industrialization." Moss (1965) lists several dozen reasons which have been suggested as antecedents of early marriage, and most of them have a negative ring to them. In general we are led to expect that people who marry young have unusual problems, tend to choose an inappropriate solution, and are uninfluenced by the usual mechanisms of social control. It is the old belief that "evil causes evil" (Cohen, 1955).

The family of orientation is viewed as a major source of the forces which lead to early marriage. Such marriages are often viewed as an effort to escape an unsatisfying home environment; or the home may be seen as responsible for some form of personality inadequacy which leads to the choice of this inappropriate solution. The family can also act as a facilitator of these marriages. The parents are seen as the major barriers to youthful marriages, and if they are ineffective in fulfilling this function the family can be tagged with the responsibility even if it is not the main motivating factor.

The family, however, is not saddled with all the blame. The schools, the mass media, the economy, religion, and general social trends can all be tied to this view. Obviously, we will not be able to test the idea completely, but our data will permit us to cast some light on the key issues: (1) To what extent are differences in age at marriage within the black community due to differences in cultural norms, and to what extent are the differences due to situational factors? (2) Do people who marry young come from deviant backgrounds? (3) What is the relative contribution of family and nonfamily factors?

We cannot test the cultural view directly, but it seems reasonable to suggest that if any segments of the black population have norms favoring early marriage they would be found in the South, in rural areas, and in the lower-status group. If people in these categories do marry at an early age, this would provide some support for the idea.

Region of birth and size of birthplace are not related to age at marriage, and those who left the South after 16 but before they married also fail to show an early age at marriage. Those who were residents of the South at the time of marriage did tend to marry young. The difference is about 2 years ($r = .24$). These findings taken together suggest a situational rather than a cultural explanation. If in the South there were a norm which favored early marriage, persons who were brought up there would show an early age at marriage regardless of where they were living when they married, and they do not.

Early marriage is often viewed as a lower-status pattern, and most, but not all, studies of white couples support this notion (Moss, 1965; Burchinal, 1965). For blacks the correlation between age at marriage and parental SES is only .05 for men and .07 for women. Lower-status people do not show a strong propensity toward early marriage.

These data, though not conclusive, do not support the view that early marriage arises from deviant norms. Does the hypothesis that early marriages arise out of deviant backgrounds take us any further?

The relationship between stability of the parental home and age at marriage seems an appropriate place to begin, for a broken home has a logical relation to all three of the postulated intervening effects. It could bring about a desire to escape, it could cause the personality inadequacy that is postulated, and it could indicate a relative lack of parental control.

Utilizing a simple classification of "parental home ever broken" versus "parental home never broken," we find a very slight tendency for respondents from broken homes to marry earlier. The correlation is .08 for males and .10 for females. In general, for the total samples and for each PrSES group separately, respondents from stable homes marry 7 to 10 months later, on the average, than do respondents who have known a break in their family of origin. There is clearly a difference here, but it is obviously not of very great significance.

When we look at the various kinds of broken homes separately the difference becomes larger, particularly for males, but we find that people from the supposedly most deviant family form do not have the earliest age at marriage. Men from "female only" families marry on the average at 22.3 years, those from expanded homes at 21.4 years, and those from reconstituted homes quite early, at 20.4 years.[1] Though these findings do not fit the "deviance produces deviance" idea, they do make sense. We are quite prepared to assume that for males the presence of a stepfather increases the likelihood of conflict and a desire to escape. On the other hand, a female-headed home may be financially insecure but quite desirable in other respects. In addition, in a female-headed household the mother is more likely to oppose her son's marriage at an early age because of her financial and emotional needs. And under such circumstances the opposition is likely to be effective. In reconstituted and expanded homes these seem less likely. Thus, for men from female-headed homes the motivation to marry

1 A reconstituted home is one in which there was a remarriage. An expanded home is one in which the respondent and the parent with whom he was living lived with other adults, including at least one person who was of different sex than the parent. For example, the respondent and his mother went to live with her father.

early is likely to be low and barriers to doing so are likely to be strong.

This would suggest that the basic mechanisms which were noted are valid, but it is wrong to assume that the existence of those forces is predictable on the basis of the evil-produces-evil rule.

For women, those from female households also have a late age at marriage (19.6), and both types of two-sex households have the same average (18.7). The explanation of these facts would be similar to the one just proposed.

Family size and birth-order position are among the family variables which have been suggested as possible influences on age at marriage. The idea is that these variables affect the relative attractiveness of marriage and continued residence in the family of orientation, and at the same time they are relevant for the strength of parent-child bonds and the personality of the respondent. Thus they, too, are of potential significance for all the postulated factors.

Our data do not support de Lissovoy and Hitchcock's (1965) finding that people who marry young are likely to come from large families. In all the SES and sex subgroups the correlation between size of family of origin and marriage age is about zero. We have seen in Part One that large families do affect satisfaction and personality, and it also seems likely that ties are weaker in such families. The differences, however, are clearly not enough to affect age at marriage.

Schulz's (1969) discussion suggests that first-born girls who have younger siblings frequently have an early and heavy responsibility for their rearing and are therefore less anxious than other girls to enter marriage and child-bearing.

At first glance, the evidence does not seem to give any support to Schulz's view. In the total sample, women who were the oldest girls but not the youngest children married on the average at 19.6 years. The average age at marriage for the rest of the women in the sample was 19.5. When the parental SES groups are handled separately, differences do not increase. This is, however, a weak test of Schulz's idea, for we would not expect birth-order position to make much difference in small families; the processes he describes would be likely only in families with many children. The data show in fact that for families of 7 or more children, first-born girls do marry later, 20.7 years as compared with 19.5. However, there is no difference among those from families of 4 to 6 children, and we would think that such families would be large enough to show the postulated effect. We must conclude that the evidence supporting Schulz's hypothesis is weak. It seems likely that there are opposing forces operating here. Probably being the first born does mean responsibility for siblings, and this may make marriage and motherhood somewhat less attractive. But for some it develops a taste for "mothering." Also, there are disadvantages in being the oldest, and this may represent an impetus to escape.

Birth-order position does, however, seem to influence the age at marriage of men. In medium-sized families those who are first born marry about 6 months earlier than other men, and in large families they marry about 2 years earlier. This relation is not completely stable, in that the difference is reversed for middle-sized broken families. In general, though, it seems plausible that the oldest son in a large family is given a lot of responsibility for the family's welfare, and some seek to escape this burden by founding their own families.

In general, we have a problem which is common in studies of birth order, and which we have discussed in the previous chapter. Though one's position in the family does influence one's experiences, the influence is not very strong; it varies somewhat from case to case; and opposing trends follow from particular positions. Therefore, the relative failure of these hypotheses is not all that surprising.

As we saw when the matter was considered before (see p. 32), in most discussions of early marriage among whites premarital pregnancy is given a central place. "Premarital pregnancy probably is the single most compelling factor affecting the timing of a young marriage" (Burchinal, 1965: 247). The reasons for this seem obvious. It is a powerful motivation in cultures which have strong attitudes against illegitimacy, in this case marriage seems to be an appropriate response, and it can turn parental opposition to early marriage into parental encouragement or even insistence. The question is, does this hold for blacks?

As we have already noted, our index of premarital pregnancy is inexact, but it is sufficiently accurate for our present purpose. It tells us, first of all, that premarital pregnancy is by no means universally present when there is an early marriage. Depending upon the respondent's sex and social status, between two-thirds and three-fourths of the early marriages were probably not preceded by a premarital conception. Most youthful marriages involving blacks are not "forced" marriages.

Even more striking is the fact that in all but one of the subgroups those who marry later are the ones most likely to have been involved in a premarital pregnancy. For example, the data show that 32 percent of the men who married young were involved in a premarital pregnancy, but 45 percent of those who married later in life fathered children out of wedlock. Furthermore, many of these children were fathered years prior to the respondent's marriage. We reiterate here our previous conclusion that premarital pregnancy is neither necessary nor sufficient for early marriage.

There is one interesting reversal of this pattern. Among higher-status women those who marry late are quite unlikely to have been pregnant prior to marriage. For these women, the rate of premarital pregnancy is probably low, and most who become pregnant marry soon after. Pregnancy is sufficient to bring about marriage in this group, and since most of these pregnancies occur at an early age, premarital pregnancy does lead to early marriage. However, even here premarital pregnancy is not a necessary factor. Only one-third of early marriages involve premarital conception.

There is some evidence to indicate that early marriage may be a reaction to an unsatisfying school situation. As is the case with whites (Havighurst, 1961), people who marry young report lower grades in high school. This is particularly the case for males. The correlation with parental SES partialed out is .16. For females the comparable figure is .08.

The data suggest in general that black people who marry young are not particularly distinctive. At least, at the level of social characteristics, the associations are generally weak. Furthermore, they are not particularly deviant. In some instances a characteristic generally considered undesirable is associated with early marriage, but this is by no means always the case.

Most of our results can be explained in terms of the motivation and facilitating factors we discussed, but it is difficult to suggest beforehand whether a particular characteristic will have a net impetus toward later or earlier marriage. The same trait may have opposing effects on motivation, and sometimes a trait may motivate toward early marriage at the same time that it strengthens the effectiveness of parental opposition. This suggests that if the theory is to be useful, it must be developed and specified a great deal more than it is at this point.

The answer to our final question is rather unequivocal. A regression analysis (see Table 10.1) indicates that all our factors combine to

Table 10.1.   Effects of Family and Nonfamily Variables upon Age at Marriage by Sex (Ever-Married Respondents)

	Beta Weights	
Variables	Males	Females
Parental marriage unbroken *	.11	.11
Number of siblings	−.01	.01
Oldest son or daughter	−.07	.00
Premarital conception	.15	.04
Parental SES	.00	.02
High school grades	.20	.12
In North at time of marriage	.20	.29
R	.33	.32
R^2	.11	.10

* For the nonnumerical variables a positive beta means that the response indicated is associated with a later age at marriage.

explain only 10 or 11 percent of the variance in age at marriage, and the bulk of the explained variance is attributable to the nonfamily factors. When the family factors are entered first, they explain 1 percent of the variance for males and the same amount for females. Premarital pregnancy adds 2 percentage points for males, but here the trend is for men who have been involved in premarital pregnancy to marry later. The 8 or 9 percent of the explained variation which remains is a function of high-school grades, which we take as an indication of how the respondent was getting along in school, and region of residence at marriage. With parental SES held constant the results are unchanged, except for the fact that premarital pregnancy does lead to an early age at marriage for higher-status women.

fertility differentials

Previous studies of black fertility suggest that the major dimensions of differential fertility among blacks are similar to those which have long been known to be associated with differences in fertility among whites. From U.S. Bureau of the Census publications (1971a) we learn, for example, that nonwhites from rural areas have higher fertility than those in more urbanized areas, and Southerners have higher fertility than those in other parts of the country. Also, the higher the income and the higher the education, the less the fertility; women in the labor force have lower fertility than those who are not working outside the home, and, of course, older persons have more children than younger persons. From another source we have learned that higher fertility is associated with marrying young and with stable marriages (Kiser, et al., 1968).

Instructive as these data may be, they suffer from the basic problem that the various factors are correlated with each other, and it is quite possible that the data contain many spurious correlations. What is needed is a regression analysis which will tell us the independent effects of each factor.

The only analysis of this kind is that done by Reynolds Farley (1970) on the basis of the 1/1000 sample from the 1960 census. He found that for women in the North and West, he could explain 8 percent of the variation in fertility on the basis of 3 factors: years of schooling (beta $= -.15$), age at marriage (beta $= -.23$), and marital stability (beta $= .09$). Farley's study is obviously not the last word on the matter. It is limited by the small number of variables he used and his failure to control for age or number of years since marriage. We will introduce additional variables in an attempt to add to our understanding of the factors which influence fertility among black women.

The zero-order correlations presented in Table 10.2 generally support the findings of previous studies. Large families tend to be associated with Southern origin, an early age at marriage, a lower-status background, poor education, premarital pregnancy, etc. Our data disagree with previous findings only in that they suggest that there is no relationship between stability of marriage and number of children.

As was suspected, however, these correlations turn out to be misleading, for some of them are redundant. Several of the variables are intercorrelated so that more than one variable is explaining the same part of the variance. The major independent effects, aside from years in the married state,[2] are attributable to premarital pregnancy and age

2 This is the sum of the length of each marriage the respondent had.

Table 10.2. Effects of Family and Nonfamily Variables upon Ever-Married Women's Fertility

	Zero-Order Correlation	Beta Weight
Number of years married	.33	.33
Parental marriage unbroken *	−.10	−.06
Number of siblings	.12	.09
Oldest daughter	.08	.06
Age at marriage	−.24	−.12
Premarital conception	.29	.32
Number of broken marriages	−.02	−.01
Parental SES	−.14	−.02
Family income	−.11	−.05
Born in urban area	−.06	.07
Born in South	.11	.09
Age moved North	.11	.03
Education	−.32	−.11
R	.55	
R^2	.30	

* For the nonnumerical variables a positive relation means that the response indicated is associated with a larger number of children.

at marriage. Smaller effects are connected to number of siblings and education, but all the other variables have trivial independent effects.

The many reductions in the size of the correlation cannot be attributable to the effect of any particular variable. Each time we enter a new variable into the equation, the values of the other associations change somewhat. There are no dramatic increases or decreases.

The whole list of variables explains about 30 percent of the variation in fertility, but this is certainly claiming too much. Eleven points of that is the variation explained by number of years married, and it hardly comes as a surprise that the number of children increases as the years go by. A more appropriate measure of our success in explaining variation in fertility would be to ask, how much of the remaining variation is explained by the other variables after number of years in marriage has explained all the variation it can? The answer to that question is about 21 percent.

In contrast to the situation with regard to age at marriage, family variables account for a considerable part of the explained variance in fertility. Three family-of-orientation variables add 5 percentage points to the variance explained by number of years married; age at marriage adds another 2 points; premarital pregnancy, 11 points; and marital stability has no additional effect. Thus the nonfamily variables add only 2 percentage points to the explained variance if the family variables are entered into the equation first. If the nonfamily variables are entered first, they add 7 points to years married and the family variables add 12. Education is the only nonfamily variable which has anything more than a trivial independent effect upon fertility, and even this effect is not large. Nonfamilial variables are associated with fertility, but these associations seem to be due to the fact that these variables are in turn associated with family variables that appear in the equation.

In general, our findings make sense in terms of general fertility theory (Hill, et al., 1959). Variations in family size are a function of variations in the biological capacity to produce children, length of exposure, desired family size, and ability to control births. The translation of our findings into these terms is generally a simple matter so we will not belabor the point here. A few comments on matters which are perhaps not so self-evident will suffice.

First, we would note that the high fertility of those who have borne a premaritally conceived child is not due to the fact that by definition such women cannot be childless and other women can. When we limit the analysis to women who are of proven fecundity, since they have at least one child, there is considerable difference in total fertility between those who have had and those who have not had a child from a premarital conception. There still may be differences in the extent of fecundity, but this probably does not account for the difference reported. The fact of a premarital pregnancy may be taken as an indication that there was little desire and/or ability to avoid conception. Though people obviously change on these dimensions after marriage, the fact of a premarital pregnancy probably says something about later differences in desired family size and contraceptive practice.

The positive correlation between number of siblings and fertility may be taken as an indication that people do to some extent repeat in their family of procreation their experiences in the family of orientation. The difference is probably largely due to differences in definition of what the ideal family size is.

We would note in closing the relative unimportance of parental SES and region or size of birthplace as independent factors. This would suggest that these variables do not have a direct effect on the general variables. They are correlated with fertility largely because they are related to length of marriage, premarital conception, age at marriage, and education. These are the most direct indices of fecundity, length of exposure, desired family size, and contraceptive effectiveness.

conclusion

The cultural-norm idea, which says that segments of the society differ in their definition of the proper age for marriage, provided no help in explaining variations in age at marriage in our black sample. There was weak support for an alternative explanation which suggests that early marriages are motivated by the desire to solve personal problems and occur when the usual social barriers to such marriages are weakened. Some of the hypotheses are supported, but not everything that has been suggested as an antecedent of early marriage is in fact related to it among blacks. Of particular interest is the fact that involvement in a premarital conception is a cause of early marriage only for high-status black women. The blacks who married early do not seem to be particularly distinctive, but when they differ from others it is usually in the direction postulated by the theory.

Our findings on the correlates of differential fertility seem to fit existing theory more closely. High fertility tends to be associated with number of years since marriage, premarital conception, age at marriage, region of birth, education, number of siblings, etc., and these differentials seemed tied to fecundity, length of exposure, definition of ideal family size, and contraception effectiveness.

The data on fertility differ in an important way from those on age at marriage. Family variables are important determinants of fertility but they have little relevance for age at marriage. This is, of course, subject to change; most of the variance in these two variables has not been explained, and when additional factors are discovered the conclusion may need revision. But for now it seems that the family is not as important a determinant of other family traits as some would contend, and not as irrelevant as others suggest.

chapter eleven

sources of variation
in internal
and external
family relationships

Theories of family power abound in the literature, but most of them can be encompassed in a threefold classification. The first category includes those ideas which suggest that variations in husband-wife power relations are a result of differences in traditional norms. This view, which we will call the normative approach, suggests that Mr. Jones is more powerful than Mrs. Jones because in their society people are taught that men should be dominant in marriage. If we learn that in another marriage Mrs. Smith is more powerful, this view would lead us to suspect that the Smiths are the products of a different tradition. The assumption here is that arguments end when one or the other says, or implies, "It is *right* that I decide."

The other two theories differ from the first in that they emphasize some situational or personal factor as the determinant of power. They do not say that traditional norms are irrelevant; the norms may set limits. But these theories assume that a power arrangement emerges as the result of a bargaining process which can be understood only through knowledge of the characteristics of particular couples.

One theory of this type considers relative competence to be the key. It says that decisions will be made by the person who is *thought* to be best able to make them. Numerous hypotheses have been derived from this notion: persons who exceed their spouses in status will win a disproportionate number of disputes; the power of spouses will vary depending upon the issue involved, etc. In general, the assumption is that arguments are won when one spouse can make stick a claim to "knowing what is best."

Both these theories have in common the fact that they are not conflict theories. They assume consensus, for arguments can be settled along these lines only if the two parties agree that one should decide or that one is better able to decide. The third theory, which has been labeled the relative contribution theory, has some place, at least, for the exercise of coercion. Here it is suggested that the one who has the most to give can get the most. The person who can make the greater contribution has the greater power. In one version this is another consensus theory. The greater contribution is translated into greater power because one of the partners claims that he or she *deserves* to win, because "I'm such a good husband (wife)"; and the other accepts the claim as valid.

In another version, however, we get a clear view of a different side of marriage. In this view the victory is gained by the explicit or implicit use of the threat to withdraw the resources that one contributes. Here the argument ends when one implies "If I don't win, I won't . . ." If the threat of withdrawal is a credible one, if the other cannot top it by threatening the withdrawal of a greater contribution, the argument is over.

a test of the three theories

Before we present the data bearing on the theories, we should emphasize that they are by no means mutually exclusive. All three processes could contribute to a difference between groups. By the same token, if certain differentials are caused by a particular process, it does not necessarily follow that all differences have the same source. Or, to reverse the statement, a theory which we find to have little explanatory value may nevertheless prove useful in explaining a different set of comparisons.

As it is usually applied to the black family, the normative approach suggests that since slavery women have exercised an inordinate amount of power. This is attributed to the frequent absence of a male, to the poor economic position of many black men, etc. Regardless of the original source, the point is that as time went on the actual became, if not the ideal, at least the acceptable. Because people were accustomed to the exercise of power by women they came to accept it as

Table 11.1.   Tests of the Normative Theory of Family Power (Respondents from Intact Families)

		Percent Responding: Mother Made Decisions	*Weighted Base N*	*Gamma*
Age of respondent	21 to 28	49	698	
	29 to 36	55	635	−.06
	37 to 45	45	746	
Region of birth	North	51	677	
	Border	45	134	−.02
	South	50	1,235	
Size of birthplace	Urban	52	1,072	−.06
	Rural	48	974	
Mother's education	Grammar Sch.	50	1,013	
	Some H.S.	48	425	
	H.S. Grad.	51	333	.00
	College	51	156	
Father's education	Grammar Sch.	48	1,212	
	Some H.S.	51	327	
	H.S. Grad.	55	188	.00
	College	32	111	

appropriate; or at least, to accept it as the way things were done. Thus there developed a subcultural value quite different from the modified patriarchy of the larger society that suggests that there should be relative equality between husband and wife with the male somewhat more equal.

If the normative view is applied to the black family, we would expect that female power would be highest in segments of the black community which are most traditional and most isolated from influence of the larger society. Specifically, we would predict that older respondents and respondents originally from the South and rural areas would report more female power in their families of origin. Similarly, those whose parents were poorly educated should report higher levels of mother control.[1]

The data to test these hypotheses are presented in Table 11.1, where the dependent variable is responses to the question, "Thinking

1 These are the same predictions that Blood and Wolfe (1960) made when they were looking for the locus of the traditional white family.

back now, who do you think made the important decisions in your house when you were a child?'' [2] The table shows, first of all, that there is no consistent relationship between female control in the family of origin and respondent's age. Since older respondents do not report the greatest female dominance, this finding is inconsistent with the normative-tradition idea, for it seems reasonable to suggest that older respondents would be the best representatives of a unique cultural tradition.

The results also indicate that blacks from the various regions do not differ in their reports, and persons of rural birth do not report more maternal dominance than those who come from urban families. In fact, among those born in the Northern and border states, urban backgrounds are associated with greater female control ($\gamma = .18$, $\gamma = .38$). In general, none of these findings is consistent with the normative idea.

Our next assumption was that education would decrease traditionalism, and from that it would follow that the power of the male would be high when the parents were highly educated. The evidence says, however, that this is not true for mother's education. In regard to father's education we find some support for the hypothesis. There is no general trend, but college-educated black males wielded relatively great power.

The last finding should be added to the negative evidence that has been brought forth to this point. If education were relevant for power because of its influence on traditional norms, it should work for women as well as men. Our conclusion must be that the normative theory is of little value in understanding variations in black family power. The power arrangements in traditional black groups do not differ in a meaningful way from those in less traditional groups. Either there is no matriarchal tradition or it is retained even in nontraditional groups. Whichever is true, the relevant conclusion is the same: we must look elsewhere if we wish to predict or explain variations within the black group.

---

2 Persons from broken homes and those who said they could not decide who made the major decisions are eliminated from consideration. The application of the theories to broken homes is unclear, and the inclusion of such data would unnecessarily complicate· the analysis. As for "can't decide," its meaning is ambiguous, and fewer than 10 percent of the respondents gave this answer.

The obvious next place to look is at the theory of relative competence. This theory suggests that family decisions are made by the person who is considered better able to make them, by the person who is perceived to be more competent. In the present case, the best indicator of competence that we have is education. We hypothesize that the decision-making power of each sex will be at a maximum when the partner of that sex has greater education than the other.

In Table 11.2 the results of a test of this hypothesis are presented. For the husbands the hypothesis gains some support: those who have more education than their wives have a little more control over decisions than is usual. Furthermore, this is true at both the higher and

Table 11.2.   Percentage Distribution of Responses to the Question, "When You Were Growing Up, Who Made the Important Decisions?" by Mother's and Father's Relative Level of Education (Respondents from Intact Families)

Who made the decisions?	Mother's Education Higher	Mother Equals Father *	Father's Education Higher
Mother	45	55	38
Father	55	45	62
Weighted N	730	871	211
Gamma	−.04		

* A couple is included in the "equal" category if the difference between their educational levels is no more than one year.

lower educational levels. It is not merely a function of the fact that husbands who have a high level of education are also more likely to exceed their wives in education. On the other hand, male power is not at a minimum when men have less education than their wives.

In regard to wife's power the situation is somewhat complicated, for the results vary depending on how an equal education is defined. In the table it appears that the wives who have higher education than their husbands have less power than do those who have about the same education as their spouses. If an equal education is defined within broader limits, there is no difference between the "wife higher" and "equal" groups. They are both near 50 percent.

The crucial point is, however, that regardless of the cutting point used, the wives with higher education never have *greater* than average control. Either added education is not perceived as bringing extra competence to a wife, or wives who exceed their husbands in education do not take advantage of this weapon. Obviously, these findings do not provide unqualified support for the relative competence theory. Greater "competence" leads to greater power only under certain circumstances. At best the idea holds in the black group only for husbands.

The final theory we will consider, the relative contribution theory, would suggest that wives who worked exercised greater power than those who did not, for the contributions of the former are probably defined as greater. The data of Table 11.3 shows this to be true for the

Table 11.3.   Percentages Reporting Mother Made the Important Decisions by Employment Status of Mother and Father by Parental SES (Respondents from Intact Families)

		Total Sample	Lowest PrSES	Middle PrSES	Highest PrSES
Mother's employment status	Worked	54	56	56	43
	Did not work	46	45	47	42
	Gamma	.18	.22	.18	.02
Father's employment status	Unemployed	54	54	60	36
	Generally employed *	48	49	48	44
	Gamma	.13	.11	.24	−.17

* A man was classified as "generally employed" if he had never been unemployed for as long as one month.

total sample. However, when we control for parental socioeconomic status we see that the relationship is found only in the two lower categories. In the highest parental SES category, working wives did not have greater control. Only lower- and middle-status males lose power when their wives work.

The relative contribution idea also suggests that a wife's power would be increased when her husband has been unemployed, for then he makes an unusually small contribution to the family. When we tested this idea we found the expected relationship in the total group and in the two lower parental SES categories. Here, the wives of unemployed husbands are more powerful. In the highest PrSES group few husbands were unemployed, but the small group which was does not seem to suffer a power loss. In fact, their wives have a little less power than is the case for those of their "generally employed" peers. Given the small numbers, however, we would not make much of this last point. The important conclusion is that highest-status males seem to be able to ward off the effects of unemployment.

When these two variables are combined to produce a measure of comparative work participation (CWP), it appears that there is a danger that the previous material may be slightly misleading. They suggest that a woman can gain power either by working or by having an unemployed husband, and the data of Table 11.4 show that this is not quite the case. Father's unemployment (columns 1 v. 2, 3 v. 4) is important only if mother worked. Mother's working (columns 1 v. 3, 2 v. 4) is important only if the father was unemployed. This says that a man has to have everything going against him before he gives up control to his wife. She has to make an unusually high contribution and he has to make an unusually small one before there is a significant power shift.

In view of the previous findings it would be desirable to know if high-status males avert a power loss even when they experience unem-

Table 11.4.   Percentages Reporting Mother Made the Important Decisions by Comparative Work Participation of Mother and Father by Parental SES (Respondents from Intact Families)

Who Made the Decisions?	1 Mother Worked, Father Unemployed	2 Mother Worked, Father Not Unemployed	3 Mother Didn't Work, Father Unemployed	4 Mother Didn't Work, Father Never Unemployed
	Total Sample			
Mother	64	50	44	46
Weighted N	287	678	281	840
Gamma	.16			
	Lowest PrSES			
Mother	67	52	44	45
Weighted N	147	374	166	353
Gamma	.20			
	Middle and Highest PrSES			
Mother	62	47	46	46
Weighted N	140	304	110	483
Gamma	.12			

ployment and their wives are employed. The table shows the relationship holds for those in the middle and highest groups combined, but the key members of this combined group are those with the highest parental SES. Since it is rare for high-status men to be unemployed and have working wives, the weighted N of this column is only 30. This is too small to be of any real value, but we can't resist noting that though these males have less power than is average for high-status males, the difference is quite small—about 7 percentage points. The highest status males seem fairly immune to a power loss.

The implications of these data for the theory are clear. They generally support the notion that a person who makes a greater contribution is going to increase his control and the person who doesn't make the usual contribution is going to lose power. They also indicate that the shift is not very strong and occurs only toward the extreme. When the two factors we investigated were both present, a significant change occurred, but highest status males may "even survive" this.

If all this has a vaguely unfair ring to it from the point of view of the women, our next finding will only serve to make the ring clear. If there is any justice in the world the woman who has a large family should have that counted as a considerable contribution, and she should be able to increase her power in accordance with the principles we have been considering. The fact of the matter is that family size has a weak relation to family power, and the differences favor the women with the smallest families.

To summarize, it seems beyond debate that the normative idea does not help to explain differences in family power within the black group. The relative competence idea receives slim support, for the data do not consistently favor it, and the relative contribution theory works only at the extremes. None of the theories is completely satisfactory.

Part of the problem lies in the fact that the exercise of control requires more than the possession of certain traits which represent a source of power. The other has to recognize the legitimacy of the claim and/or the possessor of the trait has to be willing to push it. The relative competence and relative contribution ideas probably point to the objective sources of potential power, but they do not go far enough. They tell us nothing of the factors which influence the likelihood that the objective traits will be translated into actual control.

A partial explanation may be found in a revision of Waller's (Waller and Hill, 1951) "Principle of Least Interest": he who has the least to lose is most likely to control a relation. In the present case it works out as follows: pushing a claim to control decisions in a marriage may threaten the relationship. Thus, people are unlikely to insist on the right to control unless they are pretty sure it will not lead to a breakup or unless they do not care if one occurs. Thus, the person who has alternatives and the person who sees the relation as safe, because the other has more to lose if it does break, is more likely to translate his potential power into real power. A working wife who has an unemployed husband is likely to push her claim, but a well-educated woman cannot because she has a lot to lose, since there are relatively few acceptable marriage partners available to her. The mothers of large families do not gain from their great contributions to the family because many children increase their dependency and limit their alternatives. In fact, men, regardless of their characteristics, have less to lose from the breakup of a relationship and therefore are more likely to control it. A truly powerful person is one who has a "legitimate" claim, many alternatives, and a spouse who has few.

In general this discussion presents a picture which is quite at variance with the usual image one gets of the black women who rule the roost because "that's the way it's supposed to be." Rather we see a situation in which the power arrangement in any particular family is determined by their particular circumstances. Further, it seems quite probable that males have an easier time in the competition for control. They gain power by high education and by exceeding their wives in education, but the reverse is not true. They lose power only when they are out of work for long periods and their wives work. If they are of high SES, they may retain a goodly share of the power under almost all conditions. And, finally, their wives don't gain power by producing, and presumably raising, a large family. This doesn't quite sound like a matriarchy.

Because of the nature of some of the variables, a regression analysis would not be particularly informative; but it is clear in any case that the variables we have explain very little of the variance in family power. At best, the differences are small, and several of the variables are totally unrelated to the dependent variable. It could be argued that the family variables are more relevant than the nonfamily variables, but the difference is one between weak and almost nonexistent correlations. Neither side in the controversy can cite these results to support their position concerning the relative significance of family and non-family variables.

the antecedents of companionship and role integration

In our earlier discussion of spousal companionship and integration, we came to the conclusion that the importance placed upon them varied among subgroups and that this was the reason their relationship to satisfaction and self-evaluation differed in different segments of the sample. We will now consider whether value differences also explain the incidence of companionship and spousal integration, or whether we can make better sense of the data by looking at situational factors.

In regard to the kind of recreational activities which make up our indices, it seems likely that situational factors do not have strong influence. Many of the activities do not involve expenditure of money, and anyone who wants to can find the time to take a walk or go to the movies with his or her spouse. Therefore, we will adopt as our working hypothesis the conclusion that Komarovsky (1962: 317) reached in her study of working-class white families: "Differences in the extent of joint social life appear to be explained less by external obstacles than by attitudes toward it."

If this idea is correct, we would expect that education would have a stronger independent effect upon spousal interaction than family income does. Education, if it has an independent effect, probably works through values, but if there are income differences they are probably an expression of a situational factor. Income differences would lead us back to the idea that people with little money cannot spare the resources of time and money.

For companionship, which is the total number of activities the spouses did together, the partial correlation with education is .19 when we hold income constant. The correlation between income and companionship with education constant is .06. For role segregation, which is the ratio between joint activities and total activities, the education correlation is .13. The partial correlation with income is .01. The findings clearly oppose an economic-barriers explanation, and favor an interpretation based on value differences.

Of course, there are other possible obstacles: heavy work schedules, many household responsibilities, large financial obligations or debts, nonmeshing work schedules, unavailability of baby-sitters, etc. Our data do not permit us to check all of these, but those we can look at support the value hypothesis. For example, working wives do not engage in fewer joint activities than wives who do not work (partial $r = -.04$). In fact, among lower-status women those who are employed have more joint participation (partial $r = .12$), and the greater the number of hours worked, the greater the participation (partial $r = .14$). For men, number of hours worked is not related to interaction with wife.

If situational barriers explain variation in husband-wife activity we would also expect that the parents of large families, particularly if they are young, would show less husband-wife activity, and it does appear at first glance that there is a tendency for people with large families to engage in fewer joint activities (Pearson $r = -.15$). Further analysis quickly shows, however, that this relation is largely spurious. When we control number of years since first marriage, respondent's and parents' SES, the correlation declines to $-.07$. For the sample as a whole, if other things were equal there would not be much difference between husband-wife companionship in large and small families.

When we look at each age group separately, the matter turns out to be more complicated. For people under 29 and for those over 36, family size does show a slight relation to companionship (partial $r = -.11$ and $-.10$), but for those in the middle there is no relation (partial $r = .02$). It is not at all clear why children should "interfere" with companionship in the oldest age group but not in the middle group, and we conclude therefore that the relation is tenuous and inconsistent.

Our data diverge from Komarovsky's (1962) in regard to the relevance of age for joint activities. She found that joint activities decrease with age, but in this sample neither companionship ($r = -.06$) nor role integration ($r = -.05$) differ very much by age. And it might be added that the relationship of these variables to length of present marriage is equally weak ($r = -.03$ and $-.04$). When we control for sex and SES, we find also that there is no clear nor consistent tendency for joint activities to change significantly as time goes on. We believe this is a further indication of the importance of value differences. People who have favorable attitudes toward such activities retain them and live accordingly. The vagaries of life which are associated with increasing age do not have much influence on the incidence of joint activities.

It is of particular interest that neither our data nor Komarovsky's support the common notion which suggests that young married men of the working class enter marriage strongly tied to a peer group and only become companions to their wives after a period of struggle and socialization. Actually, in both SES groups and for both sexes, the rate of marital integration is higher than average in the first 3 years. However, the differences are generally small and it is least for lower-status males. The relevant point is, however, spousal integration for lower-status males is not at a minimum in the early years of marriage.

It should also be noted that our data are not consistent with the notion that role segregation is a male problem—assuming it is a problem at all. In both SES groups the role integration indices are almost identical for men and women. The men in this sample may do things with "the guys," but their wives seem to enjoy equal privileges.

Perhaps the most influential work on the subject of role integration is that of Elizabeth Bott (1971). Though her theory does not deny the influence of general values, it may be described as a situational theory. She suggests that the immediate cause of role segregation is a highly connected network of associations outside the nuclear family. That is,

when many of the people a person knows interact with one another, that is when the person's network is close knit, the members of his network tend to reach consensus on norms and they exert consistent informal pressure on one another to conform to the norms, to keep in touch with one another, and, if need be, to help one another. If both husband and wife come to marriage with such close knit networks, and if conditions are such that the previous pattern of relationships is continued, the marriage will be superimposed on these pre-existing relationships, and both spouses will continue to be drawn into activities with people outside their own elementary family (family of procreation). Each will get some emotional satisfaction from these external relationships and will likely demand correspondingly less of the spouse. Rigid segregation of roles will be possible because each spouse can get help from people outside. [Bott, 1971: 60]

Though we cannot directly measure the density (or connectedness) of the networks in which our respondents are enmeshed, we can test

Bott's theory indirectly. First of all, we have two indirect indices of network connectedness. And, more importantly, we can measure some of the situational variables which Bott says are related to role segregation because they are antecedents, concomitants, or effects of closely knit networks. If these variables are associated with degree of role integration, Bott's theory gains support, and the value hypothesis is put in doubt. If the expected associations are not found, Bott's theory comes into question, at least as a general theory which is applicable to all groups. In this case, however, there will be an ambiguity. We will not be able to tell if the failure of the prediction arises from the fact that the situational factor is not related to density of network or if it is that density of network is unrelated to role integration. In other words, negative results will indicate a flaw in Bott's theory but will not show exactly where the problem is.

One further point should be noted. Clearly, when Bott speaks of role integration and segregation she has in mind a lot more than is implied by our list of activities. For her the term includes type of division of labor, decision-making practices etc., as well as the recreational activities which are the major components of our list. Nonetheless, she gives an important place to recreational segregation, and if her theory is adequate it should hold for our measure of role integration.

The first two variables we will utilize are not specifically mentioned by Bott, but they seem to have such a clear relation to connectedness of networks that they may serve as indirect indices.

One question asked the interviewees if they had any white friends, and it is reasonable to suggest that those who answered in the affirmative are likely to have less connected networks. In contemporary America, blacks with white friends are less likely to have a network in which the "people known by a family know and meet each other independently of the family" (ibid.: 59). Thus, according to the Bott thesis, blacks with white friends should show greater conjugal role integration.

The data give only the weakest support to the idea. In all but one subgroup the correlations *are* in the expected direction, but they are all trivial in size. Only three are above .05 (Pearson r) and the highest is only .09.

Another indirect index of network connectedness is arrived at by determining who visits the respondent. It would appear that those who have visits from either friends or relatives but not both would be more likely to have connected networks. Though ties to both friends and relatives do not preclude a connected network, such a network is probably less likely under these circumstances. Persons who receive visits from both friends and relatives should, therefore, show greater conjugal integration. And, on the assumption that networks of relatives are more connected than networks of friends, we would expect that those who receive visits from friends should show the next highest conjugal integration. Those whose visits are exclusively from relatives should have the most connected network and the least conjugal integration.

The data which test this notion are similar to those obtained for the previous variable. Though the data go in the right direction, the correlations are extremely low. Only one exceeds .07, and that is .14 for higher-status females. We would again conclude that there is little evidence here to support Bott's notion.

We now turn to a series of variables which do not purport to measure network connectedness even indirectly. However, Bott says they are related to network connectedness and therefore they should be related to role segregation if her theory is correct.

Bott states (ibid.: 92) that connectedness of networks increases as geographical mobility decreases, and this leads to several hypotheses which are testable with our data. It would follow, first of all, that people who have always lived in the same city would show less conjugal integration. The data, however, show that there is practically no relation between life-long residence in a particular city and role integration. On the assumption that people who attended more than one high school probably changed neighborhoods during their teen years, we attempted a further test of Bott's hypothesis by relating number of high schools attended to role segregation. Again, we find no relation. In fact, the small differences are generally in a direction opposed to Bott's prediction.

Geographical mobility is, of course, not the only road to unconnected networks. In Bott's view, movement along the social scale will also lead to division in a person's networks. In this case, the direction of movement is not important. The extent of movement is the key factor. Thus we related generational social mobility to conjugal integration with sign of the mobility score ignored. Again the relation proves to be small, but for males in the two social status groups $r = -.17$ and $-.12$. The direction, however, is opposed to that suggested by Bott. The greater the mobility, the lower the spousal role integration.

Further indirect tests of Bott's thesis are possible. As she presents it, one of the immediate causes of role segregation is the existence of sources of aid, sustenance, and companionship outside the nuclear family, and her view is that connected networks are the ones which are most likely to offer these. "Because old relationships can be continued after marriage both husband and wife can satisfy some personal needs outside the marriage, so that their emotional investment in the conjugal relationship need not be as intense" (ibid.: 34).

We have a measure of whether the respondent can get aid from people outside the marriage, and it would follow, if Bott is correct, that respondents who can call on others would be less likely to have integrated relationships with the spouse.

The data give no support to Bott's hypothesis. Respondents who could call upon many people do not consistently differ from those who say they could call on fewer. If anything, the correlations tend to run in a direction opposed to Bott. The same conclusion emerges when we deal with each source of possible aid separately (friends, relatives, in-laws) and when the data are collapsed into two categories, "can call on no one—can call on someone."

The same thing was found when we looked at other indices of aid from kin and friends. Those who say a friend or relative helped them get a job or could help them get one do not systematically differ in conjugal role integration from those who do not mention a friend or relative on those items. Those who say they would go to a friend or relative if they had to borrow $100 right away do not differ from those who would not. The correlation for lower-status women reaches .15, but for the other 3 sex-SES groups the correlation is negative or essentially zero. Thus another set of hypotheses does not support Bott's hypothesis.

It is perfectly obvious to us that what we have done here does not represent the last word on Bott's theory. The tests are too indirect for us to be certain that we have done the theory justice. Perhaps more direct tests will indicate it does have validity. However, the material we have presented does, at least, shift the burden of proof to those who see merit in the theory.

Our findings on companionship and role integration are largely negative, but they are no less important for that. We have given a fairly searching test to the idea that situational factors lie behind differences in these variables, and the data consistently indicate that the notion is wanting. This certainly does not prove that value differences hold the key, but they suggest that this is so.

For activities of the kind we are concerned with, it seems that anyone who wants to can participate with his spouse. All that is needed is the motivation to do so. With the possible exception of many children, there are really no effective situational barriers. As far as we can tell this is probably why Bott's hypothesis fails. No social network, no matter how connected it is, exerts an irresistible pull on a person. If a spouse "believes" in conjugal role integration, if he or she takes it as natural that marriage partners should be companions, role integration will follow. On the other hand, if marital companionship is not valued, alternative sources of companionship are easily found—this does not require a connected network.

Of the family variables we have considered, working status of the wife, number of children, length of marriage, and extent of kin aid, only number of children shows any relation to companionship and integration and that association is small and inconsistent. However, none of the nonfamily variables, other than education, is correlated with joint activities. Until we can explain more of the variance in husband-wife interaction we can say nothing about the relative contribution of family and nonfamilial variables.

external family relations: aid from kin

Despite the great interest in the subject, nowhere is there to be found a straightforward discussion of the general factors underlying variations in the degree to which kin ties are maintained. However, such a discussion is easily developed, for there are many relevant suggestions in the explanatory materials of previous studies. Our major focus will be on those factors which influence the number of relatives that could be depended on in an emergency. A relative is counted as a part of the respondent's kin group if he is available to help out in times of need. Though different from previous authors' definitions, this seems a legitimate way of defining the membership of a viable kin group.

Our first proposition will hardly strike the reader with its profundity, but it has to be mentioned because it seems likely that many of the variations we know about can be explained at least partially in such simple terms:

1. All other things being equal, the larger the number of relatives known, the greater the number who will be available to help out in times of need.

The point hardly needs elaboration, so we can pass to the second proposition, which suggests that:

2. All other things being equal, the greater the number of relatives the respondent has contact with, the greater the number who will be available to help in times of need.

This proposition may also seem rather self-evident, but it is not necessarily true. We are assuming that kinship ties can wither if they are not nourished by continuing contact and interaction, but it may be that the bonds of loyalty associated with kinship are set early in life and require no replenishment.

The next question is, what are the factors which will influence contact with kin? Our answers to that represent a set of subpropositions for proposition 2. All other things being equal, contact with kin will be increased by:

2a. geographic propinquity;

2b. social and cultural compatability;

2c. leisure time.

A third factor which will influence the extent to which kin will be available to aid the respondent in time of emergency is the value the respondent and his relatives put upon familism; i.e., the extent to which they are family oriented.

3. All other things being equal, the more highly familism is valued by the respondent and his kin, the greater the number of kin who will be available to help out in times of need.

Insofar as it pertains to the respondent's kin, this proposition requires little defense, for it is true almost by definition: if a kin member is familistic he believes he has strong obligations to his kin. As it pertains to the respondent, however, it is less evident. Why should the respondent's emphasis on familism suggest that he is more likely to be the recipient of aid?

In part, this proposition is an extension of the previous ones, for an emphasis upon familism by the respondent will lead to increased contact and that will in turn lead to an increased likelihood of aid. It goes beyond that, however. For one thing, different groups and subgroups put differential evaluation on familism; so if the respondent thinks it is important, there is a good possibility that his relatives have similar ideas. But even this does not cover it all. We believe that exchange principles work in kin relations as well as in other relations. If the respondent values familism, it is more likely that he has aided his relatives in the past, thereby putting them in his debt and increasing the likelihood that they will aid him in the future.

Proposition 4 is of the variety, "He who has, gets more," for it states:

4. All other things being equal, the less frequently a person needs aid, the greater the number of relatives who are available to help him when he does need it.

The basis of this proposition is rather simple. People who are reasonably well-off can reciprocate aid received, and are unlikely to have exhausted their credit. Though we do not deny the existence of altruistic motives, it is a fact of life that people are more willing to help others if those others have the potential to reciprocate. Furthermore, the willingness of a person to help another is limited. Too many requests will finally lead to a refusal. The principles may not work as starkly with relatives as they do with nonrelatives, but they certainly pertain in both cases.

The giving of aid as we have conceived it here includes both money and services, but whatever the nature of the specific aid needed, some people are going to be more able to spare it than others. Thus the likelihood of receiving aid will be influenced by the capacity of the kin group to provide it. Formally stated, proposition 5 says:

5. All other things being equal, the number of relatives a person can call on for aid in an emergency is a function of the relatives' ability to provide aid.

Hopefully, the reader finds these propositions persuasive and com-

Table 11.5.   Effects of Family and Nonfamily Variables upon Number of Relatives Respondent Could Call on in an Emergency by Sex (Respondents Who Are Currently Married and Live in a Nuclear Household)

| | Beta Weights | |
	Males	Females
Number of siblings	.16	.15
Visits relatives *	.19	.10
Years in present city	.12	.10
Lives in West	.02	−.02
Lives in small metropolitan area	.00	−.02
Educational mobility	.11	.06
Admired father most	.09	−.12
Familism score	.13	.13
Number of broken marriages	.00	−.22
Family income	.13	.09
Self-evaluation as offspring	.11	−.02
Father's education	.04	.16
Years since marriage	−.17	−.20
Age at marriage	−.17	−.14
R	.41	.43
R^2	.17	.19

* For the nonnumerical variables a positive beta means that the response indicated is associated with a larger number of relatives.

plete, but their evaluation depends, of course, on the test of specific hypotheses derived from them. We turn now to a test of a few of the many hypotheses suggested by this discussion.

A completely adequate test of the first proposition is not possible with the available data for we do not know whether the respondent's parents were alive at the time of the interview and we have no indication of the number of aunts, uncles, cousins, etc., he or she has. We do, however, have information on the number of siblings, and this is of considerable importance. Siblings are probably the second most common source of kin aid, and their numbers are much more variable than the number of parents.

In Table 11.5 we present a regression analysis, and it may be seen that with many other variables held constant, there is a clear positive relation between number of siblings and number of relatives the respondent believes he could call on in an emergency. The beta is .16 for males and .15 for females.[3]

3 The dependent variable is the base 10 logarithm of the number of relatives mentioned. This transformation tends to normalize the distribution when there are a few extremely

Proposition 2 states that aid is dependent on continuing contact, and that suggests that people who receive visits from relatives would be able to call upon more relatives than those who are not in contact with any of their kin. The beta for males is .19 and for females it is .10.

Further analysis shows that the male-female difference is largely due to the fact that some women who receive no visits maintain an extensive kin network. Very few men report that. Women have a little less need to feed the ties of kinship. In both sexes, however, most people expect to receive some aid even in the absence of visiting.

Two subsidiary propositions hold that contact with kin, and therefore aid from kin, will be increased when the kin and respondent are close geographically and compatible in personality, values, and interests. The first of these suggests that those who have lived a long time in their present city should receive more aid, since recent migrants are less likely to have relatives in their immediate vicinity. This proposition also suggests that the number of respondents who report that many relatives will help should decrease as you go cross-country from the East Coast to the West, for people in the latter region are, in this sample, more likely to be migrants. A third hypothesis would suggest that people in the smaller metropolitan areas have more relatives to aid them than people in the larger cities. This hypothesis is based largely on Klatzky's (n.d.) finding from a white sample that there is greater contact with parents for persons in smaller cities.

To summarize, this argument would suggest that years of residence in present city, region of residence, and size of city should be related to number of relatives available for aid with "all things except extent of contact" held constant. The relationship should be reduced when extent of contact is controlled. Operationally this suggests we look at the beta weight without visiting included and then with it included. At the same time that we formulate these hypotheses, we should hasten to add that it is unlikely that any of them will be strongly supported. Region, size of community, etc. are poor indicators of geographical propinquity; geographical propinquity has only a slight relation to kin contact, and kin contact has a weak relation to the availability of aid.

Two of the variables, region and size of city, do not even provide

---

high values. The use of the transformation seems particularly appropriate because there is probably a tendency to guess high when there are a large number of people available.

weak associations supporting the hypothesis. Years of residence, which is the best index we have of kin availability, does, however, show a clear relation to the dependent variable. With the "visiting" variable excluded from the equation, the longer a person has lived in the city of present residence, the greater the number of relatives who are available to help in an emergency (beta = .14 for males and .12 for females).

Our analysis would also suggest that measures of propinquity have no relation to kin aid when contact is held constant. Given the indirect nature of our measures we would hardly expect the correlation to be reduced to zero, but we would hope that the addition of the "visiting" variable to the equation would lead to some reduction in the association of kin aid with years of residence. As it turns out, there is a slight reduction in the beta when the visiting variable is introduced. The drop is small, about 2 points, but that is just what we would expect.

Despite the existence of data from whites which show that social mobility does not affect contact with parents (Klatzky, n.d.: 41–43), we hypothesized that social mobility, in either direction, leads to assimilation into new reference groups and new cultural patterns which may discourage interaction with the family of orientation (ibid.: 39–40). If this is so, it would then follow that social mobility is negatively related to kin aid, and the relation should go toward zero when visiting is controlled.

The data indicate that for men educational mobility has a weak association with number of relatives available to give aid, and the direction of the difference shows that the educationally mobile can depend on more relatives. For women the difference is about half what it is for men.

Further study shows that the failure of this hypothesis is not due to the inapplicability of proposition 2b. Mobile men are, as the theory predicts, less likely to receive visits from their relatives (beta = −.15). Despite this they can call on more of them. Mobility predicts lack of contact, but something about being a mobile man makes up for the lack of contact.[4] What this is is not at all clear.

If there is to be visiting between families, there has to be compatability, particularly between persons of the same sex. This implies that

4 This is also seen in the fact that for men the beta is raised when the visiting variable is added. If visiting were equal, mobility would be even more strongly related to aid.

if the respondent gets along particularly well with the parent of the same sex there is more likelihood of contact with the parents. In that situation the person will have a head start in accumulating relatives who will aid him. The evidence tends to support this—men who say they most admire their fathers have more relatives they can call on, and this diminishes slightly when visiting is controlled. For females, those who most admire their mothers have more people to call on, and there is a similar slight reduction in the beta when the "contact" index is added.

In general, though our ability to operationalize our concepts is weak, there is some suggestive evidence that contact is a relevant factor in determining the extent of kin aid.

Proposition 3 suggests that groups and persons who emphasize familistic values will have more aid forthcoming, partially because of increased contact, but largely because familism leads one to help others and this leads to reciprocal aid. The data using a factor analysis score of familism [5] show a tendency for people with familistic characteristics to report more relatives available to help (beta = .13 for both sexes).

Number of broken marriages, which may also be related to familism, shows a negative relation to the dependent variable for women (beta = −.22), but for some inexplicable reason there is no association for males. This last point notwithstanding, the results do tend to support the point that family orientation is associated with higher levels of kin aid.

The next proposition, which suggests that those who are economically best off have the greatest number of relatives willing to help, receives limited support. Family income is clearly, if weakly, related to number of relatives available (beta = .13 for males and .09 for women).

5 The familism score is a factor-analytic score which is composed of the following items: (1) Number of joint activities with spouse. (2) Number of children the respondent would have if he "had it all to do over again." (3) Response to: "Since you have been married, do you think you had your best times when you were doing things with your husband(wife) or when you were with friends but without your husband(wife)?" (4) Response to: "If you had your life to live over, would you marry or not?" (5) Response to: "When do you think that the average man has the best times in his life—when he is married or when he is single?" (6) Response to: "When do you think that the average woman has the best times in her life—when she is married or when she is single?"

The notion behind the proposition is that those who have given or can give to others in the future and those who have not used up their credit with others are more likely to have many people willing to help out. One should not be misled, however, by the use of economic indicators, for our conception of the exchange is much broader than this. All kinds of goods and services would be involved.

We don't have any direct indicator of the respondent's capacity or willingness to provide these other aids, but we do know how the respondent evaluates himself as a child to his parents. Working from the well-established theory that a positive self-evaluation depends on favorable evaluations received from others, and going a step further to suggest that favorable evaluations are forthcoming if one is willing to help out one's relatives, we arrive at the suggestion that people who think they are performing well in their kinship roles will say they have more relatives available to help them if they need it. The data support the prediction for males (beta = .11) but not for females (beta = .02).

The sex differences tend to support a suspicion that the provision of aid to men is more a contractual matter than it is for women. Women seem to be able to maintain many kin-aid relationships even with little contact, and now we see that having less to offer may not stand as a barrier to reporting many relatives would help. It seems that women may get, even when they don't give.

The fourth proposition says the better off the relatives are, the more aid they will give. Using father's education as a rough index of the social standing of relatives, we find clear support for the hypothesis among females (beta = .16) and no support for it among males (beta = .04). This, too, is consistent with our view of the situation. The aid available to a man is a function of his relation to the potential donors. The aid available to a woman depends on the resources available to the kin.

A number of the propositions come together to support the view that those who have been married a long time would have fewer relatives they could call on. Their parents are less likely to be alive (1), and they are more likely to have lost contact with some of their relatives (2). Their relatives are not as likely to be well-off (4), because of aging and the fact that older blacks have not benefited as much from recent increases in economic well-being. Two of the propositions lead in the opposite direction—people who have been married a long time are probably more familistic, and in this sample, which has a top age of 45, they are probably at the top of their earning power. But we control for these variables, and therefore we would predict the longer the time since marriage, the fewer the relatives available. This is what the data say: beta $= -.17$ for men and $-.20$ for women.

Our final finding should be reported, though it was not predictable on the basis of the theory. With all other things equal, those who marry young have more relatives they can call on: beta $= -.17$ for men and $-.14$ for women.

A completely adequate test of our theory has not been accomplished, for our measures are generally too indirect. Nonetheless, the results are encouraging. The facts are that most of the predictions were supported and we have been able to explain almost 20 percent of the variance despite the flaws of the measures. This clearly suggests that it is worthwhile to push forward along the path we have laid out.

These data, if rearranged, can also cast light on the general question underlying this part of the book. Depending on when they are introduced into the equation for males, family variables contribute between 12 and 14 percentage points to the 17 percent of the variance which all the variables explain. For females, the figures are 13 to 16 out of 19 percent. This is the clearest indication we have had so far that family variables have more important causal effects upon other family variables than do nonfamily variables.

conclusion

The data show rather clearly that variations in husband-wife control of family decisions are best explained in terms of a relative contribution hypothesis. We were unable to discover ''pockets of traditionalism'' in which female power was high, and the idea of relative competence also did not cast much light on the differences we observed. However, the person who makes an unusually great or small contribution to the family often does have his or her control affected accordingly. We also see indications that the potential power that is associated with certain characteristics is not always used. In order to explain this we added a corollary of the ''principle of least interest'' to our explanation. This new element states that in marriage the utilization of potential power will be more likely when there are alternatives to the relationship or when the relationship is not important. The exercise of power may threaten the relation, and cautious people will give up a claim to power unless they see the relationship as safe or unless they don't care about it. The addition of this idea clears up some of the points left unclear by the explanations we began with.

Though female control is common, we do not see signs of a "matriarchal" system. What is suggested is that under normal circumstances the male is more powerful, and the factors we have been discussing push the power balance in one direction or the other. Men, however, have a head start in the competition for control.

In regard to companionship we find no support for theories such as Bott's which suggest that situational factors determine the extent to which husbands and wives participate jointly in recreational activities. Though we cannot provide direct proof of it, there seems to be a strong probability that the differences we observed are due to differences in the value given to joint participation. The activities included in our list are not particularly time-consuming or expensive, and thus the only reason for a lack of joint participation is a lack of desire.

In our attempt to explain variations in the number of kin who would help out in an emergency, we emphasized differences in the extent of contact with relatives, the value given to familism, the frequency of the respondent's need for aid, and the ability of relatives to supply it. In general, predictions based upon this theory are supported by the data, and though our measures are flawed and indirect we can explain 20 percent of the variance in kin aid by considering factors suggested by the theory.

Our attempts to account for variation in power and companionship do not explain enough for us to point to family or nonfamily variables as being more important. Neither side of the controversy finds support. Both the family and the nonfamily variables which are usually considered have little causal significance in this area. In regard to kin aid the situation is different. We have discovered some of the key factors, and it seems the family variables are more relevant than the nonfamily factors.

chapter twelve

marital instability
    and
remarriage

Discussions of marital instability empitomize the split between those who look to the family itself and those who look outside it when they wish to account for the family characteristics of blacks. In regard to instability the group which looks beyond the family tends to focus on economic factors. The ultimate cause is thought to be racism, but the extreme economic problems facing many black couples are considered a basic source of marital instability. Black marriages break up because a racist society makes it difficult for a black to obtain and hold a good job, because it forces him to migrate, and because it leads him to live in substandard housing. Billingsley states it as follows: "Family income has a most powerful effect on the structure and function of Negro family life" (1968: 88); "The men were encouraged to go north, get settled, and send for their families later. While most of them did, in the meantime, the period of estrangement . . . exerted definite strains on family solidarity and organization" (ibid.: 78). "For the Negro families in the northern urban areas, housing is perhaps their chief external badge of inferiority . . . it is little wonder that family life in the urban ghetto is grossly circumscribed" (ibid.: 91).

    Another group looks for the roots of marital instability in the family experiences of blacks. Here the focus may be on characteristics of the family of origin which are assumed to affect marital values and general personality, or on characteristics of the family of procreation which influence the nature and extent of the problems faced by a couple. We have already dealt with a specific form of this approach when we considered the transmission-of-instability idea (see pp. 109–118).

    It should be emphasized before we go on that these explanations are not at all incompatible. They differ mostly in their focus and emphasis. Few would insist that one kind of variable held the whole answer, and most recognize that family and economic factors are interrelated and intertwined.

In Table 12.1 we see that there is little correlation between the economic situation of the parental families of the male respondents and the number of broken marriages they have experienced. For

Table 12.1.   Effects of Family and Nonfamily Variables upon Number of Broken Marriages (Ever-Married Males)

	Pearson Correlation	Final Beta Weight
Number of years since marriage	.37	.44
Parental SES	−.09	−.03
Father was unemployed *	.00	−.02
Mother worked	.08	.07
Respondent's income	−.10	−.12
Education	−.11	.04
Level of present job	−.07	−.04
Level of first job	−.11	−.06
Number of jobs in last 5 years	.04	.04
Born in South	−.02	−.07
In South at time of marriage	.05	−.03
Age at marriage	−.24	−.12
Parental marriage broken	.08	.03
Number of children	−.11	−.26
Premarital conception	−.16	.01
R		.50
R^2		.25

* For the nonnumerical variables a positive association means that the response indicated is associated with broken marriage.

parental SES Pearson $r = -.09$, for length of time father was unemployed the association is zero, and for working status of the mother it is .08. Moreover, the parental SES correlation is misleading. The likelihood that there has been a broken marriage is strongly related to the number of years which have elapsed since first marriage, and when we partial that variable out we find that the parental SES correlation is −.04. Contrary to what many assume, men from higher-status backgrounds do not have much more stable families.

The adult socioeconomic characteristics of the respondent are somewhat more consistently, though not strongly, related to the respondent's marital history. Income [1] has a − .10 correlation with number of broken marriages, education − .11, and occupational level − .07. Level of first job has a − .11 correlation and number of jobs in last 5 years .04. Controlling for years since marriage reveals that two of the correlations were being suppressed. The partial correlation for income is − .14 and for number of jobs it is .10. On the other hand, the correlation for education is reduced to zero.

Of course several of these variables are correlated with each other, so these figures do not give an accurate picture of the effect of each factor. This information is provided by considering the betas when all the economic factors are included in the regression equation (plus years since marriage and region respondent grew up in). Then we see that present income is the "strongest" economic factor (beta = − .11), followed by number of jobs held in last five years (beta = − .07). Of the family-of-origin traits only working status of mother shows even a weak relation to respondent's marital history. Those whose mothers worked have slightly greater marital disruption rates (beta = .07). We also see that being born in the South and living in the South at time of marriage have very weak favorable effects on marital disruption rate (beta = − .07 and − .05).

None of these factors seems very important taken individually, and all together they add only 4 percentage points to the variance explained by number of years since marriage. It seems clear that their significance for marital stability has been grossly exaggerated.

Our findings on the relation between economic factors and marital stability will be disappointing to those who see them as the key factors, but the results from the family variables will not give much more satisfaction to the adherents of the opposing view.

A few family traits do have the expected relation to instability: age at marriage ($r = − .24$), broken parental marriage ($r = .08$), and number of children ($r = − .11$). Premarital fatherhood, on the other hand, is not associated with broken marriages, which is directly opposed to generally accepted notions ($r = − .16$).

Again, however, there is the problem of intercorrelation, and to

1 Of necessity we use respondent's current income. As we noted earlier, the relevant figure is the income earned by the "broken marriage" respondents at the time of their broken marriage and the income of the other respondents at comparable points in their marriages. Since the comparison here is limited to males, it is acceptable to use current income as a rough index of earlier income.

understand what is going on we must turn to a consideration of the betas. We see first that the relation between premarital fatherhood and broken marriage is misleading. With other family variables constant, the beta is only $-.03$, and when the economic factors are added in, it drops to almost zero. A closer scrutiny of the data shows that these men who fathered children prior to marriage have lower broken-home rates in part because a shorter time has passed since marriage. With years since marriage controlled the relation drops from $-.16$ to $-.09$. Also they have a higher total number of children, and such men have more stable marriages. Controlling for total number of children reduces the relation to practically nothing.

Age at marriage is not as strongly related to marital breakup as originally appeared, but it still shows a clear association when the family variables are introduced (beta $= -.16$) and this influence is reduced only slightly more when economic factors are also included (beta $= -.12$). Number of years since marriage is greater for people who marry young, and this is the major reason that the zero-order correlation is higher than the beta.

The strongest relation we find in the analysis is between number of children and marital breakup. The zero-order correlation is $-.11$, but that is an underestimation of the independent effect. People with many children have been married longer, and this longer period of risk hides some of the benefits associated with children. When number of years since marriage is controlled we find a beta of $-.26$.

The problem here is that we cannot be sure of the exact nature of the relationship between family size and marital history. For one thing, people who do not get divorced have greater exposure to the possibility of fathering a child. We control for years since marriage, but it is possible that a man who was married twenty years ago has been married for only a few of these years. In such a case the chances of his being the father of a large family are slim. Divorce may "cause" family size rather than family size influencing the likelihood of divorce.

The issue can be resolved by controlling for number of years the respondent has been in the married state. This ensures that any relation between number of children and marital stability is not due to the fact that those who have stable marriages have more opportunity to become fathers. When this is done we find that the previous data somewhat exaggerate the importance of children, but there still seems to be an effect. The correlation between family size and marital breakup is $-.09$ with number of years married held constant. The previously reported relationship is not entirely due to differential exposure, but some part of it is.

It is still not certain that children "protect" against divorce. Another possibility is that people who are likely to divorce are likely to want few children. To separate these alternatives is not possible. We have to leave it at this; there is a relationship between family size and marital stability, and it is not due to number of years married.

All the family variables add 8 points to the variance explained by number of years since marriage, a figure which is double that explained by the economic and geographical factors when they are put into the equation first. All together, the model explains 25 percent of the variance, but 14 points of that is accounted for by years since marriage. One is not impressed by the explanatory value of the variables suggested by either camp. Those who put the blame on the kind of family factors we have dealt with are really no closer to the truth than those who point to general economic conditions.

Given our earlier discussion of the relative lack of relationship between parental marital stability and respondent's marital stability (see pp. 115–18), it is not necessary to go into a lengthy discussion of the inadequacies of the two viewpoints we have considered here. They both consider factors which are often quite distant in time from the events they wish to predict, and given the fact that they represent only a small part of the relevant factors, it is hardly surprising that the correlations are low. These variables do not affect marital stability directly, and their relations to the intervening variables are weak. They may push in a particular direction, they may make the situation a little more difficult, but they do not determine whether or not the couple will face unusual problems. They may tell us a little about the probable success that the couple will have in solving the problems that emerge, but again their relevance is limited. And, of course, people who escape the push toward trouble that some of these factors represent will end up with marital troubles anyway because of other factors that operate independently of these and have the same consequences.

We could reiterate that though studies at the level of the present analysis are worthwhile, they will never account for the bulk of the variance. An earlier comment is appropriate here too. "Marriage is a relationship and a process, and its outcome is determined not only by the characteristics each individual brings to it but also by the relationship between the traits of the married pair and by the details of the situation in which they interact." Further progress must wait until such studies become available.

remarriage

The evidence we provided earlier (see chapter 8) tends to support the idea that it is in the individual's and the society's interest to have most divorced women reabsorbed into the ranks of the married. With the partial exception of those who live with other adults, mothers without spouses have a rather difficult time of it. Despite this, however, not all such people remarry, and this naturally brings up the question of why some do and some do not.

The answer provided by Bernard (1956) and Goode (1956) says in general that the factors which select for remarriage fall into three categories: motivation, opportunity, and acceptability. Simply stated, the chances for remarriage are lower: the lower the desire for remarriage, the lower the opportunities for meeting potential mates, and the lower the ability of the person to win acceptance from a potential mate.

These factors are somewhat interrelated, to be sure. For example, people who have a strong desire to remarry are more likely to find opportunities to meet potential mates, etc. Nonetheless, the factors are conceptually distinct, and they exhaust the logical possibilities. They are, however, rather general and a more specific set of postulates is needed. What are the antecedents of motivation to remarry? Which women have greater opportunities to meet potential mates? And so on.

Again following suggestions to be found in Bernard and Goode, we may say that a woman's motivation to remarry is influenced by her attitudes toward her experiences in her previous marriage, and her attitudes toward her postbreak situation. These would combine to develop in her a feeling of satisfaction or dissatisfaction with the unmarried state and an estimate of her chances of bettering that situation by a remarriage. More specifically, the relevant factors would include expectations and standards that arise from previous experience, particularly in the family of origin, the economic situation during and after marriage, cause of the break in marriage, availability outside marriage of such "marital services" as companionship and sexual partners, the attractiveness of potential marriage partners, etc.

There are, of course, problems involved in meeting a second mate which were not present the first time. Since most men of the appropriate age are already married, the cohort from which a choice can be made is limited, and because men live less long and remarry at a faster rate, the sex ratio is against the woman who wishes to remarry—particularly since some of the eligible men in her age bracket are pursuing younger women. To this must be added the fact that previously married women have less access than younger women to places where eligible men are often to be found: schools, places of recreation, and the homes of unmarried friends.

For the woman who has been married the chances of meeting a potential new mate are increased greatly if she has access to a large circle of friends and kin who can provide introductions. Her chances are further improved if she holds a job which brings her into contact with men, and she is in the best situation if she has in addition to these two characteristics the time, freedom, and money which are required to take vacations, etc.

The characteristics which make a previously married women attractive as a potential spouse are similar but not identical to those which are relevant for the unmarried. Youth, physical beauty, and pleasing personal characteristics are useful regardless of previous marital status, but when men choose among the previously married they undoubtedly use additional criteria. The absence of children would seem to be an advantage, though Goode's (1956: 281) data do not show that women with fewer children marry at a faster rate. Financial concerns are also important in a second marriage. The absence of debts, a good job, and a little property undoubtedly increase the attractiveness of a previously married woman.

This may not be systematic enough to be considered a theory, but it will serve adequately as a framework for the presentation of our data. We will consider a number of subgroup differentials in remarriage rates and attempt to account for them in terms of this discussion.

Before we turn to factors which have more theoretical significance,

Table 12.2.   Effects of Family and Nonfamily Variables upon Remarriage for Women Who Have Had a Broken Marriage

	Pearson Correlation	*Beta Weight*
Years since end of first marriage *	.50	.46
Parental marriage unbroken	−.01	.05
Parents divorced, not widowed	−.09	−.10
Brought up in female-only home	−.12	−.14
Mother worked	.00	−.03
Father was unemployed	.01	.01
Number of jobs held by father	−.11	.01
Parental SES	−.01	.03
Preferred father	−.02	−.03
Father made major decisions	−.05	−.12
Education	.04	.12
Age at end of first marriage	−.33	−.20
Length of first marriage	−.26	.12
First marriage broken by death	.06	.06
Number of children from first marriage	−.20	.06 †
Wife working at end of first marriage	.06	.00
Husband working at end of first marriage	.05	.00
R	.56	
R²	.31	

* For the quantitative variables a positive association means that a high score is associated with a tendency to remarry. For the nonnumerical variables a positive association means that the response indicated is associated with remarriage.

† For technical reasons some of the items listed above had to be eliminated when we calculated the beta for this item. The value is therefore only approximate.

we should note that the variable which is most strongly related to likelihood of remarriage is simply number of years since the end of the first marriage (beta = .46). We will enter this variable into the regression equation first, and then determine how much additional variance is explained by the other variables (see Table 12.2).

Family Background and Remarriage. There is good reason to predict that parental marital history is related to remarriage, since the respondent's experiences in her family of origin may very well affect her perception of marriage and the unmarried state. At the same time, it is not particularly surprising to find that there is no general relationship between living with both parents until age 16 and remarriage (r = −.01). This measure does not tell us very much about the nature of the relevant experiences. More appropriate are the questions relating to the cause of the break and the nature of the living arrangements after the break in the parents' marriage. There we begin to see some relationship emerging.

Women whose parents' marriage was broken by divorce are somewhat less likely to remarry than are women who experienced a parental death ($r = -.09$). In addition, we see that women who were brought up in female households are somewhat less likely to remarry ($r = -.12$). Further analysis reveals, in addition, that these associations are not spurious. When these variables are entered into a regression equation with many other variables we see that their independent effects upon remarriage are about the same as the zero-order correlations: beta $= -.10$ for cause of break, and $-.14$ for sex composition of household.

It seems obvious that the relevant factors underlying these findings are not those which have to do with ability to meet and attract a new mate. The explanations must be in the area of motivation, and it seems reasonable that women who have known divorce in their parental family as well as in their own marriage would be somewhat more likely to believe that marriages just don't work out. Thus they might be rather leery of moving back into the married state. We believe that those from female-headed homes show a tendency to remain unmarried after their own marriage breaks up because they are less likely to consider the female-headed household abnormal, since that was what they grew up in. We also assume that their ability to adapt to the role of spouseless mother would have been improved by their childhood experience.

It seemed to us at first that other aspects of the respondent's mother's marriage might have an effect on the respondent's motivation for remarriage, since they would also influence her view of marriage. The betas do not, however, indicate that the variables we have available are very relevant. Whether the mother worked or not is unrelated to remarriage, as are father's employment history and parental SES. It does not matter whether the respondent preferred her mother or her father, but with other variables held constant, the respondents who came from father-controlled homes are less likely to remarry (beta $= -.12$). Though this fits in with our idea that women will be more likely to remarry if their mother had a "good deal" in marriage, it cannot overweigh the contradictory evidence.

Factors such as these last ones probably have only minor effects on attitude toward marriage. At least after the fact, it seems likely that the respondent's own marital experience is the most important determinant of her view of marriage. These experiences tend to overshadow all but the strongest of the parental family variables.

Social Status. The best measure of the respondent's socioeconomic status is her education; all our other indices are as much effects of remarriage as they are causes. The Pearson correlation suggests that education is not related to remarriage, but when other variables are held constant we see that this is misleading. Length of time since divorce is a major suppressor. When this and other variables are controlled we see that better-educated women are in fact more likely to remarry (beta = .12).

We would guess that this finding is the result of a complex relation among the three general factors. It seems quite likely that the higher-educated woman is more strongly motivated to remarry. The situation of being formerly married is more unusual for this group than it is for those with less education, the "comedown" from the married state is probably greater, etc. However, the relation is not very strong because of the difficulty such women have in meeting *acceptable* potential mates. The well-educated black woman who insists upon having a husband with equal or greater education may never marry. The previously married woman in this situation is even more likely never to find the right man, for there are relatively few unmarried educated black males of the requisite age.

Characteristics of the First Marriage. As might be expected, the original architects of this study did not gather much information about the characteristics of previous marriages, but we do have some information which is worth considering. First let us look at some of the basic demographic facts of the first marriage.

Women who contracted their first marriage at a younger age are more likely to remarry if that marriage is broken ($r = -.21$). Similarly, the chances for remarriage are greater if the first marriage was shorter in duration ($r = -.26$) and if the respondent was younger at the time of the break ($r = -.33$).

We must, of course, be very careful with these findings, for the overlap among these variables is great and they also relate to number of years since the break in the marriage. It might be, for example, that length of marriage is related to remarriage and length of marriage is related to age at break. The opportunities for spurious correlations are numerous.

The correlation of age at marriage with remarriage does in fact appear to be spurious. Age at marriage correlates with remarriage because it is correlated with age at break. Given this, we can drop age at marriage from further consideration. Let us enter the other factors in the regression equation and look into the matter more deeply.

We see first of all that with other variables held constant, age at breakup retains its influence on the likelihood of remarriage. All other things being equal, women whose first marriage broke up at an early age are more likely to remarry than those who were older at time of break.[2] All three mechanisms are probably at work here. Younger women probably have greater motivation, opportunity, and attractiveness.

For length of marriage, controlling for age at break and other variables reverses the direction of the association. All other things being equal, the *longer* the first marriage, the greater the likelihood of remarriage. The Pearson correlation is in the opposite direction because women with short first marriages are likely to be younger when they become eligible for a possible second marriage. The major factor is probably motivation. Women whose first marriage survived for a longer time are probably more anxious to rejoin the ranks of the married.

It is generally known that the divorced are more likely to remarry than the widowed, and this is generally assumed to be largely a function of age. The divorced are typically younger and thus more likely to remarry. Data presented by Leslie (1973) show that for women under 45, which is also the age limit of this sample, the divorced are more likely to remarry even when age is controlled. For this sample of black women the opposite is true. Though the difference is very small, with age and other variables controlled, the widowed are more likely to remarry than the divorced (beta = .06).

It has been suggested by Goode (1956) that white women survive

2 The situation is a little more complex than is indicated here. Controlling for number of years since breakup of marriage reduces the correlation between age at break and remarriage to − .13, but controlling for the other variables increases it again.

divorce with their faith in men and marriage unimpaired. They made a mistake with a particular man and a particular marriage. Widows, on the other hand, often retain ties to their dead husbands, which may reduce their motivation to remarry. We would guess that the same is true of widows in the black group, but some black divorcees may not consider the problem in their marriage a special case. Given the high rates of broken marriages around them, the breakup of their own marriage may convince them marriage is very risky and their motivation to marry may be reduced below that of the widowed. The data do, in fact, show that among the currently unmarried, the divorced and separated are more likely than the widowed to say that they would not marry again if they had it to do all over again (partial $r = .20$). The basis for this opinion, however, is not clear. The divorced and separated are a little less likely to agree that a woman's best time is when she is married (partial $r = .08$), but in regard to the statement, "Most men make good husbands," the difference is trivial and in the opposite direction (partial $r = -.05$).

Another commonly held notion suggests that children are a barrier to remarriage, but it is not at all certain that this is so. Bernard (1956: 62) cites evidence from 1949, which shows that the childless are more likely to remarry than those with children; but a later study (Glick, 1957: 38) shows that those with from 0 to 3 children marry at about the same rate. Goode (1956) found, in contrast, that those with 3 children remarried at the greatest rate. Sixty-one percent of this group was remarried by the end of 26 months after the divorce, as compared with 45 percent of those with 1 child.

Our data suggest still another conclusion. Like Bernard (1956), we find that women who had children at the time their first marriage broke up are less likely to remarry (30 percent v. 57 percent). We also find, going beyond Bernard, that as the number of children increases, the likelihood of remarriage decreases ($r = -.20$). The matter does not, however, stop there. When this variable is entered into the regression equation the relationship is washed away, and in fact slightly reversed (beta $= .06$). Black women who had many children when their marriage was broken are less likely to remarry because they were older at the time of break and because less time has passed since the break. If such factors are held constant, their chances of marriage are at least equal to those of other women. They may be less attractive to potential mates because several children come as part of the package, but their increased motivation to marry probably compensates.

Women who were working when their marriage broke up have insignificantly higher rates of remarriage ($r = .06$) and the same is true for women whose husbands were working when the break came ($r = .05$). In fact, even these trivial relations exaggerate the true influences of these factors. The betas are zero. This is rather surprising, for we assumed that a working woman would be a more attractive and a more willing potential spouse, and a woman who had had a working husband would not have as negative a view of marriage.

Further investigation reveals that there is something to the idea, but it has only limited applicability. For the first years after the marital breakup those women who were working at the time of the breakup are more likely to have remarried ($r = .23$), and this is also the case for those whose former husbands were working at the time of the break ($r = .19$). It would seem, therefore, that the effect of these variables tends to "wear off" after a time, and this seems reasonable. For example, working prior to a marital breakup is of significance largely because of what it tells us about the situation of the woman after the break. After a few years, the connection between the prebreak and postbreak situations is probably quite tenuous.

In general, the predictions of the theory are supported, though our test has had to be less than searching. We would conclude at this point that the basic framework proposed by Bernard and Goode is a useful tool. The question is, how much is explained, and how much remains to be done?

Taken as a group, the variables we have considered explain almost a third of the variance, but this, is of course, misleading, for number of years since breakup accounts for all but 6 points of the explained variation if it is entered first. Or to put it another way, the other variables account for about 8 percent of the variance which remains after number of years since breakup of the marriage has explained all it can. Again, the variance explained by factors associated with the family of origin is very small, but socioeconomic factors do not do any better. Both are related to remarriage, but not strongly. In general, the simplest variables seem to hold the key. If a woman is given enough time and if she is not too old, she will probably remarry. We have found some of the other relevant factors, but many remain to be discovered.

conclusion

The debate over the sources of black marital instability revolves around the question, "Are economic or family factors more important?" a question which is a specific form of the general question being considered in Part Two. Our data on black men suggest that the decision should go to the family factors; these factors explain more of the variance than the economic ones do. However, the issue is by no means settled. The strongest family factor is number of children, and there is an indication that the association is not entirely due to the causal effect of family size upon marital stability. If this variable is ruled out, there would not be very much difference in the relative effects of family and nonfamily variables.

Perhaps the most appropriate conclusion is that the assertions of neither camp receive much support. The factors we have explain 25 percent of the variance, but 14 points of this are attributable to the variable, "How many years have elapsed since marriage?" All the other factors account for only 13 of the remaining 86 percent. We are able to measure many of the variables which have been considered important in the past, and there is relatively little measurement error. Yet, the associations, though clear, are weak. The reason is, we think, obvious. Focusing on individual characteristics rather than on characteristics of couples and their interaction situations will always leave much of the variance unexplained.

In our investigation of remarriage our search was directed by suggestions of Bernard (1956) and Goode (1956) that variation in remarriage rates for women are a result of differences in motivation, opportunity, and acceptability. In general, the data supported the specific hypotheses we formulated, but most of the explained variance is accounted for by a rather trivial factor, number of years since breakup of the marriage. All our other variables explain about 8 percent of the remaining variation. Again, neither family nor nonfamily variables seem more relevant. In fact, such a simple matter as the age of the woman when she divorced is the second strongest factor. It seems in general that most blacks will remarry if they are given enough time and if they are young enough. Those who do not remarry are not all that distinctive, though we can pinpoint some of the factors which set them apart.

chapter thirteen

sources
of
black family structure

Though much of the literature on the black family is concerned with the consequences of various structures, there is a secondary interest in the antecedents of these family traits. Through the years a variety of explanations has been put forth: the family practices of blacks are considered to be a residue of the matrilineal societies of Africa, a part of the legacy of slavery, a result of the disorganization of Reconstruction, etc.

In recent years, however, two perspectives have predominated. One of these sees the black family as a closed system in which family structures are themselves the cause of other family structures. Such a view informs the tangle-of-pathology notion as well as the idea which speaks of the transmission of marital instability within families. The second approach looks toward nonfamily, particularly economic, variables. According to this view the black family has the traits it does because of pressures caused by poverty, discrimination, etc.

The group which looks outside the family puts considerable stress upon the respondent's socioeconomic background, but we found that the various indices of parental SES had almost no association with characteristics of the respondent's family. With other variables held constant, measures of parental SES had trivial or inconsistent correlations with age at marriage, marital stability, remarriage, and kin aid. Fertility is about the only variable which fits expectations. It is related to parental SES ($r = -.14$), and the major reason for this seems to be that women of lower-status background are characterized by low education and a higher likelihood of premarital pregnancy. These characteristics are in turn importantly related to fertility. This is just the kind of causal chain that this view suggests, but we cannot make too much of it, given the lack of association found for the other variables.

The respondent's own social standing seems to be more important than parental SES. Education and/or income are related to fertility, conjugal integration, aid from kin, marital stability, and remarriage. However, these relationships do not approach the level that one would expect from the emphasis given in the literature to poverty and poor education.

This is also the case with other nonfamily variables, such as years of residence in present locality, region of birth, size of birthplace, etc. They tend to be related to the dependent variables in the predicted direction, but their influence is weak. This is best seen in terms of total variance explained. Even when they are the first variables entered into the regression equation, geographical factors, parental SES, respondent's education, and respondent's income usually explain less than 5 percent of the variance. This is particularly striking since our measures of these variables are relatively error free.

Authors who speak of lower- and middle-class black families as separate entities are sharpening a rather fuzzy distinction. The overlap between these categories is great. To use just one example; marital instability is higher in the lower class, but many people who are poorly educated and poor have never had a broken marriage. Relative affluence and a higher level of education, on the other hand, give only partial immunity to marital breakup.

Despite all this, the advocates of the other view can take little comfort. The data on the familial antecedents of black family structure are stronger, but they are not all that different. Again, a number of the variables have a clear antecedent relation to some of the traits we are interested in. Age at marriage is the factor which is most consistently related to the dependent variables, but several of the others, parental marital disruption, family size, and respondent's marital stability, also have independent effects in one or more instances. On a variance-explained basis, these variables do better than the previous set. In a few cases, the family variables explain as much as 15 percent of the variance.

If the question is merely which kind of variable explains more, the answer is clearly that we were able to go further with the family variables. If, however, the question is which type of variable holds the key to black family structure, and that is the way the issue is usually posed, we must conclude that neither camp seems to have found the answer. To bring it to the practical level, if certain economic facts were changed black families would change, but not very much. If certain antecedent family facts were changed other family traits would change a little more, but the change would still not be a major one. The specific variables that are discussed in the literature are not the major causal factors.

Since these two categories of variables exhaust the logical possibilities, continued work in this vein would, of course, ultimately lead to the "key" variables. We would suggest, however, that the distinction between familial and nonfamilial variables is not a particularly useful one. It may have some polemical value and perhaps even some practical significance, but from a social scientist's view its utility is limited. Certain values, experiences and situational factors are the immediate causes of black family structures. In some instances the ultimate causes of the values, etc., are family variables; in some instances they are nonfamilial factors. Many of the more immediate causes undoubtedly have roots in both.

It would seem appropriate to move away from the question we have been considering, and direct our attention to the nature of these more immediate factors. If we shift our attention to the more specific theories covered, these materials can be used to further our understanding of the immediate causes of black family structure. We still must use the same findings we have been using, and the explained variance will not change, but we can get more mileage out of these findings by considering their implications for theories which suggest the dynamics at work in determining the form that black families take.

The data do not support the view that people who marry young come out of a tradition which favors early marriage. We were unable to discover a segment of the black community which had such norms. The data are more consistent with the view that early marriages represent a way of solving personal problems, and that such marriages are most likely to occur when the usual barriers to them are weakened. Blacks who marry young are not all that distinctive, but their traits are consistent with this situational view.

Discussions of differential fertility usually focus on four categories of variables, differential fecundity, differential exposure, differences in desired family size, and variations in the ability to control births; and these factors also make sense of our findings. The strongest variables are number of years since marriage and premarital pregnancy. The former is simply a measure of length of exposure and the latter is probably indicative of a relative lack of desire and/or ability to control fertility. The other important variables, age at marriage, number of siblings, and education, are also easily understandable in these terms.

Theories of family power are more developed than most in this field, and our data shed light on all three types that have been put forth: normative, relative competence, and relative contribution theories. The data are, to begin with, inconsistent with the idea that variations in female power are due to differential commitment to a traditional norm which favors female dominance in decision making. The more traditional segments of the black group are not more female dominated.

The other two theories, particularly the relative-contribution idea, do somewhat better, but they do not provide a full answer. Greater competence and a greater contribution to the family's welfare are apparently the basis for staking a claim to decision-making power, such claims are, however, not always pushed, for they may represent a threat to the relationship. Therefore, it is necessary to consider the conditions under which a person is likely to attempt to translate his potential power into actuality. The key seems to be in a revision of Waller's "Principle of Least Interest" (Waller and Hill, 1951). Persons who have more alternatives to the present relationship and those who see the relation as safe are more likely to exercise their claims to control. This additional postulate does much to clear up the ambiguities of the data.

Much of the material we have gathered indicates the crucial importance of situational factors and tends to play down the importance of variations in values; but when it comes to the extent of husband-wife companionship and role integration, the opposite is true. Situational factors have little influence upon the extent to which there is joint participation in recreational activities. The major barrier to such activities seems to be a low evaluation of them.

On a more specific level, a searching investigation finds no support for Bott's (1971) hypothesis which states that the immediate cause of conjugal role segregation is a highly connected network of associations outside the nuclear family. Our indirect tests show that a number of variables which she says are related to degree of connectedness in external network are not related to degree of joint participation. It may be, of course, that the variables are not related to connectedness of networks, but it seems more likely that the lure of the connected network is not strong enough to cause role segregation when a couple holds values which make role integration important to them.

Our view of the factors which determine the extent to which the respondent can call on kin for aid in time of need leads us to look at both situational and value variables. Six propositions were presented which speak of number of kin available, extent of contact with kin, frequency of need, ability of kin to provide aid, and the respondent's familism. On the basis of these ideas a number of specific hypotheses were formulated and tested. In general the tests were successful. Despite the fact that our measures are indirect and permit us to test only a few of the hypotheses suggested, we can explain 20 percent of the variance in kin aid. It seems clear that our propositions do point to relevant considerations.

Starting from suggestions in Bernard (1956) and Goode (1956), we arrive at the view that the factors which select women for remarriage after a broken marriage fall into three categories: factors which affect motivation to remarry, those which influence opportunities to meet eligible men, and those related to the woman's acceptability to potential new mates. We then described the specific factors in each category and formulated testable hypotheses. As previously, the hypotheses are generally supported, and the framework we presented helps to make sense of the data. In this case, however, the findings are not very strong. This is due, we believe, to the fact that most black women who have a broken marriage ultimately remarry if they are relatively young when the break occurs. Thus, the most distinctive characteristics of those who have not remarried are that their marriages broke up fairly recently and that they were relatively old at the time. Their other traits are not so different from the remarried group into whose ranks most of them will ultimately go. The other differences which exist are, however, consistent with expectations.

In general, it would seem that the data enlighten us regarding the antecedents of black family structures. Though in no instance do we explain the bulk of the variance, the findings take on added weight because they are consistent with specific theories and frameworks. Much remains to be done on an empirical level, but the data we have give us some confidence that the approaches we have laid out represent appropriate roads to follow. They do not flow into a single highway leading to an all-encompassing conclusion, but given the present development of theory in the field we may ultimately get further by taking it slow and easy on these narrow winding roads.

are the causes of black family structures unique?

There is a rather strong tendency in the literature for the causes of black family structure to be treated in a manner which is basically different from that used in discussions of white family structure. Only rarely are the characteristics of white families explained in terms of events which occurred a hundred years ago, but we still find discussions of black families which speak of the importance of slavery, Reconstruction, and the northward migration. Our previous materials, have, of course, dealt with the antecedents of the black family in the same way that white families are treated. We have considered the experiences of people who are living today. A question still remains, however, as to whether or not the forces which shape the two family systems are the same. Are the antecedent variables the same, in both instances? At a more general level the question becomes, ''Are these theories, which explain variations in black family structure, also applicable to white families? We now turn to a consideration of these issues.

Control of Decisions. In regard to family power we have directly comparable data for the two groups, and they indicate, to begin with, that the normative-tradition theory is no more useful for whites than it proved to be for blacks. Using variables such as age, father's education, generation in the United States, and Southern residence at some time in life, we found no indication that variation in family power can be tied to closeness to a presumed *patriarchal* tradition. Like Blood and Wolfe (1960) we find that men do not have more power in the more traditional white groups.

In regard to differences in education, our measure of relative competence, the results exactly parallel those reported for blacks. If the male has greater education, his power is increased, but greater education for a woman does not always increase her power. It depends upon how narrowly an equal education is defined.

The patterns in regard to the relative-contribution variables are also the same for whites as blacks. In fact, the relationships are even stronger—though we must be careful here, since the items are not exactly the same as those used for blacks and there were only 14 white men who had long periods of unemployment. Be that as it may, the unemployed males had low power ($\gamma = .71$) and the working wives had high power ($\gamma = .24$). Also, most studies show that female power decreases among whites as the number of children increases (Campbell, 1970). This is just what we found for blacks.

The existing literature on family power among whites is very large, and we will not attempt to survey it at this point. The data are quite complex and by no means consistent. Nonetheless, it does appear that the relative contribution theory is the leading contender in the field. However, that theory does not account for all that is known, and it seems clear that a more sophisticated theory will ultimately be needed. Safilios-Rothschild (1970) seems to suggest that a desirable path to follow would involve integrating it with an exchange theory such as Heer's (1963). Exchange theory as used here turns out to be very similar to the principle of least interest which we previously found useful in improving our understanding of black family power.

Fertility. The data on the antecedents of white fertility are quite similar to those we obtained for black women. With other variables controlled, disruption of parents' marriage, parental SES, and respondent's marital stability show at best weak associations with fertility in both races. The same is true for Southern birth for blacks and Southern residence at some time in life for whites.

There are, however, several differences of magnitude. Age has a stronger influence on fertility for whites (beta = .12 for blacks and .27 for whites), and education is somewhat more influential for blacks (beta = $-.27$) than for whites (beta = $-.19$).[1] In neither case, however, is the difference so great that we would reach a different conclusion

---

1 It should be noted that when additional factors are held constant the beta for education decreases to $-.11$ for blacks. See Table 10.2.

for the two races. That is not true for family income. Here there is an effect for white women (beta = − .10), and none for black women.

Two of the other fertility differentials we found among blacks are consistent with those generally reported for whites. At least among Protestants, people from large families tend to have somewhat larger families (Westoff, et al., 1963) and people who marry young have larger families (Kiser, et al., 1968). In general, fertility differentials are the same in both races.

Aid from Kin. The white respondents were asked the number of relatives they could call on in an emergency, but unfortunately we have no data from them for a number of the independent variables which proved to be important in the black group. We do not know the size of the respondents' families of origin, their age at marriage, the number of years they have lived in their present area, whether they visit their relatives, and their attitudes on several of the familism items.

The remaining variables do not show the same patterns in the two groups (see Table 13.1). Respondent's age shows perhaps the greatest consistency. For males and females of both races, there is an inverse

Table 13.1. Effects of Family and Nonfamily Variables on the Number of Relatives White and Black Respondents Can Call on by Sex (Currently Married Respondents)

| | Beta Weights | | | |
| | Males | | Females | |
	White	Black	White	Black
Age	−.12	−.12	−.10	−.16
Lives in a small metropolitan area *	−.16	−.03	.01	.00
Lives in West	.05	−.03	.12	−.03
Father's education	.29	−.06	.20	.08
Family income	.13	.11	−.03	.10
Educational mobility	.24	.07	.13	.00
Preferred father	−.08	.11	−.23	−.16
Self-evaluation as offspring	.06	.15	.05	.02
Number of broken marriages	.03	.04	−.05	−.19
R	.36	.27	.35	.35
R^2	.13	.07	.12	.12

* For the nonnumerical variables a positive association means that the response indicated is associated with a larger number of relatives.

relationship between age and number of relatives available for aid. We would also note that size and region of residence do not have the predicted relationship to kin aid in the white group, and they also do not support the hypothesis in the black group. This statement hides, however, the fact that the patterns which lead to these conclusions are different in the two races.

On most of the other variables the patterns are not even this similar. In some cases—father's education, for example—the hypotheses are more strongly supported in the white group then they were in the black. In other instances—income is an example here—the data of the black group are more consistent with theoretical expectations. On several of the other variables, 3 of the subgroups indicate a particular conclusion and one opposes it.

It is not possible to carry this much further. It is obvious that there is a lack of clear-cut parallelism between the races. But the implications of this are not certain because we do not have white data on the key variables. The fact that we must question the general relevance of variables such as respondent's income somewhat reduces our confidence in the generality of our theory of kin aid. It does not destroy that confidence, however, because income is not that important in the black group either. Evidence that parental family size, for example, also did not show a consistent pattern would probably lead us to conclude that the theory was limited to blacks. For now we can merely note the possibility that it might be.

For the other variables, either we have no responses for whites or we cannot analyze the data because the N's in a particular category are too small. We must therefore turn to the existing literature in the search for an answer to our question.

Age at Marriage. Since our basic ideas come from studies of white marriages, it is not surprising to find that our portrait of the person who marries young holds in general outline for both whites and blacks. The factors which motivate and facilitate early marriage are similar for the two groups. However, the theory seems to work out less well for blacks. Some of the variables which apparently have considerable causal significance for whites are of trivial importance for blacks. Included here would be premarital pregnancy, socioeconomic background, and family size.

These findings do not suggest to us the necessity of revising the basic notion that young marriages are attempts to solve particular difficulties and that they are facilitated by a breakdown of the usual barriers to them. The problem is that the paths to this situation are not the same in both groups, and our data focus on those which lead white youth to the point where they want to escape by marriage. For blacks other factors also lead to this situation, and we do not have information on them. The general principle may be the same, but the specific factors which put the principle into effect may differ.

Conjugal Integration. Though many of the studies which investigate conjugal integration in white couples have been inspired by Bott's theory, we do not as yet have a clear idea as to whether or not it is valid for whites. Many of the studies which purport to test her views do not in fact do so, and others do not bear directly on the key issue. The studies which are pertinent are, to add to the problem, rather contradictory in their findings.

It seems rather clear that working-class communities tend to be characterized by tightly knit networks and conjugal segregation (Bott, 1971), but the strong possibility remains that the two are not causally related. Both may be reflections of general working-class values, or each may result from totally disparate causal paths. These studies by no means show that tightly knit networks interfere with husband-wife companionship. Several authors (Bott, 1971: 265) found, however, that geographical mobility, which has the effect of breaking up closely knit networks, is associated with an increase in conjugal integration. This may be taken as support for Bott's hypothesis.

Of most value to us are studies which actually attempt to quantify and measure the key concepts in Bott's theory, and the results of such investigations are in general mixed. As Bott (1971) describes them, Udry, Hall, and Aldous and Straus do not support her position, Turner's study and Nelson's do, and the meaning of Blood's findings is debatable. The data we have do not convince the writer of the general validity of Bott's hypothesis, but the issue is by no means settled. It is clear that better research is needed before we can be sure.

Even if this research also fails to produce supporting data, we need not discard the hypothesis entirely. It might hold in some cases even if it does not in general. Aldous and Straus (1966), for example, believe that the theory may only hold for extreme cases of tight or loose-knit social networks, and Bott seems to agree at least partially (Bott, 1971: 290, 301). Aldous and Straus (1966) also suggest that better results might be obtained if consideration were given to whether the networks of the husband and wife were separate or joint. We would add that it might also be advantageous to measure the strength of the person's connection to the network. This seems to be one of the intervening variables between network connectedness and conjugal integration, and since it is closer to the dependent variable it might give stronger findings. It might also be that the Bott notion is most pertinent when the relevant values are weak. If people are rather neutral in their attitudes to "togetherness" these situational factors may operate freely. We do not believe, however, that they are sufficient to overcome a strong predisposition in either direction.

All this be as it may, the fact remains that the data from whites do not give firm support to Bott's hypothesis as it now stands. There is more support here than we found for blacks, but that, of course, is not saying very much.

Marital Stability. Bumpass and Sweet's (1972) study of marital instability among whites is concerned with the marital history of women, and the data we presented earlier related to men. However, their study is so similar to ours in method and sample that it seems appropriate to shift our focus to accommodate their data. The two sets of findings are quite similar. They find a clear effect of age at marriage upon marital instability with other variables held constant, and so do we. The beta is $-.10$. They find a zero-order relation between education and instability, and the association is altered when other variables are controlled. For blacks, the original relation is smaller (Pearson $r = -.07$), but it also changes when other variables are held constant (beta $= .03$).

They report that with other variables not controlled premarital pregnancy has a weak relation to marital instability, and when other factors are controlled the relationship disappears.[2] In our sample, the zero-order correlation is trivial, and when other variables are controlled it becomes practically zero. Our data agree with theirs in regard to the small effect of parental marital disruption upon respondent's

2 Those few who had premarital *births,* on the other hand, have high rates of broken marriage.

marital instability. Finally, they report that women with farm origins and those from the South are only a little less likely to have a broken marriage. We find that neither variable has a significant relation to stability. As far as these data allow us to go, there appears to be similarity between the antecedents of broken marriages in the two groups.

Remarriage. When it comes to remarriage, we cannot make the precise comparisons that were possible in the previous section; but even without them we may have fair confidence that there is great similarity between the groups in this matter. Bernard's (1956) and Goode's (1956) studies of predominantly white samples present data which are generally consistent with ours. Again, there is not an absolute parallelism. For example, black divorced women are less likely to marry than the widowed, with age controlled. For whites divorced women are more likely to marry. Such facts notwithstanding, there is a great deal more similarity than difference.

Taking all the dependent variables into account, we see an impressive degree of similarity between the dynamics of white and black families. Certainly they are not identical. Some variables do have different effects in the two groups. Usually, however, the patterns are unmistakably similar. It seems clear that the black and white families work under similar principles, and the explanations which hold for one group hold for the other. At least this is so in the areas we have considered. And when there is a difference, it seems to be not so much a difference in principle but rather a difference in the application of the principle. In both groups the occurrence of a particular event will increase the likelihood of a particular structure, but the antecedent of the event may be different for blacks and whites. We are suggesting that the immediate causes are the same in some cases even when the antecedents of these immediate causes are different.

summary

In Part Two we considered the antecedents of the family variables whose consequences were considered in Part One. Our material leads to the following conclusions:

(1) A major issue in the field concerns whether family or non-

family traits lie behind variations in the family characteristics which are our central concern. The data indicate that the family traits explain somewhat more of the variation in the dependent variables, but the difference is not great. More importantly, the specific traits which are usually suggested as the keys to black family structure explain only a small proportion of the variance. Advocates of neither position have pointed to the crucial factors.

(2) The data tend to support the standard theories which attempt to explain the sources of variation in family structure. An exception to this is the lack of support found for Bott's theory of conjugal role segregation.

(3) The theories referred to above were worked out with white families in mind, and the fact that they hold for blacks suggests that the antecedents of family structure are similar in the two races. Direct comparison of data from the two groups gives additional support to that conclusion.

postscript

The political proposals which gave birth to the recent interest in the black family are now dead. We are hardly likely to implement Moynihan's 1965 call for a program designed to enhance "the stability and resources of the Negro American family," as a means of bringing "the Negro American to full and equal sharing in the responsibilities and rewards of citizenship." Nonetheless, the viewpoints upon which that suggestion was based still exist, and in concluding we may be permitted to go beyond our researcher role and to offer a few comments on the implications that our work has for such programs.

Several things seem particularly clear. An attack upon the "family problems" of blacks in this country would, if successful, alleviate some of the problems they face. At the same time, however, it is apparent that the gain would be small. The family is not the main source of these problems, and a "perfect" family situation in the present reality of America would not change very much. Such a program would not only be relatively ineffective, it could be disastrous if it directed attention away from the real sources of the problem. The problem does not start in the black community, but in the white. The real source is racism with all that it implies: discrimination, derogation, and prejudice.

If this is so, of course, a focus on black family problems would not merely fail to achieve the long term goals: it would also fail to accomplish a marked change in black family life. The critics are not particularly explicit about the nature of the family aid program; the Moynihan report does not attempt to suggest concrete proposals. Nonetheless, one gets the feeling that any program of that kind could not succeed. The inadequacy of such cosmetic measures should be readily apparent. Undoubtedly they will help in individual cases. But if we have properly located the sources of black problems it is clear that such approaches do not get to the core, and family problems "won't stay licked."

At the same time that we express our doubt about the appropriateness of family-aid programs, we must also insist that all is not well with the black family anymore than it is with any family system. Those who play down the difficulties are doing a disservice to those who live under conditions they themselves consider undesirable. In combating the exaggerations of some, we must not throw out the elements of truth in their positions. For example, our data show that female-headed households do not produce all the terrible consequences which have been attributed to them. The critics clearly exaggerate in this matter. However, this does not justify defenses of the black family which seem to say that such arrangements are without problems. Contrary to what some suggest, the female household is not a perfectly functional pattern which is integrated positively into the dynamics of black life. One does not have to use middle-class white standards to come to that conclusion. Our data say that all you have to do is ask the black women who are living in such families.

Finally, we would note what seems to be an element of undue optimism regarding the black condition. This lies in the apparent assumption that changes in social status will immediately cause important changes in the black family. One of our more surprising findings is the relatively weak relation between objective socioeconomic indicators and black family structure. Moves to improve the economic position of blacks in this society require no justification. It is a matter of simple justice. We should not expect, however, immediate changes of great magnitude in family life. Ultimately economic changes will help, and the improvement will probably be speeded if more general conditions change along with the economic. A few extra dollars in the paycheck is, however, not sufficient to accomplish what many apparently think it will.

glossary

Associated bias. A third variable which is the source of an association between two other variables. (C is an associated bias if A and B are related because C influences both A and B.)

Beta coefficient (beta weight). The amount of change in a dependent variable which is associated with a standard unit change in one independent variable with other variables held constant.

Dependent variable. The phenomenon which is to be explained: the factor which is affected by the independent variable.

Factor analysis. As used in this book, a method for determining if the responses to a series of items reflect a basic underlying factor.

First-order partial correlation. A partial correlation in which one variable is held constant (*see* Partial correlation).

Gamma (γ). A measure of the degree of association between two variables. It ranges from -1 to $+1$.

Intervening variable. A variable which mediates the effect of an independent variable upon a dependent variable. (B is an intervening variable if A affects C because A affects B and B affects C.)

Multiple classification analysis. A procedure which permits one to predict how far a particular category would deviate from another category (or the mean) in regard to some dependent variable if several other variables were held constant.

Multiple correlation coefficient (R). A measure of the strength of the relationship between a dependent variable and several independent variables. When squared (R^2), it indicates the proportion of the variance in the dependent variable which is accounted for by the variance of the independent variables.

N (number). The number of cases in the sample.

Partial correlation (partial r). A measure of the association between two variables when one or more other variables are held constant.

Pearson correlation (r, Pearson r). A measure of the degree of association between two variables. Synonymous with zero-order correlation.

r. See Pearson correlation.

R, R². *See* Multiple correlation coefficient.

Regression analysis. A method which produces an equation (regression equation) which permits one to estimate the value of a dependent variable from knowledge of the independent variables.

Spurious correlation (*spurious relationship*). A relationship between two variables which is not a causal relationship but is due to their relationship to one or more antecedent factors. (The relationship between *A* and *B* is spurious if an increase in *A* is associated with an increase in *B* only because *C* is causing both *A* and *B* to increase.)

Standardized rate. The rate at which a characteristic would occur in a group if that group had a specified distribution on some other trait or traits.

Statistical interaction. A relationship between two variables which is different in different categories of a third variable. (There is a statistical interaction if *A* and *B* are positively related for males and there is no relation for females.)

Tabular control. A means of holding one or more variables constant. It involves relating two variables in each of the categories of the control variable.

Weighting a sample. Counting persons with certain characteristics more than once. This is done to correct disproportions in a sample or to make two samples equivalent on a particular trait.

Zero-order correlation. *See* Pearson Correlation.

γ. *See* Gamma.

references

Adams, Bert N. 1970. Isolation, function, and beyond: American kinship in the 1960's. *Journal of Marriage and the Family* 32: 575–98.

—— 1971. *The American Family.* Chicago: Markham.

Aldous, Joan. 1969. Wives' employment status and lower-class men as husbands-fathers: support for the Moynihan thesis. *Journal of Marriage and the Family* 31: 469–76.

Aldous, Joan, and *Murray A. Straus.* 1966. Social networks and conjugal roles: a test of Bott's hypothesis. *Social Forces* 44: 576–80.

Bartz, Karen W., and *F. Ivan Nye.* 1970. Early marriage: a propositional formulation. *Journal of Marriage and the Family* 32: 258–67.

Baughman, E. Earl. 1971. *Black Americans.* New York: Academic.

Bernard, Jessie. 1956. *Remarriage—A Study of Marriage.* New York: Dryden.

—— 1966a. *Marriage and Family among Negroes.* Englewood Cliffs, N.J.: Prentice-Hall.

—— 1966b. Marital stability and patterns of status variables. *Journal of Marriage and the Family* 28: 421–39.

Billingsley, Andrew. 1968. *Black Families in White America.* Englewood Cliffs, N.J.: Prentice-Hall.

Blood, Robert O., Jr., and *Donald M. Wolfe.* 1960. *Husbands and Wives.* Glencoe, Ill.: Free Press.

—— 1970. Negro-white differences in blue collar marriages in a northern metropolis. *Social Forces* 48: 59–64.

Bossard, James H. S. 1954. Security in the large family. *Mental Hygiene* 38: 529–44.

Bossard, James H. S., and *Eleanor S. Boll.* 1955. Personality roles in the large family. *Child Development* 26: 71–78.

Bossard, James H. S. and *Eleanor S. Boll*. 1956a. *The Large Family System.* Philadelphia: University of Pennsylvania Press.

—— 1956b. Adjustment of siblings in large families. *American Journal of Psychiatry* 112: 889–92.

Bossard, James H. S., and *Winogene P. Sanger*. 1952. The large family system—a research report. *American Sociological Review* 17: 3–9.

Bott, Elizabeth. 1971. *Family and Social Network.* 2d ed. New York: Free Press.

Bridgette, R. E. 1970. Self-Esteem in Negro and White Southern Adolescents. Unpublished Ph.D. dissertation, University of North Carolina at Chapel Hill. Cited in Baughman, 1971.

Bronfenbrenner, Urie. 1967. The psychological costs of quality and equality in education. *Child Development* 38: 909–25.

Bumpass, Larry L., and *James A. Sweet*. 1972. Differentials in marital instability: 1970. *American Sociological Review* 37: 754–66.

Burchinal, Lee G. 1959. Adolescent role deprivation and high school age marriage. *Marriage and Family Living* 21: 378–84.

—— 1960. Research on young marriages: implications for family life education. *Family Life Coordinator* 8: 6–24.

—— 1965. Trends and prospects for young marriages in the United States. *Journal of Marriage and the Family* 27: 243–54.

Burton, Roger V., and *John W. M. Whiting*. 1961. The absent father and cross sex identity. *Merrill-Palmer Quarterly* 7: 85–95.

Campbell, Frederick L. 1970. Family growth and variation in family role structure. *Journal of Marriage and the Family* 32: 45–53.

Carter, Hugh, and *Paul C. Glick*. 1970. *Marriage and Divorce: A Social and Economic Study.* Cambridge, Mass.: Harvard University Press.

Centers, Richard, Bertram H. Raven, and *Aroldo Rodrigues*. 1971. Conjugal power structure: a re-examination. *American Sociological Review* 36: 264–78.

Christensen, Harold T. 1968. Children in the family: relationship of number and spacing to marital success. *Journal of Marriage and the Family* 30: 283–90.

Cohen, Albert K. 1955. *Delinquent Boys.* New York: Free Press.

Crain, Robert L. 1970. School integration and occupational achievement of Negroes. *American Journal of Sociology* 75: 593–606.

—— 1971. School integration and the academic achievement of Negroes. *The Sociology of Education* 44: 1–26.

Crain, Robert L., and Carol S. Weisman. 1972. Discrimination, Personality, and Achievement: A Survey of Northern Negroes. New York: Seminar Press.

de Lissovoy, Vladimir. 1973. High school marriages: a longitudinal study. Journal of Marriage and the Family 35: 245–55.

de Lissovoy, Vladimir, and Mary Ellen Hitchcock. 1965. High school marriages in Pennsylvania. Journal of Marriage and the Family 25: 263–65.

Duncan, Beverly, and Otis D. Duncan. 1969. Family stability and occupational success. Social Problems 16: 273–85.

Farley, Reynolds. 1970. Fertility among urban blacks. Milbank Memorial Fund Quarterly 48 (Part 2): 183–206.

Farley, Reynolds, and Albert I. Hermalin. 1971. Family stability: a comparison of trends between blacks and whites. American Sociological Review 36: 1–17.

Frazier, E. Franklin. 1939. The Negro Family in the United States. Chicago: University of Chicago Press.

—— 1957. The Negro in the United States. New York: Macmillan.

Glick, Paul C. 1957. American Families. New York: Wiley.

—— 1970. Marriage and marital stability among blacks. Milbank Memorial Fund Quarterly 48 (Part 2): 99–116.

Goode, William J. 1956. After Divorce. Glencoe, Ill.: Free Press.

Hannerz, Ulf. 1969. Soulside. New York: Columbia University Press.

Havighurst, Robert J. 1961. Early marriages and the schools. School Review 69: 36–47.

Hays, William O., and Charles H. Mindel. 1973. Extended kinship relations in black and white families. Journal of Marriage and the Family 35: 51–57.

Heer, David. 1963. The measurement and bases of family power: an overview. Marriage and Family Living 27: 133–39.

Heiss, Jerold. 1972. On the transmission of marital instability in black families. American Sociological Review 37: 82–92.

Herzog, Elizabeth. 1966. Is there a ''breakdown'' of the Negro family? Social Work 11: 3–10.

Hill, Reuben, J. Mayone Stycos, and Kurt Back. 1959. The Family and Population Control. Chapel Hill: University of North Carolina Press.

Hill, Robert B. 1972. The Strengths of Black Families. New York: Emerson Hall.

Hyman, Herbert H., and John Shelton Reed. 1969. ''Black matriarchy'' reconsidered: evidence from secondary analysis of sample surveys. *Public Opinion Quarterly* 33: 346–54.

Inselberg, Rachel M. 1962. Marital problems and satisfaction in high school marriages. *Marriage and Family Living* 24: 74–77.

Jackson, Jacqueline J. 1973. Family organization and ideology. In *Comparative Studies of Blacks and Whites in the United States,* ed. Kent S. Miller and Ralph M. Dreger. New York: Seminar Press.

Johnson, Miriam. 1963. Sex role learning in the nuclear family. *Child Development* 34: 319–33.

King, Karl. 1967. A comparison of the Negro and white family power structure in low income families. *Child and Family* 6: 65–74.

Kiser, Clyde V., Wilson H. Grabill, and Arthur A. Campbell. 1968. *Trends and Variations in Fertility in the United States.* Cambridge: Harvard University Press.

Klatzky, Sheila R. n.d. *Patterns of Contact with Relatives.* Washington, D.C.: American Sociological Association.

Kohn, Melvin. 1959. Social class and parental values. *American Journal of Sociology* 64: 337–51.

—— 1969. *Class and Conformity.* Homewood, Ill.: Dorsey.

Komarovsky, Mirra. 1962. *Blue Collar Marriage.* New York: Random House.

Ladner, Joyce. 1971. *Tomorrow's Tomorrow. The Black Woman.* Garden City, N.Y.: Doubleday.

Leslie, Gerald R. 1973. *The Family in Social Context.* 2d. ed. New York: Oxford University Press.

Lewis, Hylan. 1955. *Blackways of Kent.* Chapel Hill: University of North Carolina Press.

Lincoln, C. Eric. 1971. The absent father haunts the Negro family. In *The Black Family,* ed. Robert Staples. Belmont, Calif.: Wadsworth.

Mack, Delores E. 1970. The Husband-Wife Power Relationship in Black Families and White Families. Unpublished Ph.D. dissertation, Stanford University. (*Dissertation Abstracts International* 31: 1889.)

—— 1971. Where the black matriarchy theorists went wrong. *Psychology Today* 4 (no. 8): 24, 86–87.

—— 1974. The power relationship in black families and white families. *Journal of Personality and Social Psychology* 30: 409–13.

Middleton, Russell, and Snell Putney. 1960. Dominance in decisions in the family—race and class differences. *American Journal of Sociology* 65: 605–9.

Moss, J. Joel. 1965. Teen age marriage. *Journal of Marriage and the Family* 27: 230–42.

Moynihan, Daniel P., Paul Barton, and *Ellen Broderick*. 1965. *The Negro Family: The Case for National Action*. Washington, D.C.: Office of Policy Planning and Research, United States Department of Labor.

Nye, F. Ivan. 1957. Child adjustment in broken and unbroken unhappy homes. *Marriage and Family Living* 18: 291–97.

Nye, F. Ivan, and *Lois W. Hoffman*. 1963. *The Employed Mother in America*. Chicago: Rand McNally.

Nye, F. Ivan, John Carlson, and *Gerald Garrett*. 1970. Family size, interaction, affect and stress. *Journal of Marriage and the Family* 32: 216–26.

Parker, Seymour, and *Robert J. Kleiner*. 1966. Characteristics of Negro mothers in single-headed households. *Journal of Marriage and the Family* 58: 507–13.

Parsons, Talcott. 1942. Age and sex in the social structure of the United States. *American Sociological Review* 7: 604–16.

Pearlin, Leonard I. n.d. *Class Context and Family Relations*. Boston: Little, Brown.

Pearlin, Leonard I., and *Melvin L. Kohn*. 1966. Social class, occupation, and parental values: a cross national study. *American Sociological Review* 31: 466–79.

Pettigrew, Thomas F. 1964. *A Profile of the Negro American*. Princeton: Van Nostrand.

Rainwater, Lee. 1970. *Behind Ghetto Walls*. Chicago: Aldine-Atherton.

Rainwater, Lee, and *William Yancey*. 1967. *The Moynihan Report and the Politics of Controversy*. Cambridge, Mass.: M.I.T. Press.

Rohrer, John, and *Munro Edmonson*. 1960. *The Eighth Generation Grows Up: Cultures and Personalities of the New Orleans Negroes*. New York: Harper and Row.

Rosenberg, Morris. 1965. *Society and the Adolescent Self-Image*. Princeton: Princeton University Press.

Ryan, William. 1972. *Blaming the Victim*. New York: Vintage.

Safilios-Rothschild, Constantina. 1970. The study of family power structure: a review, 1960–1969. *Journal of Marriage and the Family* 32: 539–52.

Scanzoni, John H. 1971. *The Black Family in Modern Society*. Boston: Allyn and Bacon.

Schooler, Carmi. 1972. Childhood family structures and adult structures. *Sociometry* 35: 255–69.

Schulz, David A. 1969. *Coming Up Black.* Englewood Cliffs, N.J.: Prentice-Hall.

Staples, Robert. 1971a. Letter to the editor. *Journal of Marriage and the Family* 33: 7.

—— 1971b. Towards a sociology of the black family: a theoretical and methodological assessment. *Journal of Marriage and the Family* 33: 119–38.

Templeton, Joe A. 1962. The influence of family size on some aspects of teenagers' attitudes, behavior, and perceptions of home life. *Family Life Coordinator* 11: 51–57.

TenHouten, Warren. 1970. The black family: myth and reality. *Psychiatry* 33: 145–73.

Udry, J. Richard. 1966a. Marital instability by race, sex, education, and occupation using 1960 census data. *American Journal of Sociology* 72: 203–9.

—— 1966b. Marital instability by race and income based on 1960 census data. *American Journal of Sociology* 72: 673–74.

—— 1974. *The Social Context of Marriage.* 3d ed. Philadelphia: Lippincott.

U.S. Bureau of the Census, 1964a. Census of Population: 1960. *Subject Reports—Persons by Family Characteristics* Final Report PC(2)-4B. Washington, D.C.: U.S. Government Printing Office.

—— 1964b. Census of Population: 1960. *Subject Reports—Families.* Final Report PC(2)-4A.

—— 1971a. Current Population Reports. Ser. P-23, no. 36, *Fertility Indicators: 1970.*

—— 1971b. Current Population Reports. Ser. P-23, no. 38, *Social and Economic Status of Negroes in the United States: 1970.*

—— 1972a. Census of Population: 1970. *General Social and Economic Characteristics.* Final Report PC(1)-C1. United States summary.

—— 1972b. Current Population Reports. Ser. P-20, no. 233, *Household and Family Characteristics: March, 1971.*

—— 1973a. Census of Population: 1970. *Detailed Characteristics.* Final Report PC(1)-D1. United States summary.

—— 1973b. Census of Population: 1970. *Subject Reports—Age at First Marriage.* Final Report PC(2)-4D.

—— 1973c. *Statistical Abstracts of the United States: 1973.*

—— 1973d. Census of Population: 1970. *Subject Reports—Family Composition.* Final Report PC(2)-4A.

—— 1973e. Current Population Reports. Ser. P-20, no. 248, *Birth Expectations and Fertility.*

—— 1973f. Current Population Reports. Ser. P-20, no. 254, *Birth Expectations of American Wives.*

—— 1974. Current Population Reports. Ser. P-23, no. 48, *The Social and Economic Status of the Black Population in the United States: 1973.*

Waller, Willard, and *Reuben Hill.* 1951. *The Family—A Dynamic Interpretation.* Rev. ed. New York: Dryden.

Westoff, Charles, Robert G. Potter, Jr., and *Philip C. Sagi.* 1963. *The Third Child.* Princeton: Princeton University Press.

Winch, Robert F. 1943. The relations between courtship and attitudes towards parents among college men. *American Sociological Review* 8: 164–74.

—— 1962. *Identification and Its Familial Determinants.* Indianapolis: Bobbs-Merrill.

author index

subject index

Age at marriage
—as antecedent of: companionship of husbands and wives, 37–38, 47, 153; economic situation, 32, 36–37, 46, 153; education, 32, 35, 154; family factors, 217; fertility, 35, 45–46, 154, 172–73, 175, 219; kin relations, 32–33, 36–37, 153–54, 199; marital dissatisfaction, 39; marital instability, 29–32, 47, 135, 153, 203–4, 226; multigenerational households, 32, 36; remarriage, 210-11; satisfaction, 39–40, 42, 45, 47, 153; self-evaluation as parent, 39; self-evaluation as spouse, 39; visiting patterns, 33, 38
—among blacks and whites, 14–15, 27, 133–34, 153–54, 224
—as consequence of: birth-order position, 168–69; family factors, 170, 175; family size, 168, 224; nonfamily factors, 171; parental marital stability, 167; parental SES, 166–67, 216, 224; premarital conception, 32, 34–35, 169–71, 175, 224; region of birth, 166; region of residence at marriage, 171; school grades, 170–71; size of birthplace, 166
—cultural theory of, 165–67, 175, 218
—and indictment v. black family, 7, 28–29, 47, 133–35
—situational theory of, 165–67, 175, 218, 225
—summary of findings on, 47, 133, 135, 159, 175

Black family structure: consequences of,

155–58; sources of, 163–65, 217–18, 228; see also specific family traits
Black and white families, compared: 8–16, 133–36, 141–42, 148–55, 221–27; see also specific family traits
Broken homes
—as antecedent of: age at marriage, 167; aid from others, 127; attitudes toward men, 128–29, 137; economic difficulties, 123–25; family income, 124–25, 131–32, 136–37; family size, 172–73; formal group ties, 128, 137; frustration, 131–32, 137; marital stability of offspring, 109–19, 137, 153; self-evaluation of attractiveness, 130; self-evaluation as mother, 130–31; social activity, 125–29, 131; son's behavior, 101–3, 119, 154; sons' education, 104, 107; son's income, 104–8, 119, 153; sons' masculinity, 98–101, 119; son's occupation, 104; visiting patterns, 127
—among blacks and whites, 25–26, 133–34, 153–55, 226–27
—as consequence of: age at marriage, 29–32, 47, 135, 153, 203–4, 226; economic factors, 201–3, 205–6, 214, 217; education, 203, 217, 226; family factors, 201, 203, 205–6, 214, 217; family size, 203–5, 214; income, 201–3, 217; maternal control, 79–81, 84, 136, 152; number of jobs, 203; occupational level, 203; parental marital stability, 203, 226–27; parental SES, 202, 216; premarital conception, 204, 226; region of birth, 203, 227; size of birthplace,